The secrets of the universe are within you

The Taoists have a saying that to die at 120 years is to die young. When you master the art of Chi Gung, not only will you add quality years to your life, but your life will become more magickal.

Chi Gung is a book of magick unlike any you've seen before. There are no spells, incantations or exotic equipment. Instead you will find a variety of simple yet challenging exercises that allow you to open the secret power of the cosmos within you.

By learning to coordinate your breathing with various postures and conscious awareness, you can increase your personal chi supply so that you can slow the aging process ... alter your metabolism ... heal yourself of minor ailments ... communicate with plants and animals ... move objects with your mind ... withstand cold, heat, and pain ... even read someone's spirit.

Ultimately, you can manipulate chi without focusing on your breath or moving your muscles in specific patterns. In fact, eventually you can learn how to move and transmit chi instantly, anywhere and anytime, using only your mind.

This book reveals the secrets of the universe. These secrets—known to mystics, magicians, witches, sorcerers and shamans throughout the ages—are so simple that anyone can learn them. Yet they are so powerful that seers and sages spend lifetimes to master them. In ancient China, knowledge of these secrets required payment of either a king's treasury or life itself.

Your secret store of unlimited power is waiting to be opened. Unlock it today with *Chi Gung*.

About the Author

L. V. (Lily) Carnie has devoted her life to the study and daily practice of Two-Spirit (Berdache) shamanism and the ancient Chinese art of Chi Gung. She has found that these two esoteric disciplines have helped her realize her potential as both a healer and energy specialist. She lives her art in everything she does. Her expertise in Chi Gung comes from practicing the art on a daily basis while learning from a variety of teachers.

In addition to Chi Gung, her interests include practicing a variety of indigenous esoteric magickal systems, as well as Tanzanian Drunken Chimpanzee-Style Monkey Kung Fu. She likes belly dancing, fencing, stunt kite flying, and sewing, and enjoys playing musical instruments such as the Celtic lap harp, fiddle, and penny whistle for the animals and plants living in wild places.

She spends the majority of her time healing plants, animals, and people as she encounters them. She also teaches Chi Gung and Two-Spirit shamanism to anybody who is interested in learning.

To Write to the Author

If you would like to contact the author or would like more information about this book, please write to her in care of Llewellyn Worldwide. We cannot guarantee every letter will be answered, but all will be forwarded. Please write to:

L. V. Carnie
℅ Llewellyn Worldwide
P.O. Box 64383, Dept. K113-9
St. Paul, MN 55164-0383 U.S.A.

Please enclose a self-addressed, stamped envelope for reply or $1.00 to cover costs. If outside the U.S.A., please enclose an international postal reply coupon.

L. V. CARNIE

CHI GUNG

Chinese Healing, Energy, and Natural Magick

1997
Llewellyn Publications
St. Paul, Minnesota 55164-0383, U.S.A.

FIRST EDITION
First Printing, 1997

Cover design: Tom Grewe
Illustrations: Wendy Frogge't
Editing: Tom Crone
Book design and project management: Amy Rost

Library of Congress Cataloging In-Publication Data

Carnie, L. V., 1961–
   Chi Gung : Chinese healing, energy, and natural magick /
L. V. Carnie. — 1st ed.
      p. cm.
   Includes bibliographical references and index.
   ISBN 1-56718-113-9
   1. Ch'i kung. I. Title
RA 781.8.C35 1997
613.7'1—dc21   97-32002
                                                          CIP

Publisher's Note

Llewellyn Publications
A Division of Llewellyn Worldwide, Ltd.
P.O. Box 64383, Dept. K113-9
St. Paul, MN 55164-0383, U.S.A.

~

Dedication

This book is dedicated to my partner Annie for
believing in me,

to Dwight for teaching me about curiosity and
scientific exploration,

to Doug and Doug for all the late-night talks,
and extensive letter reading,

to Robert and April for showing me what true
friendship really means.

and to Randall, my chi buddy.

I would also like to thank my editor, Amy Rost,
for all her help, advice, and friendship.

~

Contents

Part Two

Part Three

Exercises

PART
ONE

Introduction

For thousands of years, people from around the world have realized that the Earth is a mysterious place where anything can happen. As civilizations everywhere progressed, the magick and secret knowledge of the ancients were hidden and in some cases lost. But now is the time in history when many of the training secrets, innovations, and creative concepts are once again becoming known. One of the most advanced and thorough areas of esoteric knowledge comes from China and is called Chi Gung. The particular style that I practice is called The Flowing.

Chi Gung (also spelled *Chi Kung* or *Qigong* and pronounced *chee goong*) is an art that emphasizes learning how to deliberately develop and utilize the energy that is within your own body. This energy, called chi by the Chinese, permeates our bodies, the environment in which we live, and even the wildest reaches of our imagination. Scientific studies in China and abroad have shown that chi consists of a variety of forms of energy such as infrared radiation, static electricity, infrasound, and magnetic fields. Basically, chi is a complex form of energy that manifests itself in your vitality, your spirit, and your very life. Without chi, you die.

Chi Gung involves coordinating your breathing with your conscious awareness. The way it works is that your mind moves your chi and the chi moves your blood and oxygen, and therefore your metabolism is changed. This book will explain some of the ways you can increase your own personal energy. Most people who practice Chi Gung use chi to balance the internal energy of their bodies so that they can achieve physical, mental, and spiritual health. There is a lot more to it than that, however, because with proper training and consistent practice, you will find that the potentials of Chi Gung are limited by your own imagination and skill.

As you skim this book's table of contents, you will notice that it is divided into three parts, each with main chapters that are sub-divided into sections. Each chapter, from the physical training chapter to the end of the nature training chapter, can be read and practiced independently of the others. This unique feature means that you will not have to read the entire book cover to cover. Instead, you can open it up at any chapter, read it, then try the exercises suggested. In this way, even the reading of this book becomes a lesson in the art of Chi Gung.

As you read through the book and practice the various exercises, you will learn to follow your own interests and intuition as you flow from topic to topic. Hopefully, this will be a fun and relaxing way for you to learn. I suggest that you take the time to read all of the chapters in Part One before beginning your training from the rest of the book. However, if you are in a hurry to begin your training and you don't want to take the time to read the four chapters titled "Introduction," "Beginning Principles and Theories," "The Three Regulations," and "Beginning Exercises," then turn to the section entitled "How to Do Still Wai Dan Chi Gung." By following the exercise called "Hugging a Tree," you can begin your training today, even though you are still learning what you are doing and why you are doing it.

Reading the first five chapters before starting on the rest of the book should make you familiar with the basics of Chi Gung. This should help you in subsequent chapters as you experiment with the various skills and techniques. If you want to truly excel in this art, try to practice all of the different concepts and exercises from each of the chapters. That way, you gain a tremendous variety of small skills, which when added together will give you one of the simplest yet most complete energy systems ever developed.

The one chapter that is a little different from the others is called "Tips, Tentations, and Tales." Though it contains some exercises that you can attempt, it mostly deals with a variety of stories and observations based on my own personal experiences with chi. These stories should give you a few ideas of the types of things that can be experienced at advanced levels of training.

Learning from this book could be compared to trying to master the game of tennis. In order to become a better tennis player, you could buy a new racket, get better shoes, or practice your back swing. But to become a champion tennis professional, you would need to do a lot more. You would need to practice every tennis skill you knew, use the most advanced pieces of equipment available, and learn a wide variety of tactics and strategies. Even this would not be enough. To truly become the best, you would also have to start exploring minute details, such as sun intensity, wind direction, and court density. To become even more skilled, you would probably investigate playing desire, goals, and ultimately how to tie everything together so that your peak effort occurred precisely when you needed it to happen.

Just like the tennis player, the Chi Gung practitioner has a variety of training options based on the desired level of skill. For instance, you could just breathe—which, by the way, is not only the most basic skill, but paradoxically, the one of the most advanced. You could also just practice postures. However, if you really plan to excel, you need to achieve an edge. In other words, you need to gain as many advantages for yourself as possible by practicing everything, even the simplest, smallest, most mundane skills.

So go ahead, finish Part One, then start reading anywhere in Part Two. Part Three contains advanced material. You can read it now, but it is best for you to wait until you have experience with the basics before attempting most of the advanced exercises.

Remember to practice consistently, but when you do practice, don't necessarily strive for any particular results. Let things happen as they happen. It is the natural way of life. Be patient and you will indeed experience things you never imagined. The key to success with Chi Gung is learning to have fun and enjoy all that you do and experience. When you are happy, you are relaxed; when you're relaxed, your chi flows, making it easier to reach your goals.

History and Definition of Chi Gung

Ancient Origins

The study of Chi Gung goes back about 4,000 years, and over the centuries it has attracted more and more practitioners. Today, there are more than sixty million people in China alone who practice the art.

Nobody knows for sure who the first Chi Gung master was. About 4,000 years ago, however, people living in central China near the Yellow River began a variety of exercises and dances that someone developed after apparently noticing that when the muscles and joints of the body were heated by movement, many symptoms of arthritis, rheumatism, and other discomforts (caused by the damp air in the area) disappeared.

The first book that contained information about Chi Gung was written sometime during early 700 B.C. This book was called *The Yellow Emperor's Classic of Internal Medicine*. It listed a variety of breathing and stretching exercises and mental visualizations that could keep people healthier.

The *Jade Pendant Inscriptions of Chi Direction* were recorded on an artifact around 380 B.C., and about 150 years after that, Hua Tuo, the "Father of Chinese Medicine," created a form of exercise called "Five Animal Play." This new series of movements taught people how to maintain health and strengthen their bodies by mimicking animals. The five animals were a monkey, a bird, a deer, a bear, and a tiger.

More than 600 years later, sometime during early A.D. 500, a Buddhist monk from India named Da Mo traveled to China and developed a series of exercises to make monks stronger and healthier. He wrote two books, *Muscle and Tendon Changing Classic* and *Bone Marrow Washing Classic*.

Chi Gung was further developed during the Tang Dynasty in the fifth century A.D., when Sun Si Miao created the "Six Healing Sounds" after noticing the therapeutic effects of sound on the body.

Chi Gung Today

During the early part of the twentieth century, all forms of traditional medicine and exercise were banned throughout China as the Chinese government cast aside old ways and tried to develop Western technology. This ban went on until Mao Tse Tung came to power in the 1940s, during which time he organized efforts to relocate the lost knowledge of some of China's ancient healing methods. From 1966 to 1976, the Cultural Revolution took place in China and all ancient practices were once again outlawed. Throughout most of China's history, Chi Gung was only practiced by a select group of people—Taoists, Confucian scholars, Buddhist priests, martial artists, and some medical specialists. In 1979, however, this art was brought to the awareness of the general public for a couple of reasons.

First, at this time, China realized the importance of its hidden and lost knowledge, and started a massive search throughout the country in order to record as much of the old ways as possible before they disappeared forever. The second and probably more important reason for the renewed interest in Chi Gung is that China lacks enough medical doctors and medicine to adequately care for its population of more than a billion people. A highly motivated person who trains properly can learn to use external or healing chi in a minimum of about one year. It generally takes an acupuncturist two or three years of training and a traditional Chinese medicine practitioner four to six years to learn their healing techniques. All of these methods take substantially less time than the training required by a Western doctor. Since the results of both Eastern and Western medicine are often similar, the Chinese government is urgently recruiting Chi Gung specialists. Today, Chi Gung is a viable medical practice, along with acupuncture, moxibustion, and Western medicine.

Chi: The Ultimate Source

Essentially, Chi Gung is the study of energy. The basic premise of the training is that it offers people a way to strengthen their bodies, minds, and spirits with energy so that they have a greater chance of living long lives free of disease and premature aging.

In the West, we often think that merely by physically exercising we will become strong and healthy, but that is not necessarily the case. Western exercise consumes vast amounts of energy. Therefore, though this type of exercise program initially appears to provide people with lots of extra energy, in the long run, it depletes the body and actually ages it. Eastern exercise, on the other hand, concentrates on preserving energy and therefore helps make the body healthier.

The Three Types of Chi

There are three primary types of chi. These are heaven chi, Earth chi, and human chi. Heaven chi involves the energies of the universe, such as sunlight, gravity, and magnetism. Earth chi incorporates everything on the Earth, such as land, seas, wind, plants, and animals. Human chi, of course, relates to humans. Heaven chi influences Earth chi, and both of these influence human chi. It is possible, though, at extremely advanced levels of Chi Gung practice, for some Chi Gung masters and grand masters to partially influence Earth chi and a little bit of heaven chi, too.

Chi can be thought of as breath, energy, vitality, animal magnetism, charisma, personality, or even life itself. Basically, it is the energy of the universe. It is possible, through proper training, to increase your personal chi supply so that you can live longer, healthier, and in a much more relaxed state of mind. With proper training, you can even learn to heal yourself, and eventually others.

Every time you breathe, eat, or even drink, you absorb energy. An example of the utilization of chi is the digestion of the food you eat as it is converted into the energy your body requires. A happy, bubbly, fun-loving person is thought of as having an abundance of chi. Likewise, an athlete performing at her or his best has maximum amounts of chi. Some people equate chi with supernatural powers. Controlling chi to achieve psychic skills is one example of an allegedly supernatural power, but psychic skills are not truly supernatural experiences. The methods of attaining them are merely unknown by most people at this time. However, with proper training and lots of effort, many people can indeed attain these goals.

Most cultures have some form of chi or energy system in their beliefs. The Japanese call it Ki. In India, it is Prana. The ancient Picts of northern England called it Maucht. Both the ancient Greeks and the Egyptians called it the Art of Mysteries. To Christians, it is thought of as a gift from the Holy Spirit. You can even find it in Haitian Voodoo where it is called The Power or in the Appalachian Mountains where it is called The Shining. No matter what you call it, the bio-magnetic, electro-chemical energy, as we would think of it in the West, is the same everywhere. Energy, after all, is energy.

The only difference between one culture's understanding of energy and another is how they access and utilize it. Some cultures use instruments such as didjeridoos, flutes, or drums to increase their energy. Others use drugs, sensory deprivation, or even pain. Ultimately, though, they all use the same energy. The study of the energy of the various people of the world is kind of like climbing a mountain. There is one peak with many paths leading to it.

Chi is literally in everything, and it can be found everywhere. It can be controlled, provided that you have lots of practice and know what you are doing. That is what energy specialists such as shamans, Chi Gung masters, and and the Zulu healers called *sangoma* do. They have learned some of the secrets of the natural universe, and they ply them in their individual trades.

The Pathways of Chi

According to the Chinese understanding of energy, chi travels through the body along a series of twelve channels called meridians. This variable flow is based on a twenty-four-hour cycle as well as on the seasons of the year. These meridians follow pathways that correspond to the major nervous system in the human body. In addition to the meridians, there are two main vessels, one traveling down the center of the front of your body and the other going up the center of your back. There are also more than 700 cavities that are commonly used in acupuncture, acupressure, and Chi Gung. Because of variances in the natural flow of chi, it is important to learn how to increase or decrease your energy so that none of your chi cavities or meridians get blocked. When they do, that is when you are most likely to get sick.

There are four fundamental ways that you can increase your chi supply. The first way is the simplest and involves contracting your muscles in a series of exercises called Wai Dan. The next method, called Nei Dan, is the most advanced and involves using your mind. The third method requires a trained acupuncturist to place needles in the various chi cavities in your body, and the final method consists of various forms of massage. Each of these methods is effective. However, this book will concentrate primarily on the first and second methods because they enable you to increase or decrease your chi at will, anywhere, anytime, without the need of special equipment, partners, or extensive medical training.

Chi Gung, Tai Chi Chuan, and Yoga

Chi Gung, as an energy system, has some similarities to both Tai Chi Chuan and Yoga. Tai Chi Chuan originally was developed as a soft martial art for self-defense; *soft* means that the movements are based on using relaxed muscles instead of tense ones. Today, instead of practicing Tai Chi Chuan as a martial art, most people use it as a form of moving meditation and to improve their health. In fact, very few people actually know and understand its martial applications.

One of the chief differences between Tai Chi Chuan and Chi Gung is that Tai Chi Chuan, as it is practiced by most people today, focuses primarily on identifying the chi within one's body, whereas Chi Gung specializes in mentally generating, manipulating, and utilizing this energy. Tai Chi Chuan uses complicated movements that require considerable mental effort to memorize. Therefore, most people who practice Tai Chi Chuan focus on the physical aspect of moving their muscles instead on what is happening inside of their bodies. Chi Gung, on the other hand, offers more of a chance to focus on the internal feeling of chi since the movements and postures are relatively simple. Yoga specializes in holding a variety of immobile postures for improved health and for meditation. It is different from both Tai Chi Chuan and Chi Gung, because the way it is taught to most people today tends to ignore internal energy.

Varieties of Chi Gung

There are numerous styles of Chi Gung, each designed for a particular purpose. Some styles are based on following the doctrines of particular ideologies, such as Taoism or Buddhism. Others are based on the different ways that the body moves and whether you move your body yourself or someone moves it for you (as in massage). Some styles concentrate on the particular uses of chi.

Mental Chi Gung is used primarily for maintaining your mental health. Its primary emphasis is on teaching you to control your mind so that your brain is active and alert. You can become sick when your mind is weak. For example, stress can cause ulcers and fear can damage your bladder. By learning to remain calm, you can eliminate these types of problems. The way this is done is by learning how to relax and control your mind, body, and breathing through a series of regulating exercises called the Three Regulations. These exercises are extremely important and should be learned and practiced before delving into the various Wai Dan and Nei Dan Chi Gung exercises.

Medical Chi Gung is used for healing yourself, and, at advanced levels, healing others. With this style of Chi Gung, the practitioner learns how to move chi throughout the body in order for it to flow properly. The primary idea here is that physical movement is essential for the movement of chi. Therefore, a number of different physical exercises and movement patterns were developed.

Martial Chi Gung is another type. This style concentrates on learning how to fight and how to defend yourself. This training covers ways to increase your muscular strength and endurance by using internal energy. Examples of martial arts using this system are Tai Chi Chuan, Aikido, Pa Gua, Tanzanian Drunken Chimpanzee-Style Kung Fu, and Hsing Yi.

The last category of Chi Gung is Spiritual Chi Gung. Here, you strive to learn to control your emotions and spirit. This specialty offers ways to learn to live longer as well as to reach spiritual enlightenment. The Taoist monks of China used to concentrate heavily on practicing this style of Chi Gung. One of their main goals was to learn how to live forever. Sure, that is quite an ambitious goal, but the Taoists have a saying that dying at 120 years old is dying young. With lots of consistent practice, it is possible to develop high degrees of psychic skills by using some of the advanced methods of Spiritual Chi Gung.

Levels of Chi Gung Training

In addition to the various types of Chi Gung training, there are also different levels of experience. A beginner is a person who has not yet mastered Small Circulation Chi Gung. Small Circulation is a method of moving chi in a cyclical pattern throughout a person's body and head (excluding the arms and legs). It can take anywhere from a few hours to a few weeks or months to properly learn how to do this.

An intermediate-level practitioner can consciously circulate chi in the Small Circulation pattern and has begun working on moving chi in the Grand Circulation pattern. Grand Circulation involves moving chi throughout the entire body, and often takes a few months of regular practice to achieve. With extensive practice, a person can become an advanced practitioner—someone who can instantly send chi to specific areas in the body, as well as absorb chi from the environment. When a person can emit chi into others and move someone else's chi, they are generally considered a master.

You can develop a number of psychic skills using Chi Gung, including healing and psychic skills, but you might not want to focus on learning just on single skill. Personally, I prefer to work with Chi Gung as a total package rather than as a series of specialized lessons in particular categories. It is important to understand that you can go as far in this art as you desire, so long as you practice diligently and consistently. The point to remember here is that the advancement of your training directly relates to your will and determination. If you want results, the single most important thing required of you is persistence.

Is This the Real Chi Gung?

In China, each family often created its own martial arts style, and, not surprisingly, it was the same way with Chi Gung. It is hard to estimate how many different styles of Chi Gung exist today. Certainly there are hundreds, and some researchers even speculate that there are possibly thousands. The quantity of styles is not important. What is important is the similarities that tie them all together. Chi Gung is a method that you can use to cure and prevent diseases, to strengthen your overall health, and to avoid premature aging while prolonging life.

You might be wondering if there is a right way to do Chi Gung. In other words, is the style that you are reading about here the official style? Well, there really is no right or wrong style. What works for you works for you. It is that simple. That is why there are many variations of how to do the exercises. You see, Chi Gung was traditionally passed on from master to student by primarily using nonverbal lessons. The master would demonstrate lessons and also send chi into his students so that they could feel what any given lesson was supposed to teach. Unlike today, where almost any knowledge is available in books, traditional Chi Gung was seldom recorded, and when it was, it was hidden behind a language of metaphors. That ensured that only select people could master the hidden arts. Because each master had his or her own particular style, there was never any one official style. Even if some culture claimed that their style was the only way (energy training is practiced in some form or another throughout the world), who is to say that one particular way of doing it is right?

Here is kind of an imaginative example. Suppose for a moment that birds could talk to each other and that one day they got together at the local bird feeder and debated about the real way to fly. Hummingbirds would say that you have to beat your wings very fast, while vultures would say that you glide on the wind. Chickadees would say the way to fly is to dart about in short spurts while landing frequently, and albatrosses would say that flying means covering extremely long distances. Which bird really knows how to fly?

So you see, the answer to any question dealing with the right way to do anything depends on perspective. In the end, everything is relative. Because all paths are the right way, all you need to do is to forget about whether or not what you are learning is official, and instead, concentrate on the fact that any path you walk is indeed a path.

Ways to Learn Chi Gung

When learning new skills, it is very easy to find one particular source of knowledge—a book, a person, or something from nature—and stick exclusively with that teaching tool. There is a lot to be said for learning from one teacher. After all, it allows you to potentially master a specific system of knowledge. You could find one Chi Gung master and study exclusively under her or him until you too mastered that system. That actually is a very good way to learn.

Learning from a single teacher has its limitations, however. What if your teacher only knew part of a system? Then you would only learn part of a system too. What happens if you think you have learned everything? (If that is even possible, which it is not.)

I suggest you learn from as many different teachers and sources of knowledge as you can. Read a variety of books and magazines. Talk to masters. Learn from other Chi Gung students as well as from magical practitioners from every discipline. Let nature teach you. You'd be surprised how much you can learn from a single leaf. Never scoff at any teacher, because everyone and everything has some lessons to share with you. It is very important that you never place limitations on anything.

Self-imposed limitations are the reason that there are so many energy systems available today. There are thousands of variations. Each of these systems developed under at least semi-isolated circumstances, which is why each of them uses different methods of bringing forth energy. All of these systems work to some degree or another, hindering themselves merely by their own rules.

Therefore, open yourself up to studying as many different disciplines as possible while looking for analogies in everything. Once you start doing this, you will see new possibilities everywhere, every day. Not only will this increase your ability to train effectively, it will dramatically increase the speed with which you can master new skills.

Is Chi Gung the Only Way to Master Energy?

Innumerable energy systems have been developed throughout the world at various times in history. Some use crystals, scents, or colors. Others use massage, movement, or posturing. A few concentrate on sound. Many require a variety of pieces of apparatus. However, few of them are complete systems by themselves.

Often, these alternative disciplines use only one or two methods of raising or manipulating energy instead of looking at the study of energy as a whole. In other words, they approach it like the general philosophy of Western medicine as opposed to Eastern medicine. In the West, we tend to look at the symptoms of a disease, then prescribe some sort of drugs or surgery to alleviate those symptoms. For example, if you have the flu, you take flu medicine. In the East, on the other hand, they look for the cause of the disease. Their idea is based on the concept that by knowing why something happens, it is then possible to prevent it from occurring. In a similar manner, most energy systems often utilize a Western way of looking at things. They use a variety of props to raise, enhance, and control energy. Chi Gung, on the other hand, explores the basics of what energy actually is and how to use it directly.

Interestingly enough, even many of the systems of Chi Gung limit themselves unnecessarily by following given sets of movement patterns to the exclusion of all others. This occurs because, historically, a variety of different families in China developed their own systems of Chi Gung, and each family tried to make their system unique. Ironically, their very uniqueness hinders them. An eclectic approach is more valuable. It views all forms of energy as ultimately one form of universal, cosmic chi. By adopting this approach, you can open yourself to trying any form of energy system from any culture, regardless of its historical setting. You can broaden your knowledge and understanding of all types of energy, and consequently you can achieve things that followers of singular methods never even dreamed existed.

Understanding Basic Energy Systems

At basic through master levels, Chi Gung works with meridians in the body. These are long, narrow pathways, similar to the ones your nerves follow (Figure 1). Other energy systems, such as those from India, use chakras, which are whirling balls of energy located at given locations along the center line of your body (Figure 2). The third common type of energy system is based on auras. Auras are fields of energy surrounding your body and extending out beyond your skin (Figure 3). Each of these energy-raising styles contain facts, all of which lead to one truth. Because chi is universal cosmic energy, it extends beyond the boundaries placed upon it by people as they try to neatly categorize it to fit a certain set of rules. Therefore, once one passes beyond the

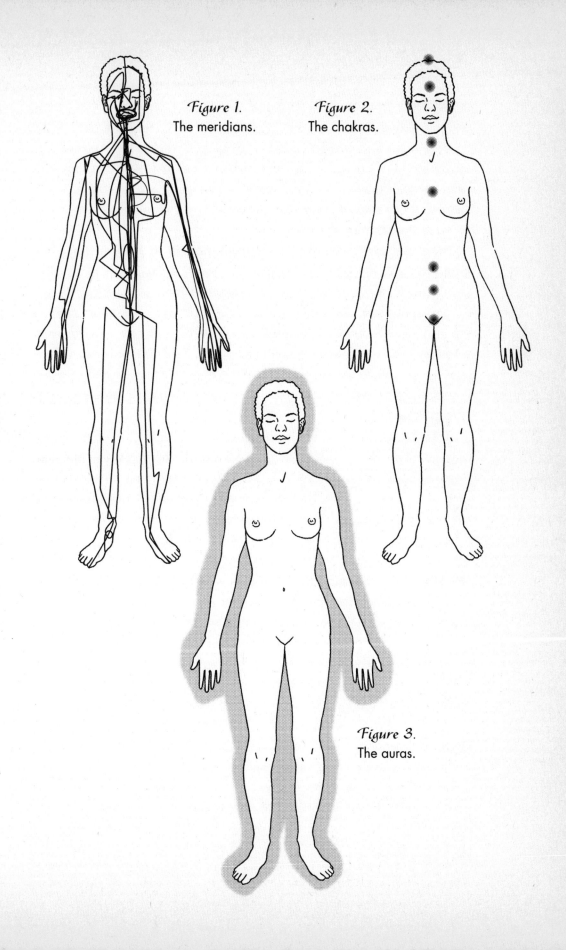

Figure 1.
The meridians.

Figure 2.
The chakras.

Figure 3.
The auras.

master level, Chi Gung branches into a broader spectrum of total energy training without restrictions.

By combining a variety of energy systems, you will be able to practice the full spectrum of existing energy training, but you first need to learn about what energy actually is and how to use it. Chi Gung is an excellent way to learn what you need. It offers all of the basic skills you will require, as well as access to almost unlimited advanced skills.

What is energy and how can you gain more of it? Energy is that substance that makes you alive. Without it, you are dead. Yet, paradoxically, even in death, we still have energy. In order to gain control over your body's energy supply, you need to open yourself up to as many possibilities as you can imagine. It is very important that you never place any limits on yourself. If you say you can't do something, then you can't. If, on the other hand, you say that you can do anything, then you just might. At least by thinking that you can do whatever you desire, you have opened yourself up to the possibility of it occurring.

Let's take a look at the development of the airplane as an analogy. Historically, many people dreamed of flying but few really thought that they could. However, a few determined and persistent people kept trying to discover how to fly until one day the airplane was invented. In fact, if you think about it, all of our modern inventions began this way. They all started with a dream and a belief. This same analogy applies to chi. You must believe that there is energy within your body and that you can eventually learn to control it. Once you believe this, you can start to ask yourself a variety of questions regarding the limits of chi generation and manipulation. Interestingly enough, you will probably come to realize that the only limits are those that you create yourself.

You see, self-imposed limits are a sign of inadequate understanding. Consider some alternative energy systems for a moment. Today is the Information Age, but it hasn't always been like this. In our past, civilizations grew based on their understanding of the world around them. In some cases, this world was limited to a particular valley, a vast jungle, or numerous mountain ranges. Ultimately, there were boundaries that limited how far a given culture could expand. Because neighboring cultures did not always share their views of life with each other, they often tended to develop in quite different manners. As already mentioned, both China and India developed energy systems, one using meridians, the other chakras. By looking beyond the specifics of their personal interpretations of energy, you will see that both cultures have the same general concept, each utilizing different means.

There are innumerable traditions for mastering energy. Each has its own set of facts. Viewed independently, they all seem dramatically different. Yet, when looked at as a whole, they all strive to connect with the one truth—universal energy. That universal energy is the energy of vibration. Because everything imaginable vibrates, everything is actually a path to understanding universal energy. That is the secret. There is no one way, because all ways are their own way. Therefore, as you gain skill in your Chi Gung training, you should eventually create your own path by following your intuition regarding what is right for you.

Is Chi Gung Magick?

The chief difference between Chi Gung and all other systems of energy manipulation is simply the depth with which it has been studied. Throughout history, various cultures have developed what are often called "magickal arts." These can be used to heal, to predict the future, to make certain events happen, and to communicate with nature. Sometimes this magick is used for good, sometimes for evil. However, it is impossible to develop as many evil chi skills as good chi skills, because at the highest levels of the arts, the utilization and manipulation of all energy requires a relaxed body, mind, and spirit. All negative emotions stress the body in one way or another and thus hinder chi flow. Therefore, good or white magick will always be stronger than bad or black magick.

How does chi fit into the field of magick? Well, chi and magick merely are different words describing the same thing. You see, Chi Gung is nothing more than the Chinese word for the study of using energy. That is also the definition of magick. Both magick and Chi Gung use the Earth's natural energy to affect our lives.

All magick stems from universal energy, which goes beyond any culture's specific rituals; every culture has different ways of tapping into this energy. Chi Gung happens to concentrate on using breathing and increasing your sensory awareness through various exercises instead of focusing on using tools or special locations. That is not to say one system is better than another. It is merely different. The advantage of Chi Gung is that it can be done anywhere, anytime, by anyone, with anything or nothing. However, Chi Gung, just like any system, often follows a particular training program. This is so individuals can be sure they are learning all of the steps needed to progress in their skills safely and efficiently.

Where does magick fit into all of this? Magickal systems often require verbal spells, incantations, special movements, secret locations, and specially created tools. Each of these things is a method of training you to focus your mind and to increase your energy. The key is focus. Studying magick is a wonderful way to build your Chi Gung skills. It gives you specific ways to build your concentration, and it enables you to learn to believe in yourself by gaining confidence in using certain rituals. If you decide to follow a particular magickal tradition, choose one you feel drawn to naturally. Some will want to follow traditions that bring many people together. Others will want to work by themselves. Some will want to use fancy equipment. Others will want simple, natural tools. Some like drums. Others like rattles. No matter what magickal tradition you decide to practice, stick with it. As you gain deeper understanding, you will see how all magickal traditions are related. Sure, there are external differences, but ultimately they all call upon and use universal energy.

Just as Chi Gung transcends some magickal arts by not requiring a lot of paraphernalia, at very advanced levels, it transcends itself. Ultimately, you can manipulate chi without focusing on your breathing and without moving certain muscles in specific patterns. In fact, you can eventually learn how to move and transmit chi instantly, anywhere, anytime, using only your mind.

What Can You Do With Chi Gung?

Chi Gung can be used for a variety of different purposes, and everyone seems to have his or her own reason for starting training. Most people practicing Chi Gung probably begin because they are interested in learning how to lead healthier lives, but there are a variety of additional reasons. Some people, for example, want to increase their fitness level and become better athletes. Others are interested in martial arts and want to learn how to defend themselves against attack. A number of people are interested in developing paranormal abilities. A handful (more than those who are willing to admit it) are interested in increasing their sexual capabilities. A few want longevity or even immortality. Finally, a very small group practice Chi Gung for spiritual development.

Let's take a look at each of these primary reasons for practicing Chi Gung. Maybe you will find that one of them is the reason you felt the call to practice Chi Gung.

Healing Power

I know many of you are interested in learning how to heal yourself. At the basic level, you will be shown a variety of postures you can practice that should help the chi to flow more smoothly through your body. After all, the primary goal of Chi Gung is for your chi to circulate regularly and strongly throughout your entire system. By achieving a smooth flow of energy, your body has a greater chance of healing itself of minor inconveniences such as headaches, backaches, stiff muscles, colds, sleeplessness, congestion, and general fatigue. Many of these symptoms can be eliminated in one to three days. For more serious illnesses, it may take as long as a few weeks to a couple of months for a skilled practitioner to see results.

When you reach the intermediate level of training, you should be able to have some degree of control over your chi flow so that you can direct it to some of the general areas within your body. This should enable you to concentrate chi in areas such as an arm or a leg to help heal a bruised major muscle. The increased chi flow in such an area can help the damaged tissue to heal quickly. With lots of consistent practice, you can eventually reach the advanced level where it is possible to heal a number of diseases and traumas by learning to send chi into or out of specific damaged areas of the body. Sometimes healers will lay their hands directly on their patients while healing them, but at extremely advanced levels, preceded by extensive practice, actual touching is not necessary. There are a few Chi Gung masters (fewer than you can count on one hand) who are able to heal others from as far away as they can imagine with their minds. This skill requires the most dedicated practice of all. Chi Gung masters at this level have successfully treated rheumatism, tumors, muscular dystrophy, and even cancer. Chinese clinics report there are more than 100 diseases that can be cured by the skilled use of Chi Gung.

Fitness

If you are interested in increasing your overall fitness level, you will find that Chi Gung is a great addition to any training program. One of the first things you will learn as a beginner is proper breathing. By breathing properly, you should notice increased energy, strength, coordination, and awareness. At the intermediate level, you will use a variety of postures held for longer and longer time periods; these will increase not only your muscular endurance, but also your internal energy flow and control. At this level, you should find that proper training gives you an edge in some of your physical activities.

As you progress in your training, you will learn ways to increase your energy level so you will not tire as quickly. In addition, you will discover ways to convert extra energy into strength and increased flexibility. This means proper Chi Gung training can help you to exercise harder, longer, and safer. At advanced levels of training, a few athletes, particularly in China, have used Chi Gung to help them win medals in the most recent Olympic Games, and help them succeed in professional sports, such as volleyball, gymnastics, and baseball.

Personal Defense

Perhaps martial arts hold your interest. Wouldn't you like to know how to defeat stronger, faster, and more coordinated opponents? By using chi, you can learn how to soften the movements involved in your martial art, regardless of the style you happen to practice. Soft style means learning to move with your muscles relaxed while also using your opponent's energy against him or her. By relaxing your muscles, you will find you can move faster and more efficiently. Even if you normally practice a hard or external muscular style, you can alter it to a soft or internal system.

As a beginner, learning to move with your muscles relaxed will greatly increase your chances of maintaining your health and avoiding unnecessary injuries. Once you are in the intermediate levels of Chi Gung practice and find that you can move your chi with at least a certain degree of coordination with your mind, you will probably find your martial arts training is progressing faster than you might have otherwise expected. At this level, you will probably find yourself becoming more aware of your opponent's potential moves, which should enable you to respond to emergency or dangerous situations with greater efficiency. With lots of muscle and tendon Chi Gung training, some people have learned how to take blows from empty hands or from a variety of weapons and absorb them without damage to themselves.

At the master level, it is possible to learn how to take energy from an opponent so that they drop on the spot or how to give your opponents chi, which alters their internal body functions, thereby rendering them helpless. At the most advanced levels, you can learn to alter your opponent's emotions, and in that way, learn to fight without fighting.

Paranormal Skill Development

More and more people today are interested in developing paranormal skills, such as reading people's minds, healing at a distance, communicating with plants and animals, leaving their own body, talking with spirits, seeing the past, understanding the present, and predicting the future. Many of these skills are extremely advanced and require specialized training, but that does not mean you can't start learning the basics of some of these skills today. Some people can learn rudimentary psychic skills in as little as one year of training.

The training involves learning how to heighten your sensory awareness to new levels of perception that are broader, higher, and deeper than what you are generally used to using. As a beginner, you can practice ways to calm your mind and your emotions. Because most paranormal skills require some sort of mental effort, it is vital to learn how to control your own thoughts. One of the first ways you can do this is by learning how to concentrate. As you do a variety of breathing exercises, you will focus your mind on a spot about an inch and a half below your belly button. The Chinese call this spot the Dan Tien, and it marks the center of your body.

Once you are an intermediate level Chi Gung practitioner and know how to move your energy, you can begin to switch your concentration and awareness to various spots on your body. These locations will coincide with a variety of acupuncture and acupressure spots. When you are at the advanced level of training, you can switch your focus to the spot located slightly above and between your eyes. This area is commonly called the third eye. People who learn to send chi in and out of this cavity find they have the potential to master some of the most advanced paranormal skills. A few highly skilled people are even able to mentally move objects and read someone's thoughts.

Improved Sexuality

Some of you may be interested in learning how to increase your sexual performance. Perhaps you would like to last longer with your partner or to have multiple orgasms. Chi Gung can help you. This particular training is a bit unusual according to Western standards, and you must really feel confident in your own sexuality if you plan to pursue it.

If you are male, you can use some of these exercises to convert your own sperm into energy. Men can learn to withhold their ejaculation after they have an erection. By ejaculating, men lose their energy. If they can control themselves, they can learn to absorb their sperm inside their bodies and to change it directly into chi. Women, on the other hand, can learn how to absorb a man's chi from his sperm and convert it directly into energy. They can also learn to absorb chi from their own feminine sexual secretions. There are also some really fascinating ways to learn to send chi into your partner that can create feelings and sensations they never dreamed existed.

Longevity

If you are interested in living a long life, perhaps that is the reason you chose Chi Gung training. If this is the case, you should start practicing Chi Gung today, regardless of your current age. If you want to utilize the maximum amount of practice in a lifetime, probably the best age to start training is about seventeen years old. Some people, though, have begun as early as the age of four or five, but most children do not have the necessary patience to adequately benefit from the training. One of the chief advantages older people have is that they are often more patient and open-minded than younger generations.

Regardless of your age, the most important point to remember is to practice consistently. Once you have begun, you have to stick with it if you want to see results. Your health is quite possibly the most important thing you have and it definitely is worth your time and effort. Some people may not want to live a long life because they think old age implies disease, loss of mental faculties, and general lack of strength and endurance, but that does not have to be the case. By starting training today and sticking with it, you increase your chances of living not only a long, but also a happy, productive life.

One of the reasons the ancient Taoists practiced Chi Gung was because they wanted to live forever. Many Taoists still strive to achieve this goal. They believe that by practicing Chi Gung every day for their entire lives, they can increase their chances of experiencing eternity. Their view is that in order for people to reach this kind of an advanced level, they must learn to live on sunshine as their primary source of energy, and that once they learn to do this they will then know the way to alter their bodies' vibration patterns so they can travel to the ends of the universe. The Taoists view this as one of the highest levels of Chi Gung training.

Advanced Spirituality

Finally, you may be interested in spiritual development. Practicing Chi Gung can help you learn to control your emotions, to become in tune with all creation, and understand and respect everyone and everything. Everything your mind can think of has chi. When you understand this concept you will have started on the path to unlimited horizons, because you will start to have greater appreciation for everything you experience.

Regardless of your personal reasons for beginning Chi Gung, this book will give you a variety of solid guidelines for meeting your goals.

Training Sequence

The following is a training sequence you might follow in your Chi Gung practice. Feel free to use it as a guideline, or develop your own training sequence.

While you can try doing almost any exercise in this book at practically any time, your Chi Gung training will progress best after you have built a solid foundation of core skills, including breathing and relaxation techniques.

I. Beginning skills.

    A. Beginning principles and theories.

    B. The Three Regulations
        1. Regulating the mind.
        2. Regulating the body.
        3. Regulating the breath.
            a. Natural breathing.
            b. Buddhist Breathing.
            c. Taoist Reverse Breathing.

    C. "Hugging a Tree" exercise.

D. Chi familiarization exercise.

E. Generating chi with Still Wai Dan.

F. Expanding chi with Moving Wai Dan.

G. Further development of Wai Dan training.

H. Nei Dan.

   1. Small Circulation.

   2. Grand Circulation.

   3. Additional breathing techniques.

   4. Breathing through focus points.

I. Absorbing chi from the environment (Environmental Breathing).

J. Sending chi to the environment (chi projection).

II. Advanced skills.

III. Master skills.

Beginning Principles and Theories

This entire chapter is extremely important to read and understand because it will teach you the principles and theories behind Chi Gung, which is helpful because it gives you an awareness of what you are trying to achieve. Once you know what you are attempting to do, you have a much greater chance of actually doing it. Without this knowledge, you probably would not get anywhere with your training, so all of your efforts would be in vain. Chi Gung training directly involves your mind. Though at times it seems physical, it is in reality a mental discipline. Because of this, the three spiritual traits you must cultivate are will, patience, and endurance.

Because Chi Gung is an Eastern art based on Oriental philosophy, many Westerners are not familiar with the basic ideas necessary to practice the art. Even the act of reading this book is an example of Eastern and Western philosophies. You see, in the West we generally learn things in a left-brained fashion. That means we use a sequential order of learning where we start with chapter one, then go to chapter two, and so forth. However, one of the things you have probably already noticed about this book is that it doesn't have chapter numbers. That is because the material is ideally suited to a right-brained approach to learning. This means you can take a little from here and some more from there, because everything is interconnected with everything else.

Many people like to dive into their training immediately. You can do that, but before you do, you have to know where to start. Paradoxically, though, if you jump right in immediately, you will need to start at a different place than if you take your time.

If you absolutely cannot wait, then the section you need to read right now is called "How to Do Still Wai Dan Chi Gung." Go ahead and turn to that section (page 81) if you want to start now. Personally, if I had a book like this available when I was a beginner, I more than likely would do that too.

What Are Wai Dan and Nei Dan?

Chi Gung can be divided into two general training categories. One is called **Wai Dan** and the other is called **Nei Dan**.

Wai Dan, the Physical Chi Builder

Wai Dan involves using a variety of physical postures in order to create a surplus of chi in your arms and legs. Once the chi builds up to a high enough level in your appendages, it will clear through most any tension or blockage you might have in your body. This then enables the chi to flow smoothly and efficiently throughout your system so it can then increase your overall health. (This good chi flow is one of the reasons people who have physical jobs or who exercise on a regular basis are often healthier than sedentary people.)

Wai Dan is the form of Chi Gung most commonly used by health specialists because the physical positions are easy for beginners to learn and use. They can generally be learned in as little as one to three days, and these positions offer excellent internal healing potential. In fact, according to Chinese medical statistics, about eighty percent of patients who practice these positions are healed of their medical problems. Western medicine has proven to have about the same eighty-percent level of effectiveness.

There are two kinds of Wai Dan practice. One of them is called **Still Wai Dan** and the other is **Moving Wai Dan**. Still Wai Dan (also called Zhan Zhuang) is used primarily for the incredible health benefits it provides. In this style, you hold a particular position while you try to relax your muscles. In a typical position, you might stand with your feet shoulder width apart and your knees slightly bent while also having your arms extended straight out at

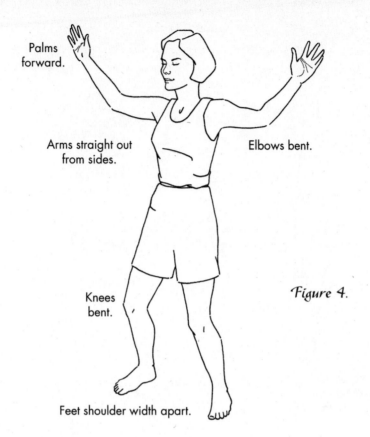

Palms forward.

Arms straight out from sides.

Elbows bent.

Figure 4.

Knees bent.

Feet shoulder width apart.

your sides at shoulder height, your palms facing forward and your elbows slightly bent (Figure 4). After standing in this position for up to twenty minutes, you will probably notice that your arms feel quite fatigued. When you lower them, the energy that has built up in your shoulders will flow down into your arms and eventually circulate through your body.

Moving Wai Dan involves repeatedly tensing and relaxing various muscle groups as you move from one position to another. When you do this kind of exercise, it is important to make sure there is as little tension in your muscles as possible so the chi has the greatest chance of moving through your various meridians. Here is an example of how to do this type of exercise. Stand in a comfortable position with your feet about shoulder width apart and your arms hanging loosely at your sides (Figure 5, page 30). Slowly raise your arms until they are level with your shoulders (Figure 6). Have your palms facing down. While you do this, try to concentrate your mind on the feeling you get as each of your muscles moves. Once your arms have reached shoulder height, lower them back down to your sides as slowly as possible. This exercise resembles a

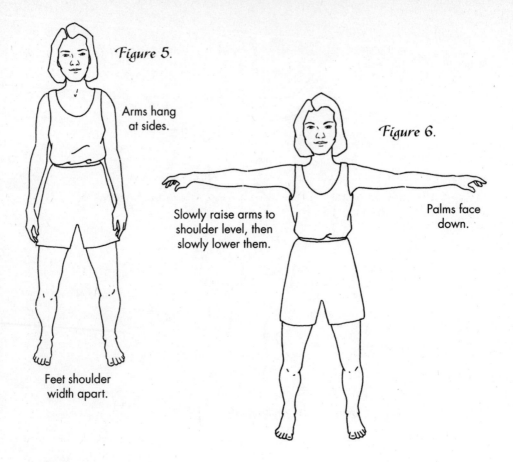

Figure 5.

Arms hang
at sides.

Figure 6.

Slowly raise arms to
shoulder level, then
slowly lower them.

Palms face
down.

Feet shoulder
width apart.

bird flapping its wings as it flies. Repeat this exercise as many times as it takes
until your arms and shoulders feel like they are starting to warm up.

Nei Dan, the Mental Chi Builder

Nei Dan, on the other hand, builds chi by using mental effort. For this reason, it is generally considered more complex and challenging to learn than
Wai Dan; it takes longer to identify the feeling of chi and also requires a
greater degree of patience and mental control. Nei Dan, however, is more
effective once you learn how to do it. The way Nei Dan works is that chi is
built up in the abdomen through a series of breathing exercises. Once the chi
has built up in this area, it is controlled and circulated through the body by
using your mind.

You can start training in both of these systems simultaneously, but as a
beginner most of your effort will probably be geared toward Wai Dan, because

it will most likely take awhile to feel the effects of Nei Dan. By focusing on Wai Dan, you should have both a quicker and a better understanding of what chi feels like than if you exclusively started with Nei Dan training. On the other hand, because Nei Dan takes longer, you might as well get started on practicing it now. That way, when you have built up an adequate supply of chi with Wai Dan, you will have a greater chance of progressing in Nei Dan at a quicker rate. Because most beginners might not really understand what chi is and exactly what it feels like, Wai Dan is an important starting point. Without this understanding, Nei Dan would be nearly impossible.

What Are Meridians and Cavities?

Once you have accepted the idea that you have chi inside of you, you need to realize that in order to maintain your health, it needs to flow smoothly through your body. In addition, it is vital that you keep a certain amount of chi inside of you at all times.

Your chi flows through your body in a series of meridians consisting of eight vessels and twelve channels. Vessels are like lakes. They act as reservoirs for your chi that empty and fill up as chi flows through your body. Channels are like rivers. They provide a means for your chi to flow from one vessel to another. Therefore, when your vessels are filled with chi, it will flow through your channels and you will be healthy. If one of your channels gets blocked, it is like damming a river or a lake. The flow changes and you get sick.

Your meridians can get blocked from the air you breathe, the food you eat, the weather, the time of day, your mind, and even your emotions. For instance, if you live in a smoggy city, it can affect your health because the air you breathe will be polluted, and your vessels and meridians will fill with weak chi. In a sense, this would be similar to a polluted river. If you eat fatty, greasy food, it also will affect your chi flow. Likewise, if you get caught outside in freezing rain, your vessels and meridians could be affected. In addition, when chi is flowing as it should, then it travels through your body at regular intervals, reaching each of your various internal organs at different times of the day. What happens to you at a given time will directly correlate to potential damage any of your organs could receive. Because chi is also affected by your mind and your emotions, it is possible that the things you think or feel could also alter your chi flow and therefore your health.

The Cycle of Chi

The twelve meridians are symmetrical on the right and left sides of the body, and they all connect with each other. When one is affected by a blockage, they all could ultimately be damaged. Chi begins its flow in the lungs, then travels to the large intestine. From there it goes to the stomach, then to the spleen. Next it travels to the heart, then to the small intestine. Next it goes to the urinary bladder and the kidneys. After this it heads toward the pericardium and the *sanjiau* (also known as the triple burner). Finally it goes to the gall bladder, then the liver, then back to the lungs where it starts its circular journey again. Assuming your chi is flowing in a normal way and that you have no blockages, it travels through each of your organs at a specific time of the day.

Lungs	3 A.M.–5 A.M.
Large Intestine	5 A.M.–7 A.M.
Stomach	7 A.M.–9 A.M.
Spleen	9 A.M.–11 A.M.
Heart	11 A.M.–1 P.M.
Small Intestine	1 P.M.–3 P.M.
Urinary Bladder	3 P.M.–5 P.M.
Kidneys	5 P.M.–7 P.M.
Pericardium	7 P.M.–9 P.M.
Triple Burner	9 P.M.–11 P.M.
Gall Bladder	11 P.M.–1 A.M.
Liver	1 A.M.–3 A.M.

The two most important meridians are the **Ren Mai** (also called the Conception Vessel) and the **Du Mai** (also called the Governing Vessel).

The **Conception Vessel** runs down the front of the body from just below the eyes, then around the mouth to the chest, to the abdomen, and finally between the legs to the perineum (Figure 7). The **Governing Vessel** goes from the perineum to the tail bone to the back of the head, over the top of the head, down the front of the face and ends near the canines in the upper jaw (Figure 8).

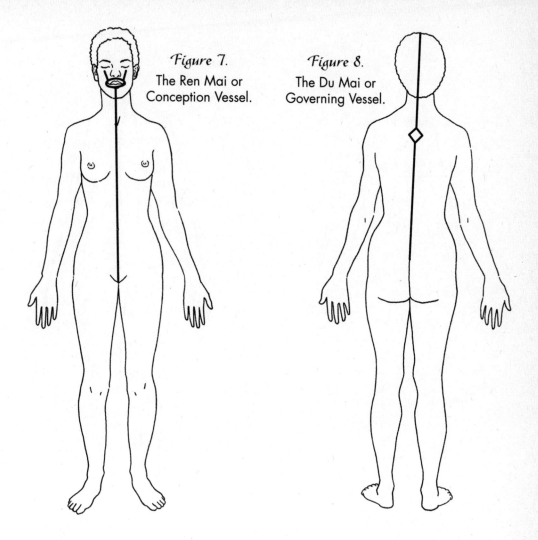

Figure 7.
The Ren Mai or
Conception Vessel.

Figure 8.
The Du Mai or
Governing Vessel.

As a beginner, you will learn to focus your attention on these two vessels as you begin practicing Nei Dan. You will first learn to build up a supply of chi in your lower Dan Tien by using Wai Dan exercises. Your Dan Tien is located in your lower belly, about an inch and a half below your belly button. You will then learn to move your chi down the Conception Vessel and up the Governing Vessel in order to complete Small Circulation training. Once you can do that, you will learn Grand Circulation, in which you move your chi into your arms and legs by guiding it along your other meridians.

These additional meridians are named after the principal organ through which they run.

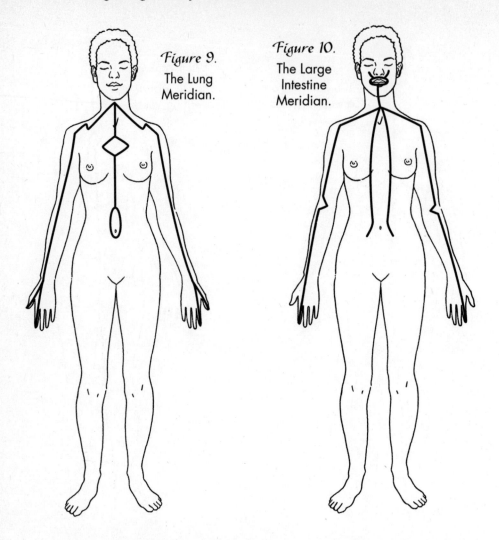

Figure 9.
The Lung
Meridian.

Figure 10.
The Large
Intestine
Meridian.

The **Lung Meridian** (Figure 9) begins in an area called the middle burner, which is near the navel. It goes down to the large intestine and then up through the lungs to the collar bone where it splits into two branches with one going down each arm. Once it reaches the hand, it splits into two more branches with one going to the tip of the thumb and the other going to the tip of the index finger where it connects to Large Intestine Meridian. Blockage in the Lung Meridian often manifests itself as coughing, skin disorders, allergies, lung disorders, or overall fatigue.

The **Large Intestine Meridian** (Figure 10) begins at the tip of each index finger and goes up each arm to the highest spot on the shoulders. There it splits into two branches. One goes down to the large intestine, and the other one goes around the mouth, then to the opposite sides of the nose where it connects to the Stomach Meridian. Blockage in the Large Intestine Meridian often manifests itself as constipation or diarrhea.

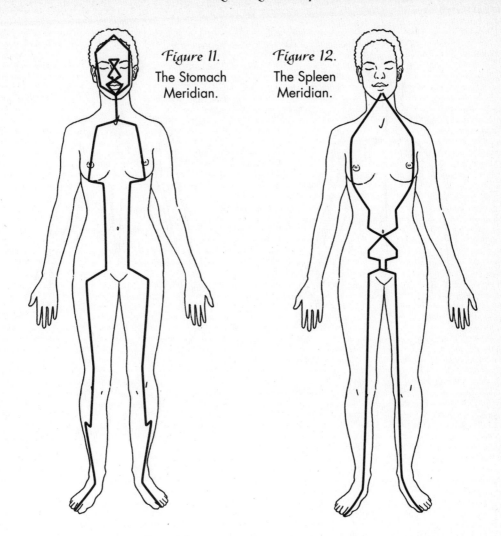

Figure 11.
The Stomach
Meridian.

Figure 12.
The Spleen
Meridian.

The **Stomach Meridian** (Figure 11) begins near the bottom outside edges of the nose. It goes up around the nose, encircling the bridge of the nose (the third eye), and at the same time goes down around the mouth and up each cheek to the forehead. It also runs from the lower jaw, down the neck to the sternum, where it splits into two branches. One branch goes down either side of the chest, belly, and stomach. They continue down past the groin; a single branch runs down each leg and ends at the tips of the second toes, where it connects to the Spleen Meridian. Blockage in the Stomach Meridian often manifests itself as vomiting, mouth sores, and nausea.

The **Spleen Meridian** (Figure 12) begins at each big toe and goes up each leg to the spleen. It then continues going up the body until it ends at the base of the tongue where it intersects the Heart Meridian. Blockage in the Spleen Meridian often manifests itself as loss of appetite, hepatitis, menstrual disorders, or fatigue.

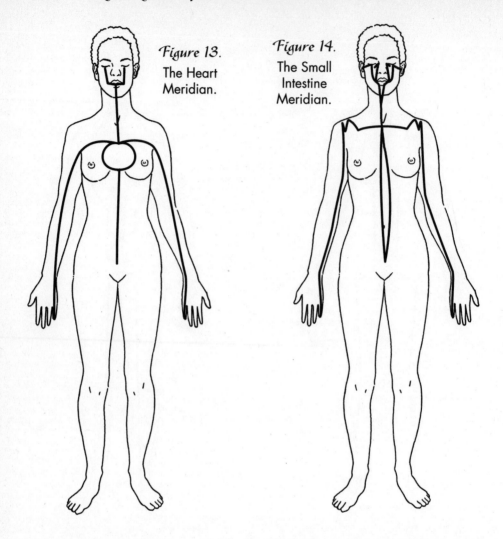

Figure 13.
The Heart
Meridian.

Figure 14.
The Small
Intestine
Meridian.

The **Heart Meridian** (Figure 13) has three branches all beginning near the heart. One branch goes to the small intestine, one branch goes up past the tongue where it meets the Spleen Meridian and then continues to the eyes, and the third branch goes down each arm and ends at the tips of the little fingers where it meets the Small Intestine Meridian. Blockage in the Heart Meridian often manifests itself as heart problems or insomnia.

The **Small Intestine Meridian** (Figure 14) begins at the outside tip of the little fingers and goes up the arms to the center of the back where it meets the Bladder Meridian and also branches into two parts. One of the branches goes down to the small intestine, while the other passes around the cheeks on the face, and also goes to the eyes and ears. Blockage in the Small Intestine Meridian manifests itself as abdominal pains or vomiting.

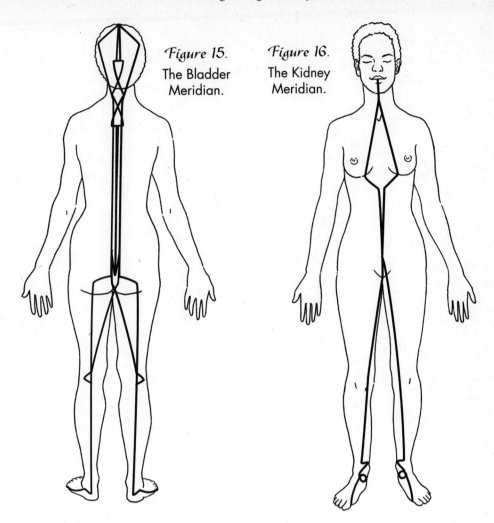

Figure 15.
The Bladder
Meridian.

Figure 16.
The Kidney
Meridian.

The **Bladder Meridian** (Figure 15) begins at the inside edge of each eye and goes up over the top of the head to the back of the neck where it splits into two parts. One branch goes down through the bladder while the other one runs along the spinal cord to the knee where the two branches intersect. They then go near the Achilles Tendon where they meet the Kidney Meridian. From here, the Bladder Meridian continues to the tip of the little toes. Blockage in the Bladder Meridian often manifests itself as incontinence or other urinary disorders.

The **Kidney Meridian** (Figure 16) begins under each big toe near the ball of the foot and goes up the legs to the kidneys where it splits into two branches. As these branches go through the chest, they meet the Pericardium Meridian. From there they go to the base of the tongue. Blockage in the Kidney Meridian can manifest itself as backaches or ear problems.

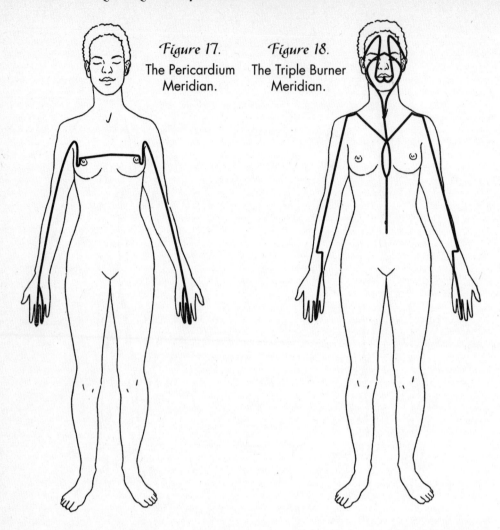

Figure 17.
The Pericardium
Meridian.

Figure 18.
The Triple Burner
Meridian.

The **Pericardium Meridian** (Figure 17) begins near the heart where it splits into two parts. One branch goes down through the body cavity while the other one goes down each arm to the palms where it splits into two. From here, one branch goes to the tip of the middle finger while the other branch goes to the tip of the ring finger, where it meets the Triple Burner Meridian. Blockage in the Pericardium Meridian often manifests itself as a variety of chest and breast problems.

The **Triple Burner Meridian** (Figure 18) is a little different from the other meridians because it is not represented by a physical organ Western medicine acknowledges. Instead, it is defined by its function. Its purpose is to circulate a water-type energy throughout the other organs. This channel begins at the tips of the ring fingers and goes over the shoulders to the chest cavity. Here it splits as one branch goes down to the middle and lower sections of the body while

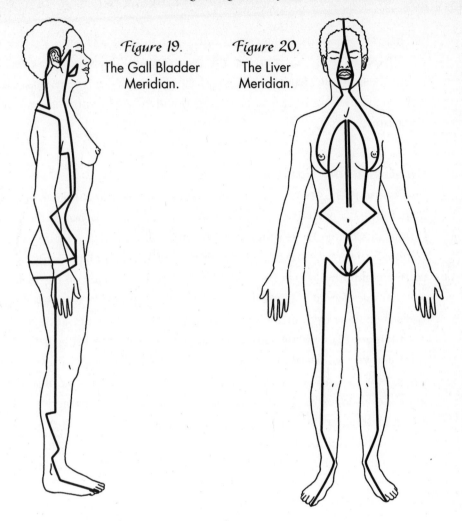

Figure 19.
The Gall Bladder
Meridian.

Figure 20.
The Liver
Meridian.

the other branch goes to the ear and then circles the face where it meets the Gall Bladder Meridian. Blockage in the Triple Burner Meridian often manifests itself as a stiff neck or water retention.

The **Gall Bladder Meridian** (Figure 19) begins with two branches near the eyes. One branch goes around the face and ears to the hips while the other branch moves across the cheeks and goes to the gall bladder where it meets the other branch. They then join as they go down the legs to the tops of the feet where it meets the Liver Meridian. From here, it continues to the tips of the fourth toes. Blockage in the Gall Bladder Meridian manifests itself as jaundice, nausea, or even a bad taste in the mouth.

The **Liver Meridian** (Figure 20) begins on the top of the big toes and goes up the legs where it circles the genitalia then moves on to the liver. From here, it goes to the lungs where it meets the Lung Meridian. Next, it goes up to encircle the mouth. It then splits into two branches, one going up to each eye. These two branches merge at the forehead, and finally run up over the top of the head. Blockage in the Liver Channel often manifests itself as dizziness, high blood pressure, eye problems, pre-menstrual syndrome, and muscle spasms.

Chi-Gathering Cavities

In addition to the vessels and meridians (or channels) in your body, you also have hundreds of cavities which are special chi gathering points along the various meridians. These spots coincide with all of the acupuncture cavities. Although there are more than 700 cavities on the human body, only four of them are important for beginners to know. Two of them are on the feet, one on each sole (Figure 21), and are called the **Yongquan Cavities** or Bubbling Wells. Two more cavities are located in the center of the hands, one on each palm (Figure 22), and are called the **Laogong Cavities** or Labor Palaces. As you train, you will learn to both send and receive chi through these four cavities. You will send chi when you are trying to heal or communicate with someone, and receive chi when you are healing yourself or gathering energy information about something.

Now that you have learned about the different meridians (consisting of vessels and channels, and the cavities), you can see how they interrelate with

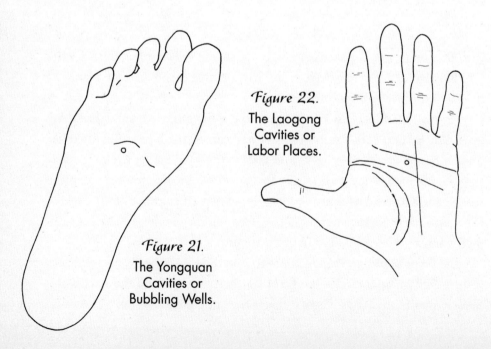

Figure 22.
The Laogong
Cavities or
Labor Places.

Figure 21.
The Yongquan
Cavities or
Bubbling Wells.

one another. By learning how to build up your chi supply and keep it flowing at a regular pace, you are able to help all of your organs to remain healthy and functioning properly. This, after all, is one of the main purposes of Chi Gung training.

What Are Yin and Yang?

Yin and *yang* are two words that describe the concept of opposites. Most things in the universe have something that opposes them, yet at the same time, provides balance for them. Without one, the definition of the other could not exist. This branch provides harmony in the universe. Examples of such opposites are light and darkness, love and hate, and male and female.

The Three Types of Chi

There are three main categories of chi. These are heaven chi, Earth chi, and human chi, and each of these three contain elements of yin and yang. In the heavens, also thought of as the sky, the universe, or space, an example of yin and yang is the moon and the sun. The moon is yin while the sun is yang. On the Earth, water is yin and earth is yang. In humans, women are yin and men are yang.

Interestingly enough, the heavens influence the Earth and both of these influence humans. For example, when the moon is full, the tides rise. In extreme circumstances, this could cause flooding on the land. A person could get trapped in this flood, get wet, and develop pneumonia.

Chi is energy and therefore really is not either yin or yang directly. When it is called yin chi or yang chi, that refers to how weak or strong it is at any given time. Yin represents ideas such as weakness, passivity, and stillness, while yang represents ideas such as strength, action, and movement.

According to Chinese medicine, there are twelve organs in your body. Half of these are considered yin. They are the heart, liver, lungs, spleen, kidneys, and the pericardium. The other six are yang and include organs that digest and excrete food. They are the large intestine, small intestine, gall bladder, stomach, urinary bladder, and the triple burner. It is important to have an awareness of how the organs relate to each other and whether they are yin or yang, because then you will have a better chance of maintaining your health.

An understanding of yin and yang is important because because according to Chinese philosophy and Chinese medicine, every aspect of our physical, mental, emotional, and spiritual lives is connected to every other aspect. If one of these is out of balance, all of them are unbalanced. Likewise, using chi to balance one of these aspects helps balance the others.

For example, let's say you are working too hard at your job and you are hardly ever home. When you are home, your spouse constantly nags you about your long hours. This leads to perpetual fights between the two of you, which then stress you so that when you are at work you can't work effectively. To compensate, you put in more hours at the office, and the cycle continues. If you want to change the situation, you need to balance it. You could balance the situation by working less, which would lead to less fighting between you and your spouse. This will keep you more relaxed, so when you do work you will be able to work at peak efficiency. Working more efficiently should enable you to cut your work hours, and therefore you will not have as much conflict with your spouse. Thus begins a positive cycle.

The Yin-Yang-Chi Gung Connection

Now let's look at yin and yang from a Chi Gung perspective. There are two kinds of Chi Gung practice, specifically, Wai Dan and Nei Dan. Wai Dan would be considered yang because it is a path of study that leads you to more physical exercises, thereby producing yang chi. Nei Dan, on the other hand, is yin because it uses mental exercises to produce yin chi.

As you can see, yin and yang are fundamental classification systems. They give you ways to figure out where you are and what you need to do about any situation you might encounter. Because the purpose of Chi Gung is to teach you how to balance or harmonize your internal energy, these two symbolic relationships provide you with guidelines on which you can base your training.

What Are the Five Elements?

According to the theories of traditional Chinese medicine, everything in existence is made of either wood, fire, earth, metal, or water. Under this premise, everything is interconnected with everything else in the same manner that these five elements interact with one another.

For example, wood is represented by spring and wind. It is windy in the spring, and this is when plants (wood) grow. Fire is represented by summer and heat. It is hottest (fire) in the summer. Earth is represented by late summer and damp. It is often damp in the late summer. Metal is represented by fall and dry. The fall of the year is when it is dry. Water is represented by winter and cold. The winter is when it is usually coldest, and this is also a time when water freezes.

Now you may be wondering how these five elements relate to people, and specifically, how they relate to Chi Gung. Well, the main purpose is to show that everything indeed affects everything else. Therefore, the food you eat, the air you breathe, and even the climate you happen to be in at the moment all affect your chi flow. For example, in the winter, you should exercise and eat less, because winter is a time in nature when everything slows down. There is less growth and less activity during the cold months of the year. The winter is a time when you would most likely practice Still Wai Dan exercises and Nei Dan exercises. By contrast, in the summer, you should exercise and eat more, because it is a time when everything in nature is growing and full of life. The summer is a time when your practice would emphasize more Moving Wai Dan types of exercises. Knowing when to practice which types of Chi Gung exercises is important, because the deeper you get into understanding how and when to exercise, the greater the chance you have of realizing how to balance the yin and yang elements of your chi if you happen to feel sick or if you need energy.

Here is an example of how such an awareness can be used. Let's say you find yourself feeling easily upset and angry. Perhaps you spend a lot of time shouting. According to the table of Five Elements (following page), your frustration is an indication of a wood situation. Your symptoms and actions could indicate you are in the process of developing a liver problem, because according to Chinese medicine, people with liver problems manifest the symptoms by getting upset easily and raising their voices in anger.

At this point you might consider seeing a traditional Chinese doctor so that he or she could interpret your other symptoms, such as the color of your eyes. You would probably want to know what you could do to prevent any potential illness. Well, your body has already taken care of that for you to a certain degree. By shouting, you relieved some of the tension and negative chi that had built up in your liver. Once you find out the location of the cause of your problem, you can do a series of Chi Gung exercises to help balance the chi flow to that particular organ. In this case, you might stand with your feet about shoulder width apart and have your knees slightly bent. Let both of your arms hang loosely at your sides. As slowly as possible, breathe in and out through your nose. Let your stomach push out as you inhale and let it pull in as you exhale. Calm your thoughts and focus on breathing. Liver problems are associated with emotional stress. By concentrating on standing in a particular pose and thinking about your breathing, you have a good chance of calming yourself and relieving some tension. The following table shows representations and relationships of the five elements.

The Five Elements

∾	Wood	Fire	Earth	Metal	Water
Direction	East	South	Center	West	North
Season	Spring	Summer	Late Summer	Fall	Winter
Climactic	Wind	Heat	Damp	Dry	Cold
Process	Birth	Growth	Change	Harvest	Storage
Color	Green	Red	Yellow	White	Black
Taste	Sour	Bitter	Sweet	Pungent	Salty
Smell	Goatish	Burning	Fragrant	Rank	Rotten
Yin Organ	Liver	Heart	Spleen	Lungs	Kidneys
Yang Organ	Gall Bladder	Small Intestine	Stomach	Large Intestine	Bladder
Opening	Eyes	Tongue	Mouth	Nose	Ears
Tissue	Sinews	Blood Vessels	Muscles	Skin/Hair	Bones
Emotion	Anger	Happy	Pensive	Sad	Fear
Sound	Shout	Laugh	Sing	Weep	Groan

The Three Regulations

The most important thing you need to learn how to do in order to have your chi flow properly is relax your mind, breath, and body. When you learn to do each of these things, you are practicing the Three Regulations.

Of the Three Regulations, the most important one is the mind, because it directly influences the others. A relaxed mind is calm and enables you to think clearly and thereby concentrate fully. To relax your body, you need to know how to pay attention to both your external self, such as your muscles, as well as your internal self, where your organs are located. Relaxing your breathing means that your breathing is slow and smooth, coordinated with your mind and body. Once you have learned to relax these three areas, you should be able to monitor your chi and eventually learn how to control it.

Your thoughts are the first thing you experience. For example, before you can walk somewhere you first have to decide that you want to go there. So the first thing you need to do is to learn to regulate your mind. You do this by concentrating your thoughts on just one thing, such as breathing, while temporarily eliminating as many other thoughts as possible. Completely focus on your breathing instead of letting your mind think about other things such as work, relationships, or what you are going to do later in the day. If you want to have any kind of success with your Chi Gung training, you need to keep your mind on what you are doing as you practice. This is particularly important for a beginner. For instance, if you are working on relaxing your body, then keep your thoughts exclusively on your muscles. Likewise, if you are practicing breathing, then center your mind on your inhalations and exhalations. The main secret to effectively working with your mind is understanding the concept of calmness. When your mind is calm, it can pay better attention to how to relax your body. A calm mind will help you control your breathing and give you a better chance to feel and identify the chi in your body.

The next thing you need to regulate is your breath. The first thing you will need to learn is how to breathe through your nose. You will want to make your breath as slow, soft, and quiet as possible. By controlling your breathing, you can influence your mind and your body. For example, it is possible to alter your heartbeat. If you breathe rapidly, your heart beats faster and you energize yourself. If you breath slowly, your heart beats slower and you calm yourself. At this point, don't worry about any particular breathing pattern—just breathe naturally. Make sure, however, that even though you are breathing slower, you do not hold your breath. Instead, you will want to make each inhalation and exhalation take just a little bit longer than they usually do.

One thing you may notice is that your breathing is directly related to your emotions. For instance, if you are upset or angry, you will probably exhale longer than you inhale. On the other hand, if you are sad, your inhalation will be longer than your exhalation. In Chi Gung, you want to try to make both your inhalation and exhalation take about the same length of time. That way they will balance each other. Also, when you inhale, you should try to make sure you never inhale more than about 80 percent of what you are capable of doing. If you inhale too much, you will tense your lungs and defeat the purpose of relaxation.

Now then, you are probably wondering how much is 80 percent. This is where you need to start monitoring your body. Try inhaling as much as possible. When you have reached your limit, try to get just a little bit more air into your lungs. Now take three more little breaths, each one drawing in just a little more air. Do you feel that tenseness in your chest? You might also notice a little stress in your throat, sort of like you might have to vomit. That is what full lungs feel like. When you fill your lungs to 80 percent you need to approximate how much air you need; you now have a scale to compare with based on the exercise you just did which told you what 100 percent capacity feels like.

Finally, you need to regulate your body. With this step, you learn how to relax your muscles while also maintaining proper postures. Even though your mind is the most important element in Chi Gung training, you need to learn how to relax your body. That is also why you should practice Wai Dan before Nei Dan. You can try this now.

Make sure you are standing in a comfortable position. You should feel steady on your feet, not leaning one way or another. Focus on your muscles, particularly the ones in your neck, shoulders, arms, and legs. If you are holding any of them in an unnatural manner, they will feel tense and quickly tire. Therefore, try to let your major muscles feel as loose as possible.

After you have completely relaxed, you can begin Chi Gung training. The reason you need to totally relax first is because if your mind is scattered or your body is tense, then you will not be able to sense your own chi. In addition, even if you could sense it, the chi would not flow strongly, because it would be hindered by your own mind and body.

There are three levels of relaxation. The first level is when you hold your body in a comfortable position while you focus your mind on your breathing. You can lie down, sit, or even stand, provided you make yourself as comfortable as possible.

The next level involves letting your mind actually sense how your muscles feel. If you have any tension anywhere, you need to focus on that spot with your mind and imagine the tension is flowing away from it each time you slowly exhale.

The final level is when you actually sense your internal organs, and even your bones and their marrow, with your mind. The easiest organs for a beginner to sense are the lungs and then the heart. With practice, though, it is possible to eventually sense almost everything that is inside of your body. This is an advanced exercise and requires the ability to direct your chi with your mind. You will have to master both Small Circulation and Grand Circulation exercises before you can do this properly.

Once you have learned how to do the Three Regulations, you will be ready to start learning how to actually generate and store chi.

Regulating Your Mind

The primary way you will develop Chi Gung skills is by developing your sense of awareness. In other words, you need to pay attention to what is happening inside of your body. Therefore, it is very important to learn how to develop your powers of concentration by regulating your mind.

Controlling Emotions and Desires

In order to have greater control over your own mental capabilities, it is important to realize that there are certain things that can affect both how and what you think. Specifically, there are seven emotions and six desires that not only can adversely affect your mind, but can also manifest themselves in your physical body as either disease or stress. The seven emotions are joy, anger, sadness, pensiveness, grief, fear, and fright. The six desires are sex, money, fame, wealth, gain, and avoidance of loss. Considering the way most of us live today, it is almost impossible for us to eliminate these thirteen mental stresses from our lives. It is possible, however, to reduce their power over us. It is extremely important to learn ways to help your mind deal with these mental intrusions.

Being aware of the existence of these emotions and desires is a large part of the battle, but you also need to know how to get rid of them once they enter your mind. In order to do this, you need to realize that you have control over your thoughts. Granted, any given thought or emotion could arise for a variety of biological or psychological reasons, but most people usually have control over how long they choose to dwell on any given thought. One thing you can do is to change your thought process once any of the thirteen mental stresses arises. One of the best ways to do this is by focusing on your breathing. Because your thoughts and emotions are partially controlled by your breathing, by changing your respiration style you can change your mental condition. What you need to do is to start to monitor your own breathing patterns under the various states of mind you typically experience. For example, when you are angry you will probably notice that you breathe at a faster and more powerful rate. Therefore, if you slow your breathing and make your breath softer and more controlled, you will discover that your anger dissipates more quickly.

Concentration

The next step is to learn to increase your ability to concentrate. Concentration will enable you to detect and move your chi. Your goal is to learn to focus your mind on your Dan Tien, or center. This is extremely important, because if you let your thoughts wander aimlessly you will never progress in your training. As a beginner, you will often notice that before you can focus your mind on a specific physical location on your body, you first need to learn to control your thoughts. You might want to try a few mental exercises as a sort of mental warm-up, similar to the way you would stretch before jogging. The reason these mental exercises can help is because most people have a tendency to get bored quickly, and if they immediately try focusing their attention on their breathing, they often find that their mind wanders within moments.

There are a number of different ways to make your thoughts more relaxed yet focused. One way is to imagine beautiful scenery. Think of some place that you have seen before or, if you want to, invent a place that you have always wanted to explore. It might be a beach, a mountain, a waterfall, or even a field covered with wild flowers. The important thing here is that the more vividly you can see this setting in your mind, the greater the benefits you derive from this exercise will be.

Here is an example. Take a moment and imagine a scene in the woods. You've just walked through a pine forest and entered a clearing that is about fifty yards in diameter. You sit down and relax. The clearing is covered with a variety of wild roses. Let your mind scan the soft pinks and the deep reds of the flowers. Notice how these colors contrast with the shades of green from the pine forest. Focus for a moment on the different scents. Try to detect the faint smell of the pines and the slightly stronger scent of the flowers. Notice how the two smells intermingle and dance together on the wind. Now listen. What do you hear? Can you hear bluejays calling in the distance?

Over to your left, behind a fallen log covered in a light green, velvety moss you can hear something moving in some field grass. You hear a thump, then quiet, then another light thump. It is almost like something slowly hopping. Turning your head to look, you can see a cottontail rabbit happily nibbling on the yellow flowers of a small dandelion patch. Watching the rabbit for a few moments, you notice it coming toward you. Can you feel your pulse increasing? Is your breath changing at all? The rabbit hops closer and jumps on your lap. Feel its weight as it settles on your legs. Reaching out your hand, you tear off a piece of the dandelion leaf that the rabbit is holding and you try it yourself. What does it taste like? Now take a few minutes and let your mind expand this scene any way that you want it to go.

Practice this type of visualization as often as you can. You can do it anywhere, for any length of time. For example, when you watch TV, imagine yourself as an additional character. When you wait in a grocery line, look around you for ideas, then let your mind wander to some other scene.

Details Are Important

Another way to increase your ability to concentrate is by paying attention to details. One way to do this is by starting to count objects. Initially, you might want to start with larger subjects, such as the items on your desk or in any given room. As you get better at it, try focusing on smaller things, such as the holes in a peg board, the cracks on a wall, or even the words on a page. Let's use reading as an example. Pick any book or magazine and start counting words. See how far you can get before your mind wanders. As soon as it does, go back and start again and see if you can get any further. On the surface, this seems like a rather simple task, but at a deeper level, you will find that this is quite challenging. Let's say that you are counting words when you suddenly hear a noise somewhere, or you notice how heavy the book seems, or how irritating the light is as it reflects off the pages. Any of these things and millions of others could distract you. You have to stick with it until all that seems to exist is you and the words you are counting.

Bodily Control of Emotions

Once you have found that you can maintain control over your thoughts, then it is time to start focusing your mind on your body. The most important place for you to become aware of is your Dan Tien. It is located about three finger widths below your belly button. As you practice your breathing by letting your belly move out as you inhale and pull in as you exhale, you should keep your mind centered on your Dan Tien. If you are having a hard time focusing on this spot, try placing one of your fingers on your center and feel it move as you breathe. Eventually, you should be able to keep your mind on your Dan Tien without actually having to touch it.

Regulating Your Body

Your health is directly related to how much tension you have. Interestingly enough, more than 80 percent of all diseases are stress related.

After you have regulated your mind, you can concentrate on regulating your body. The main part of your body you should be concerned with as a beginner is your muscles. Because you use your muscles every time you move, you should find that they are relatively easy to learn to relax.

Regulating your body means that you are trying to get all of your muscles to relax so that you do not have any unnecessary tension. The reason this is important is because wherever there is tension, your chi can get blocked so that it no longer flows smoothly and efficiently. When this happens, you can get sick, lose strength, or age prematurely.

One of the first things you should pay attention to is your posture. Whether you are standing or sitting, your back should be straight and your head should feel as though it is suspended by a string attached to the ceiling.

Although there are a variety of postures in Chi Gung, they are all based on standing, sitting, kneeling, reclining, and lying. Each of these different positions is used to help eliminate various kinds of diseases and stress within the body. The reason they work is that each position slightly alters the muscular tension of your body based on gravity. This affects your blood flow, which is related to your chi flow. If a person goes to see a Chi Gung master about a particular ailment, the position the master chooses for the patient to practice is based on the person's size, weight, overall physical condition, the specific disease being treated, and also how much time the patient can devote to doing the prescribed exercises.

Generally, the best position for most beginners to start with is lying down on your back. You might want to try lying on a bed while also having a thin pillow under your head so that you are as comfortable as possible. Try to eliminate as much noise in the area as you can and wear enough loose-fitting clothes so you do not get cold.

As you are lying still, inhale and exhale as slowly as possible through your nose while letting your stomach rise with each inhalation. Focus your mind on your Dan Tien as your belly moves up and down.

Start your relaxation process by beginning with your toes. Wiggle them and notice if there is any tension. When they feel loose, move to your feet. Alternately tense and relax your foot muscles a few times. Notice the difference as the muscles relax after each time you tighten them. Next, move to your ankles.

Rotate them clockwise and counterclockwise a couple of times. When they start to feel slightly warm, focus on your calves. Tighten them, then let them relax. If you can't isolate your calf muscles, try pulling your toes toward your shins. After this, let your mind center on your thigh muscles. Once again, tighten them a few times and then focus on letting them relax. If you are having trouble isolating your thighs, try pushing your legs and butt against the bed or floor on which you are lying.

Now switch your attention to your fingers. Wiggle them for a few moments, and also try holding them as straight as you can. Then let them slightly bend as they return to their natural position. Next, tighten the muscles in your hand once or twice before moving to your wrists. Rotate your wrists both clockwise and counterclockwise until they feel slightly warm or tired. Then move to your forearms. If you can't isolate the muscles and tighten them, try making a loose fist with your hands and bending your wrists as much as possible as if you were trying to make your fists touch your forearms. This will naturally tighten your forearm muscles. Let them tighten and relax a few times. Next, tighten and relax your upper arms. If you can isolate your biceps and triceps, go ahead and alternately tighten and relax them. Otherwise, just focus on tightening your whole upper arm at one time. You can do this by using your shoulders to push your arms against the surface.

At this point, it is time to focus on your stomach muscles. As you breathe, your stomach should rise as you inhale and descend as you exhale. As it rises, your stomach muscles will slightly tense and they will relax as you exhale. Concentrate on the feeling of relaxation you get every time you breathe out through your nose.

Next, let your mind move to your chest. Because you are using a form of belly breathing, your chest should not be too tight right now. If it is, you'll probably notice it most as you inhale. If there is any tenseness, try breathing a little slower and softer, and concentrate more on moving your belly in slow, controlled movements.

Once your chest feels relaxed, move to your neck. Notice if there is any tension anywhere in your neck, particularly in the front of your body where it meets your shoulders and also on the back of your neck where it attaches to your head. Slowly turn your head left and right a few times. If you feel any tension, hold your head in that position for a couple of breaths and concentrate on any tense muscles each time you exhale through your nose. Keep doing this until your neck feels warm and relaxed. If you are having trouble with this one, you might want to try tightening your neck by grimacing your face as much as you can or by pressing your head against the pillow.

Finally, it is time for relaxing your head. Make a variety of faces such as smiling, pouting, squinting your eyes, opening your eyes wide, and moving your forehead up and down. If you can, also wiggle your ears and your nose.

At this point, just lie still and breathe for a few minutes. Notice how relaxed your entire body feels. The reason you started with your feet and moved up your body is because most of your meridians begin in your extremities. That means your chi flows from your hands and feet before going into your body to the different organs. Therefore, you are helping your chi to flow in its natural path. In addition, because you are using your mind to relax your body, you need to keep it as active as possible by feeding your brain with chi as long as you can. If you started by relaxing your head first and then moving toward your feet, you would make it more difficult on yourself because your chi would go away from your head, and, more than likely, you would fall asleep before you finished the exercise.

Once you can do this entire exercise lying down, you should practice it in a sitting position. When you can do that, try standing as you do it. You will probably notice that when you are lying it is hardest to relax the muscles in the trunk of your body. Likewise, when you sit the muscles in your lower back and buttocks will require the most effort to relax. When you stand it will probably be hardest to fully relax your legs. Therefore, no single position offers the perfect relaxation opportunity. That is why it is important to eventually learn to relax as much as possible regardless of the position you happen to be in at any given time.

When you first start this exercise it might take you twenty minutes or so to complete it. If you can, try doing it twice a day. Good times for this are when you first wake up in the morning and also just before you go to sleep at night. Once you have gained some experience relaxing your body, you will be able to quickly determine if you have any specific areas in your body that are tense, then you can merely concentrate on loosening those muscles before beginning your Chi Gung training.

Rooting

In addition to learning how to relax your body, you also need to understand the principles of rooting, centering, and balance. For the most part, rooting deals with your legs and it is concerned with how stable you are.

Imagine, for a moment, that you are a tree. Trees have deep roots that go far into the ground in order to help them stand up. If a tree loses its roots, it can tip over. Therefore, one of the things you need to learn is to find the point where your standing position is strongest.

Try standing in a natural position and ask someone to push your chest or upper back and see if they can make your feet move. More than likely, they can. By rooting, you lower your center of gravity slightly by bending your legs a little. One way to root yourself is to imagine that you are holding a heavy weight over your head. In your mind, really try to feel its weight. Let your legs bend until they are in a position where you feel you could support the most weight that you can hold. If your legs are bent too much, they will tire. Likewise, if they are not bent enough you won't have much strength and stability. When you have found the proper position for you, you have found the standing position you should use when you practice Chi Gung. In most of the Chi Gung exercises, you will be asked to stand with your legs slightly bent, and the exercise described above will enable you to know just how far to bend them.

Centering

Next comes centering. Your center is at your Dan Tien, which is located about an inch and a half below your belly button. It is important to learn to move from your center because this helps you keep your balance and move with the best use of strength. This exercise is often a little easier for women to learn because their hips help them lower their sense of balance, while most men have most of their weight in their shoulders. Therefore, most men will have to concentrate and practice a little more to get the proper sense of centering.

The best way to learn to move from your center is by keeping your mind on your Dan Tien as you breathe. This will help keep your chi in your lower body instead of in your chest, shoulders, upper arms, neck, and head. Once you have your mind on your Dan Tien or center, you need to learn to move while keeping it there. You can try this now. Go ahead and start walking. Then, as you turn around to walk back to your starting point, let your lower body move first so that your hips turn before your shoulders do. Whenever you turn, try turning your hips first, then your shoulders, then your head.

Centering Exercise

Step 1.   Stand with your feet about shoulder width apart and have your legs slightly bent using a comfortable stance. Let your arms hang loosely at your sides (Figure 23).

Step 2.   Turn your right foot to the right until it is perpendicular to your left foot. At this point, your feet should form a shape similar to a capital letter T (Figure 24).

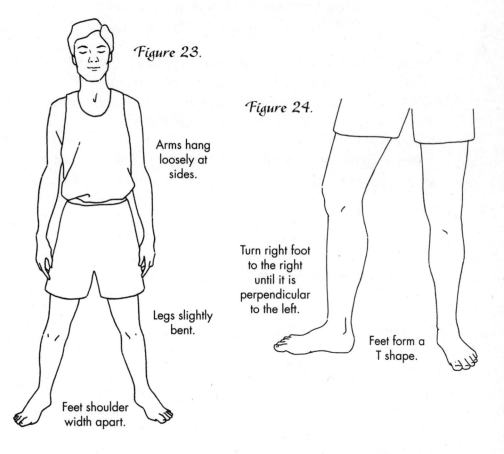

Figure 23.

Arms hang loosely at sides.

Legs slightly bent.

Feet shoulder width apart.

Figure 24.

Turn right foot to the right until it is perpendicular to the left.

Feet form a T shape.

Step 3.   Turn your body so that your belly, chest, and head all face the direction of your right foot. You should now be facing ninety degrees to your original position. For example, if you started off facing north, you should now be facing east (Figure 25).

Step 4.   Now starting with your hips, turn your waist counterclockwise as you pivot on your right foot. Let your left foot sweep the ground as it circles around behind you until it faces the direction opposite the one you were just facing. You should now be facing west with your feet in a T shape with your right foot forward (Figure 26).

Step 5.   Turn counterclockwise, pivoting at your waist as you change the positions of your feet, so that now your left foot faces forward and your right foot is perpendicular to it about shoulder width apart (Figure 27).

Step 6.   Pivot on your left foot and swing your right foot behind you as you turn first with your hips, then your chest, and finally with your head.

Step 7.   Continue this pivoting exercise, first on one foot, then on the other until you get comfortable turning your body from your center.

Balancing

Finally, you need to work on balance. Balance is a combination of both relaxation and centering. Notice, for instance, how you quickly lose your balance if you start leaning forward without allowing your feet or legs to move in order to compensate for your weight shift. It is important to work on balance because when you are out of balance, you use your muscles unnecessarily, which in turn, limits your chi flow in your body.

As an exercise for balance, try leaning in a variety of directions in order to find the exact instant where you lose your balance. You will notice there is a point where you can hold a position and another point that is just a little bit too far, because unless you shift your weight, you will fall.

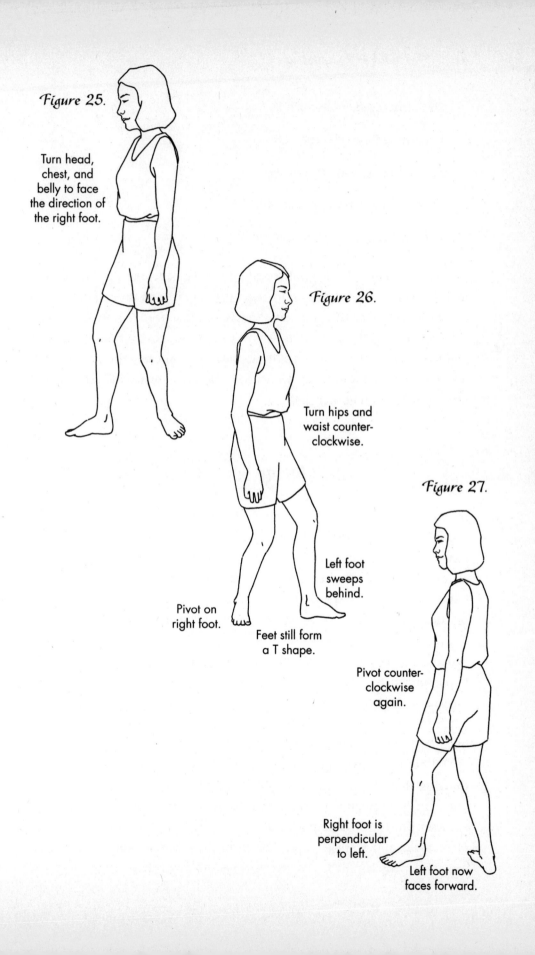

Figure 25.

Turn head, chest, and belly to face the direction of the right foot.

Figure 26.

Turn hips and waist counter-clockwise.

Left foot sweeps behind.

Pivot on right foot.

Feet still form a T shape.

Figure 27.

Pivot counter-clockwise again.

Right foot is perpendicular to left.

Left foot now faces forward.

Try balancing exercises such as:

1. Leaning forward (Figure 28).

2. Leaning sideways (Figure 29).

3. Leaning backwards (Figure 30).

4. Leaning in any direction while standing on one leg (Figure 31).

Once you have practiced both centering and balancing by just using your muscles, you can learn how to increase your abilities at these skills by also using your chi. In order to do that, though, you first need to learn Grand Circulation (see page 108). By learning how to relax your body, find your center, and know the limits of your ability to balance, you can gain more control over the muscles of your body, which will enable you to generate and manipulate your chi with greater skill.

Regulating Your Breath

In order to properly and safely practice Chi Gung, it is extremely important for you to learn how to breathe calmly, smoothly, and in a relaxed manner. In fact, this is the most important skill you will learn in practicing this ancient art. Some other types of energy systems involve breathing with great force, but make sure you never do that because it is an extremely unsafe way to practice unless you are absolutely sure of what you are doing. Breathing with too much force can lead to high blood pressure, brain congestion, or, in extreme and very rare cases, even insanity. Correct breathing is particularly important when you are a beginner, and you will also find it vital at the intermediate and advanced levels. It is only after extreme amounts of practice, when you progress beyond the master level, that you will realize how to manipulate chi without breath.

I'll bet most people go through life without spending too much time thinking about breathing. After all, it is an automatic function of the body. Therefore, you might wonder why all of a sudden you have to do breathing exercises. The reason is simply because most of us do not breathe as efficiently as we could, and as we get older, our breathing gets even worse because of a variety of inefficient habits. When we are fetuses, we receive oxygen through

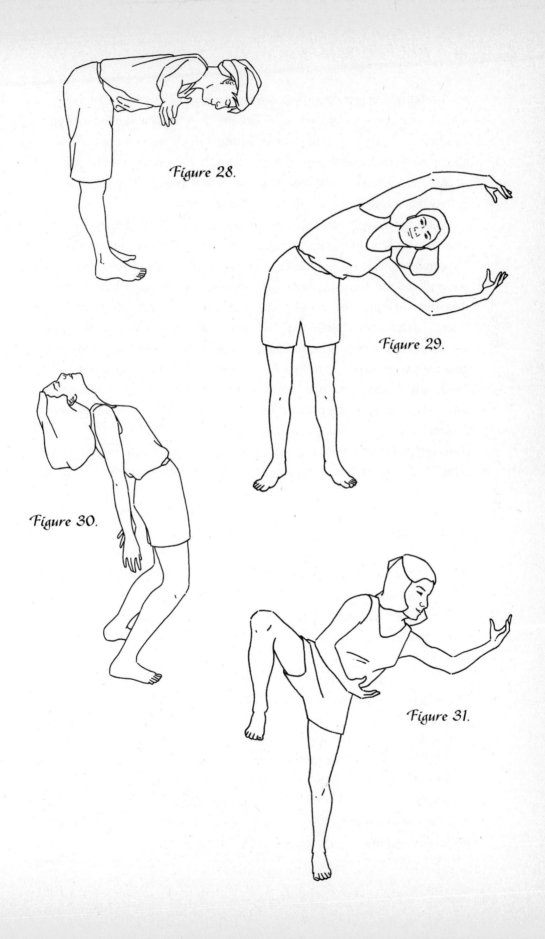

Figure 28.

Figure 29.

Figure 30.

Figure 31.

our umbilical cords by pumping our stomach muscles in a bellows fashion. Some infants breathe for a while by moving their lower abdomens. As young children, we start to breathe higher in our bellies, and by the time we are adults, our breathing has generally moved from our diaphragms to our lungs. At mid-life we often breathe more in the throat area, and by the time we're elderly our breath has often moved to our mouths.

Because we are breathing higher and higher in our bodies as we age, we tend to bring less chi, oxygen, and other vital nutrients deep into our systems. This, in turn, decreases our metabolism. In addition, our various bodily fluids not only become less nutritious, but they also lose volume, while at the same time they no longer flow to all of the places they once did. Our skin becomes drier, our hair gets brittle and falls out, our muscles lose elasticity and strength, and our organs begin to deteriorate. Learning and practicing proper breathing will counteract these effects, thus slowing the aging process.

The first thing you have to do is to calm your mind by letting your thoughts slow down. One way to do this is to think peaceful ideas, such as imagining yourself relaxing on a beautiful tropical beach or remembering some happy event in your life. This will slow your heart rate and help you to relax your muscles. You must let all of your tensions go—physical, mental, and emotional.

Next, you want to breathe deeply, fully, and very softly. Slowly inhale through your nose, drawing the air smoothly into your lungs. Remember to relax. If you feel tension in your chest, you are breathing too hard. Imagine you are inhaling a delicate silk thread and if you breathe too harshly, quickly, or spasmodically, it will break.

Continue this breathing pattern. Concentrate on being slow, smooth, and controlled. Breathe in through your nose. Then breathe out through your nose. Relax.

Over time you will notice your respiration rate has dropped. This is the first step in harnessing more energy. Most people breathe at about seventeen breaths per minute. Ideally, you should try to lower your breathing rate one step at a time. For instance, if you feel comfortable attempting this, try breathing ten breaths per minute. When you can easily do that, try for eight breaths. Eventually try for six, four, and finally, maybe even two or one breaths per minute. Continue practicing taking longer breaths until one day you can breathe with only one breath or less per minute. You will find that the slower you breathe, the greater your chi power.

Keep practicing. It is relatively easy to breathe calmly when you are in an ideal environment. Once you get the hang of breathing properly, challenge yourself by trying it when you are under just a little bit of stress. For example, one place to practice breathing is while driving your car. Another time is when you are exercising or exerting a lot of physical energy. Sure, it will be hard at first and you will probably slip back into your old breathing pattern, but your persistence and concentration will pay off in time.

The Three Breathing Styles

Breathing properly is the single most important concept in Chi Gung. It enables you to increase or decrease the amount and flow of chi in your body. There are three main styles of breathing. These consist of natural breathing, Buddhist Breathing, and Taoist Reverse Breathing.

Natural Breathing

Natural breathing is used primarily by beginners as they initially learn the various exercises of Wai Dan.

Try this quick exercise now. Stand with your feet about shoulder width apart with your arms hanging loosely at your sides. Now, allow your body and mind to calm down and relax while you focus your thoughts exclusively on standing still. Maintain this position for four minutes.

Because I didn't tell you how to breathe during that exercise, I imagine you completed it by breathing in a natural pattern. That was the whole purpose of the exercise.

Basically, natural breathing is what happens when you concentrate on the movements or positions of the various exercises while not thinking about any particular breathing pattern. The reason you do this is so that when you first learn any given exercise, you can concentrate exclusively on the details of what you are supposed to be doing without adding too many extra details.

Buddhist Breathing

The next type of breathing is called Buddhist Breathing. This is a deep breathing style that coordinates your breathing with the movement of your diaphragm and stomach muscles. As you inhale, allow your stomach to push out, and as you exhale let your stomach muscles relax so that your belly goes back to its normal position. This pumping action of your stomach muscles activates your Dan Tien, the chi cavity that is located about an inch and a half below your belly button. With practice, the very action of moving your stomach in this manner will help your chi to collect there because the muscles are being lightly exercised. Once you have an abundant supply of chi gathered at your Dan Tien, you will learn how to move it through your body using an exercise called Small Circulation. (Small Circulation will be discussed in the next chapter, "Beginning Exercises.")

Taoist Reverse Breathing

The final main type of breathing is called Taoist Reverse Breathing. This style uses the opposite movements of Buddhist Breathing. Here, as you inhale, you pull in your stomach. Then as you exhale, you relax the muscles so that your belly can return to its normal position. Because this style uses the deliberate muscular contraction of the stomach muscles, it is more powerful than the other two types of breathing. This method of breathing is used primarily for moving chi strongly through your body to achieve particular results, such as increased muscular strength or the emission of energy from your body for healing, nonverbal communication, and energy transference.

As you inhale, pull in your stomach muscles as though you were trying to suck in your gut. This will move your diaphragm and allow the air to sink even further into your body. Now you need to relax your stomach muscles, which will then allow them to move out to their natural position. Do not push them out. Instead, relax and let them move by themselves. While your stomach muscles are returning to their natural position, start exhaling through your nose very slowly. You want your inhalation and your exhalation to be about the same length, or if possible, have your inhalation slightly longer.

Additional Breathing Techniques

As you progress in your training, especially as your start your Nei Dan training (moving chi mentally), you can utilize a variety of additional breathing techiniques. There are specific breathing techniques for specific training situations. Some styles of Chi Gung training utilize a technique called Breath-Holding Breathing. You need to be careful with this technique. It takes a lot of practice to increase your lung control so that you can practice this skill safely. When you hold your breath, your chi will collect in the spot where your mind is focused, so you want to make sure you do not concentrate on your head or you will build up too much chi there. This could make you dizzy and disoriented. Instead, keep your thoughts centered on your skin as well as the soles of your feet and the centers of the palms of your hands. This will help you to energize your body as long as possible. Some people use this style of breathing for some forms of healing, such as with broken bones. Personally, though, I've found that healing takes place much quicker and more efficiently, as well as in a safer manner, if you learn to circulate your chi instead of holding it in one place.

Breathing Through Focus Points

In addition to the three main types of breathing, there are three main locations to focus your mind on while breathing. These are the Dan Tien, the hands and feet, and the skin. When you first learn Chi Gung, you will spend most of your time concentrating your mind on your Dan Tien.

After you have learned Small Circulation and begun learning Grand Circulation, you can start Four-Point Breathing by focusing on your hands and feet. In the center of each palm and also in the center of the soles of the feet are very special chi cavities. These places are the main locations where you can learn to absorb and emit chi. Try gathering chi in your hands before you try it with your feet, because your hands are more sensitive. Hold your hands about an inch apart and use Taoist Reverse Breathing. As you inhale, move your hands a couple of inches farther apart and as you exhale, move them closer together. It is as though you were holding a tiny balloon that keeps expanding and contracting. With practice, you should feel heat build up as you exhale.

Once you can do this, try the same exercise with your feet. Sit on the floor barefoot. Bring the soles of your feet within an inch or so of each other. Now use Taoist Reverse Breathing as you slowly move your feet closer together and farther apart. It might take some time before you sense heat building up, but if you stick with it every day, you will eventually sense it.

Try doing these exercises for ten minutes every day until you feel the chi building up as a feeling of warmth. Once you can send chi from your palms and soles, you can try placing a sealed balloon filled with air between your feet or hands. As you exhale and send chi out of your palms or soles, try to feel it enter the balloon. If you are doing it right, you should feel the balloon get warmer and even expand. With lots of practice, it is possible to actually pop a balloon by sending chi into it.

After learning to send chi to your hands and feet, you can then learn how to send it to the skin over the rest of your body by using Skin Breathing. The first thing you need to do is become aware of your skin. One of the easiest ways to do this is to take a cool shower and then instead of drying off with a towel, practice Chi Gung breathing. Stand in the shower after turning off the water and use Buddhist Breathing. As you inhale, pay attention to the water that covers your skin from head to foot. When you inhale, you will most likely feel a cool sensation as the water is partially absorbed through your skin and into your body. Then, as you exhale, you will feel your body warm up slightly. Practice this exercise for a few minutes every day after you take a bath or shower.

After you have learned to evaporate water off your skin, you can try drying yourself even while it is raining. I drive a Jeep and frequently have the top off. I live near Seattle, charmingly known as "the City Underwater," because it rains so much in the Pacific Northwest. You can imagine how often I get to practice warming and drying myself as I drive.

Environmental Breathing

A very advanced form of breathing is Environmental Breathing. This is an advanced form of water evaporation training. With this type of breathing, you start out by imagining a large chi circle surrounding you as you breathe. As you inhale, the circle shrinks and as you exhale, it grows.

You might try thinking of this exercise, imagining you are inside a large balloon. As you train with this type of breathing, pay particular attention to any unusual chi feelings you might get. If you are standing next to a pine tree, point your palms toward the tree and as you inhale, imagine the tree's chi entering your body, then as you exhale, picture yourself sending chi to the tree. As you do this, move your palm so it no longer points at the tree and see if you feel anything different. With extensive practice, you will be able to sense the tree's chi. Once you have identified it, you can compare it to other types of trees or to anything else that happens to be near you. Eventually you should be able to form a chi categorization system so you can identify anything simply by what type of The Flowing—the energy—it emits.

The key to obtaining success in Chi Gung breathing is to eventually get to the point where you no longer think about breathing. By thinking about it, you put a slight amount of tension in your breath. Keep practicing until you can breathe properly. Interestingly enough, the more you practice, the more you will realize there are subtle little ways you can improve your breathing even more.

Beginning Exercises

You can read all the books, articles, and ancient tomes you want. You can watch the masters of Chi Gung as they practice. But in order to really learn this art, you have to actually do it yourself. In other words, you have to put in the time and effort.

Some of the first things you need to take into consideration before you begin your training include when and where you will train and what you should wear. You will also want to take into consideration such things as going to the bathroom before training so you won't have to stop. In addition, for about an hour both before and after training, you should not eat heavily, have sex, smoke, or drink alcohol.

When to Train

It is vital that you train every day for at least twenty minutes if you want to achieve any results. Of course you can train anytime you want to, but if you are really interested in obtaining maximum results from your efforts, then there are certain times throughout the day that offer optimal training. The best time to train is between 3 A.M. and 5 A.M. It is a wonderful time of the night because the air is full of yin chi, everything is quiet, and there are not a lot of distractions. (However, I haven't found too many students who are willing to train during this two-hour period.) Other excellent times for training are between 11 A.M. and 1 P.M. and also between 11 P.M. and 1 A.M.

Because most people work during the day, the easiest times to train will be in the early morning and later at night. If you train in the morning, face the rising sun. That way, you can absorb its energy. You will want to be careful when you do this, though, because as the sun rises higher, it is not safe to look at it because you could damage your eyes. Of course, you could always practice with your eyes shut. If nighttime is the time when you can train, then you will want to face south. That way, you can get the most out of the Earth's magnetic force.

In addition to the time of day, the days of the month also contribute to chi flow. Ideally, you should train every day, but you should make a special effort to concentrate on your training three days before, during, and three days after a full moon; this is a particularly strong yin time of the month and it yields tremendous amounts of energy.

Where to Train

If at all possible, try to train outside. Preferably, find some natural setting such as a field, a lake or river, beneath a tree, or a mountain. Mountains are great places because the air is better and there are usually fewer human-made distractions. If you can't find a mountain, another really good place to train is next to a pine tree, because it gives off tremendous amounts of oxygen and chi.

Sometimes it will not be possible to train outside, and you will have to settle for an indoor environment. When this is the case, you might want to avoid areas where there are fluorescent lights because they can create a wave interference that affects some people. In addition, you might want to practice as far away from all electric appliances so their energy won't bother your concentration. Even the hum of a refrigerator can be distracting.

What to Wear

It really doesn't matter what type of clothes you wear, particularly at the beginner level. As a general rule, it is best to practice in loose, comfortable clothes, preferably made of cotton or some other natural fiber. In addition, it is important you stay warm and out of the wind as you practice.

The Beginning of Your Journey

When you first start Chi Gung training, you probably will not feel anything. Therefore, you will have to use your imagination a lot, but stick with it. Eventually, you will begin to feel the chi. It might feel warm, cool, tingly, smooth, heavy, light, flowing, surging, or it may be like a color, sound, smell, or taste. More than likely, when you inhale, the chi will feel cool and while you exhale, it will feel warm. The thing to remember is that everybody is different physically, mentally, and spiritually. Your interpretation of chi will probably differ from someone else's. In fact, as you practice and become more skilled in this art, you will notice that even your own sensory awareness of chi changes with time. The main thing to understand is that whatever you sense now will probably seem rather small and weak. With time, it will grow bigger and stronger, until one day it will feel explosive. This is not only because your chi will have increased, but also because your awareness of it has developed.

What Does Chi Feel Like?

In order for you to do the exercises in this book, you first have to have some idea of what you are trying to achieve. After all, if you don't know what something is, you can't very well do it. One of the best ways to learn to sense chi is by following a simple, seven-step exercise that can actually show you what internal energy feels like when it travels through your body.

Chi Familiarization Exercise

Step 1.   Stand in a comfortable position with your legs slightly bent and your arms hanging loosely at your sides.

Step 2.   Next, determine if you are right-handed or left-handed, then raise your dominant arm to your side until it is level with your shoulders. Have your palm facing up (Figure 32, next page). Even though you're exerting muscular tension while you support your arm in the air, try to relax as much as possible, particularly the muscles in your shoulder, your arm, and your hand.

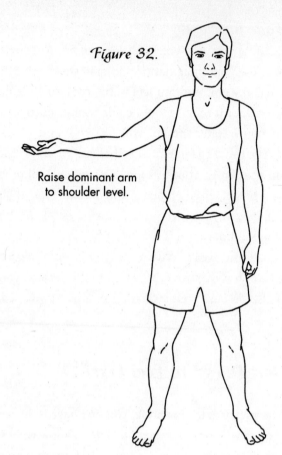

Figure 32.

Raise dominant arm
to shoulder level.

Step 3.   Place your tongue lightly against the center of the roof
of your mouth.

Step 4.   Inhale as slowly as you can through your nose, while
you pull in your stomach using your stomach muscles.
As you exhale as slowly as possible through your nose,
let your stomach muscles relax. Continue breathing in
this manner for the duration of the exercise.

Step 5.   Maintain this position for five minutes. More than
likely, your arm, particularly your shoulder, might get
tired and possibly start to hurt. Don't lower your arm
until the full time limit is up. This exercise not only lets
you feel what chi is like, it is also a beginning exercise
for training your mind to control your body.

Step 6.   After five minutes, slowly lower your arm to your side
and stand as relaxed as possible. Continue breathing as
slowly as possible, only now as you inhale, let your
stomach push out, and when you exhale let it return to
its natural position. It is important to keep your breath
rhythmic, slow, and as smooth as possible.

Step 7.   As your arm is beginning to relax while it hangs loosely
at your side, you will probably feel a massive surge of
blood, oxygen, and energy traveling down your arm and
into your hand. The sensation that you detect in your
arm will more than likely seem warm, tingly, or heavy.

I call this feeling of energy moving through your body The Flowing.
Essentially, your shoulder muscles were tense while they supported the
weight of your arm as it was held in the air. In addition, by having your palm
raised upwards, you also tightened some of the muscles in both your upper
and lower arm. When a muscle is tense, it constricts some of the blood vessels
and chi channels, thus restricting the flow of energy. When your arm is lowered, your muscles relax, and your blood vessels and chi channels fill with a
surge of new energy.

This unusual feeling of energy movement is what you will try to eventually
control at will, regardless of whether you are stationary or moving, or lying, sitting, or standing. As a beginner, you will concentrate your training on learning
how to maintain certain physical postures similar to the one you just tried.
These postures will help the chi to begin to flow more efficiently through your
body. As the chi begins to flow more freely, you will be able to sense it in your
major muscle groups, especially in your arms. At this level, as the chi flows naturally, it will help your body to maintain proper health. When you become an
intermediate-level practitioner, you will learn to direct your chi to move in
basic patterns by controlling it with your mind. As you gain experience, you
will probably begin to notice some of the distinctive patterns of chi. You
might, for instance, categorize it by speed, weight, density, movement pattern,
body location, temperature, quantity, texture, quality, effect, rhythm, color,
smell, sound, and taste. With lots of practice, you will reach the advanced level
where it is possible learn how to manipulate your chi and send The Flowing
instantly, anywhere in your body. Eventually, some people are able to learn to
send their chi from their own body into others or into the environment. It is
also possible to learn to absorb chi from anywhere or anything.

Warm-Up Exercises

This section contains a series of warm-up exercises that you should do every time prior to starting your Chi Gung exercises. You should do these exercises every day, regardless of whether you are pursuing Wai Dan or Nei Dan.

The first area of the body that should be warmed up is the muscles of the trunk—the stomach, chest, waist, and back. The main reason you want to start with the trunk first is because that is where most of your internal organs are located. If your trunk is stiff, then your organs will be affected; these, in turn will affect your chi.

Body Turning

Step 1. Stand in a comfortable position with your feet about shoulder width apart. Let your arms hang loosely at your sides.

Step 2. By rotating at the waist, slowly turn your upper body to the left as far as it will go (Figure 33), then to the right (Figure 34). When you do this exercise, try to look as far behind you as you can.

Step 3. Repeat this exercise until you have turned nine times in each direction.

Sideways Tilting

Step 1. Stand in a comfortable position with your feet about shoulder width apart. Let your arms hang loosely at your sides.

Step 2. Tilt your body sideways by bending at the waist. Move slowly and go as far as you comfortably can. First tilt to the right (Figure 35), then to the left (Figure 36).

Figure 33.

Slowly turn
upper body
to the left.

Rotate from
the waist.

Figure 34.

Slowly turn
upper body
to the right.

Figure 35.

Tilt body side-
ways to the right.

Figure 36.

Tilt body side-
ways to the left.

Step 3.　Repeat this exercise until you have tilted nine times to each side.

Forward and Backward Bending

Step 1.　Stand in a comfortable position with your feet about shoulder width apart. Let your arms hang loosely at your sides.

Step 2.　Slowly bend forward at the waist until your hands touch the floor in front of you, if possible (Figure 37).

Step 3.　Now straighten up you body, and bend backward at the waist so that you are looking at the sky (Figure 38).

Step 4.　Repeat this exercise until you have bent nine times both forward and backward.

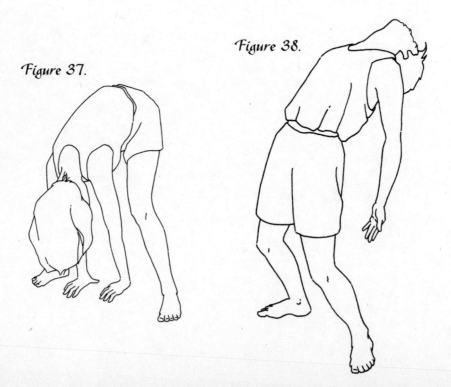

Figure 37.

Figure 38.

Neck Turning

The next area to loosen is your neck. You will be doing similar exercises to what you just did for your waist. By loosening your neck, you will increase the chi flow from your body to your head. This should help relax you as well as increase your overall health.

Step 1.   Stand in a comfortable position with your feet about shoulder width apart. Let your arms hang loosely at your sides.

Step 2.   Slowly turn your head as far to the left as it will go (Figure 39), then turn it to the right (Figure 40).

Step 3.   Repeat this exercise until you have turned nine times in each direction.

Figure 39.

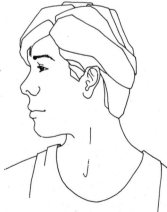

Figure 40.

Neck Tilting

Step 1.   Stand in a comfortable position with your feet about shoulder width apart. Let your arms hang loosely at your sides.

Step 2.   Tilt your head sideways until your ear gets as close to your shoulder as possible. First tilt to the right (Figure 41), then to the left (Figure 42).

Step 3.   Repeat this exercise until you have tilted nine times to each side.

Figure 41.

Figure 42.

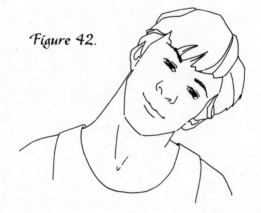

Nodding Your Head

Step 1.   Stand in a comfortable position with your feet about shoulder width apart. Let your arms hang loosely at your sides.

Step 2.   Slowly nod your head forward until your chin gets as close to your chest as it can (Figure 43).

Step 3.   Now straighten up you head and bend your neck backward so that you are looking at the sky (Figure 44).

Step 4.   Repeat this exercise until you have nodded your head nine times both forward and backward.

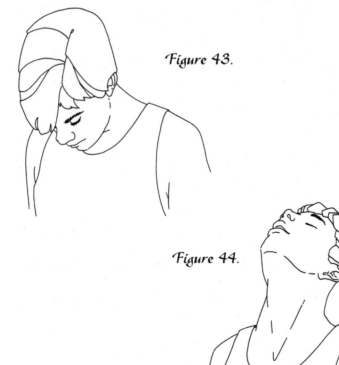

Figure 43.

Figure 44.

Now that you have warmed up your torso and neck, it is time to start loosening your arms. By warming up your arms, you are getting them ready to let chi actively flow through them. This is especially important because half of your meridians run through your arms.

Arm Circles

Step 1. Stand in a comfortable position with your feet about shoulder width apart. Let your arms hang loosely at your sides.

Step 2. Slowly swing your arms in large circles at your sides by moving them in a clockwise manner. Do this by first swinging your arms behind you, then up over your head, and finally down the front of your body (Figures 45, 46, 47).

Step 3. Next slowly swing your arms in large circles at your sides by moving them in a counterclockwise manner. Do this by first swinging your arms in front of your body, then up over your head, and finally down the back of your body.

Step 4. Repeat this exercise until you have swung your arms nine times both forward and backward.

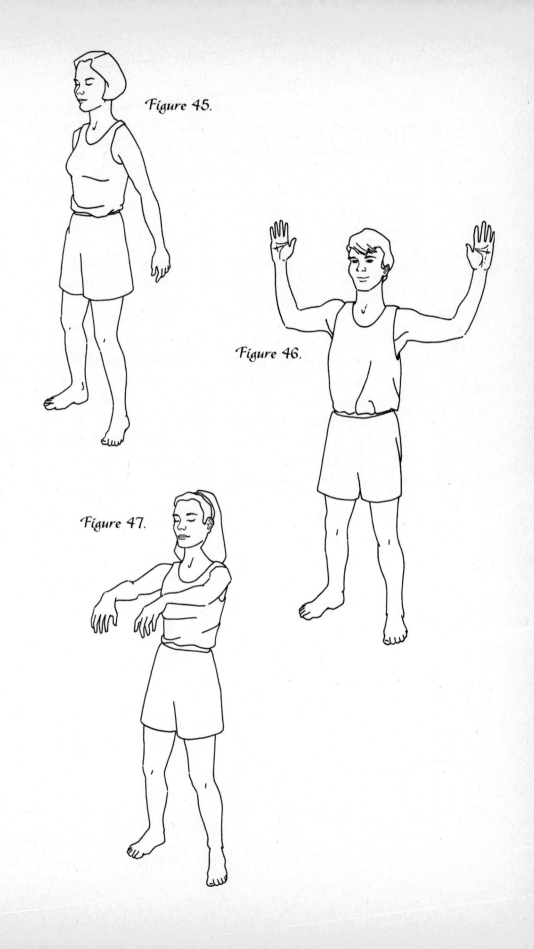

Figure 45.

Figure 46.

Figure 47.

Finally, you need to loosen up your legs. Warm-ups for your legs help your chi flow to the other half of your meridians. This is very important for the proper functioning of your organs.

Squats

Step 1. Stand in a comfortable position with your feet slightly wider than shoulder width apart. Let your arms hang loosely at your sides.

Step 2. Slowly lower your body by bending your knees until your thighs are parallel to the floor. To make sure you don't stress your knee joints, don't bend your knees more than ninety degrees (your knees should never extend beyond your toes). You may need to raise your arms to shoulder height to maintain your balance (Figure 48). After you have reached the full squat position, stand back up again.

Step 3. Repeat this exercise until you have squatted nine times.

Figure 48.

Leg Swings

Step 1.   Stand in a comfortable position with your feet slightly wider than shoulder width apart. Let your arms hang loosely at your sides.

Step 2.   Slowly raise one leg off of the floor and swing it forward (Figure 49), then backward (Figure 50) as far as you can. You may want to hold onto a chair or wall with one arm in order to help you balance.

Step 3.   Repeat this exercise with both legs until you have swung each leg nine times.

Figure 49.

Figure 50.

Lateral Leg Raises

Step 1.   Stand in a comfortable position with your feet slightly wider than shoulder width apart. Let your arms hang loosely at your sides.

Step 2.   Slowly raise your right leg off of the floor and lift it at your side as high as it will go (Figure 51). You may want to hold onto a chair or wall with one arm in order to help you balance.

Step 3.   Repeat this exercise with your left leg. Do this exercise nine times with each leg.

Figure 51.

At this point, your body should be warmed up. Now go ahead and start with the actual Chi Gung exercises.

How to Do Still Wai Dan Chi Gung

For the most part, before you begin Wai Dan training, you should read and practice the material covered in the section on the Three Regulations. This material is in the sections, "Regulating Your Body," "Regulating Your Breath," and "Regulating Your Mind." These three sections teach you how to relax and calm yourself. This state of mind and body is important because it will enable you to have a greater chance of sensing your chi.

Wai Dan means using your muscles to generate chi. When muscles are tense, the chi flow is partially cut off, so by holding your arms and legs in a variety of positions, you can build up a certain amount of pressure in any given appendage. Of the twelve meridians in your body, six of them begin at your fingers and go to your primary survival organs, including your heart and lungs. The other six begin at your toes and go mostly to your digestive and reproductive organs. Therefore, by exerting tension in your arms and legs, you can alter the chi flow in any of your organs. Whenever chi gets blocked in any of your meridians, the supply of energy is hindered. When it eventually does reach your organs, it is significantly less than it should be, and you could get sick. As you increase pressure, chi will eventually force its way through any blockage you may have had. These blockages are often caused by outside environmental factors such as food, weather, or stress. Your environment and how it relates to you is further discussed in the section called "What Are the Five Elements?" in the Three Regulations chapter.

There is, however, an exercise you can do right now. You can do it by following these six steps.

The Cormorant Spreads His Wings

Step 1.   Stand with your feet a little wider than shoulder width, and have your knees slightly bent.

Step 2.   Keep your elbows moderately bent and your wrists relaxed as you raise your arms at your sides until they are roughly even with your shoulders. Your elbows and fingers should point down (Figure 52, next page).

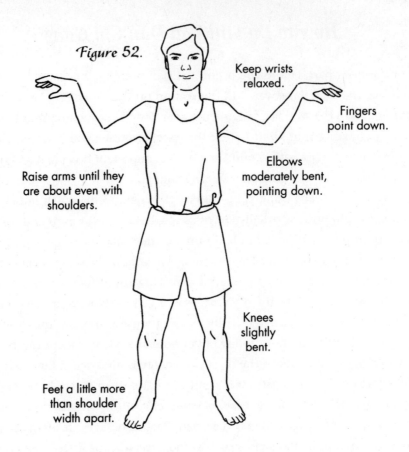

Figure 52.

Keep wrists relaxed.

Fingers point down.

Elbows moderately bent, pointing down.

Raise arms until they are about even with shoulders.

Knees slightly bent.

Feet a little more than shoulder width apart.

Step 3.   Breathe as slowly as possible through your nose using your normal breathing pattern. Also, keep your tongue lightly pressed against the center of the roof of your mouth.

Step 4.   While maintaining this stance, try to relax as much as possible. This may be somewhat difficult because your shoulders will be building up tension. Imagine it is dawn and you are a type of diving bird called a cormorant. You are standing on a fallen log overlooking a beautiful, still lake. In your mind, picture the rising sun gently warming your body, particularly your outstretched wings. Imagine your arms are covered in feathers; they are so light that even the slightest breeze causes them to gently move.

Step 5.   Hold this position for four minutes.

You should practice this position every day while trying to always hold the position for just a little longer each time. When you can maintain this position for twenty minutes, you are ready to move on to your first exercise set.

Exercises

Your first Still Wai Dan set is called "The Beautiful Flower Opens and Closes Her Petals." It consists of a series of six positions that are held for specific lengths of time based on your own breathing capabilities. In each of these initial positions, you should stand as comfortably as possible and be sure to breathe as slowly as possible through your nose. Even though you reduce the rate of your breath, try to breathe with a natural rhythm. Also, keep your tongue lightly pressed against the roof of your mouth. Practice this series of positions at least once a day, every day.

The Beautiful Flower Opens and Closes Her Petals

Position 1.   Keep your arms hanging loosely at your sides while you stand with your feet about shoulder width apart and your knees slightly bent. Try to stand in as relaxed a posture as you can. Hold this position as you breathe as slowly as possible for twenty-five inhalations and exhalations.

This is a warm-up position aimed at helping you to relax physically and mentally. Feel your tension leaving your body with each breath. Imagine you are a beautiful flower preparing to unfurl your petals in the morning sun. When you have completed the required number of breaths, slowly change to the next position.

Position 2.   Raise your arms to your sides until they are about shoulder height. Slightly bend your elbows and knees and have your wrists relaxed with your palms pointing down (Figure 53). Breathe as slowly as possible for sixteen breaths. You should feel some tension in the top part of your shoulders with this exercise.

This position keeps your arms relaxed while your shoulders exert muscular effort. The chi will start to collect in your shoulders. When you have completed the required number of breaths, slowly change to the next position.

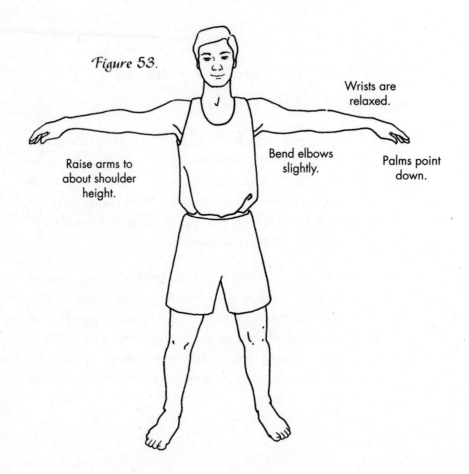

Figure 53.

Wrists are relaxed.

Raise arms to about shoulder height.

Bend elbows slightly.

Palms point down.

Position 3.   Maintain the same general pose as Position 2, only this time you turn your palms so they face up (Figure 54).

This position should put a little stress on your biceps while maintaining the tension on your shoulders. The purpose is to begin to get your chi to start to flow into your upper arms. Breathe as slowly as possible for twelve breaths. When you have completed the required number of breaths, go to the next position.

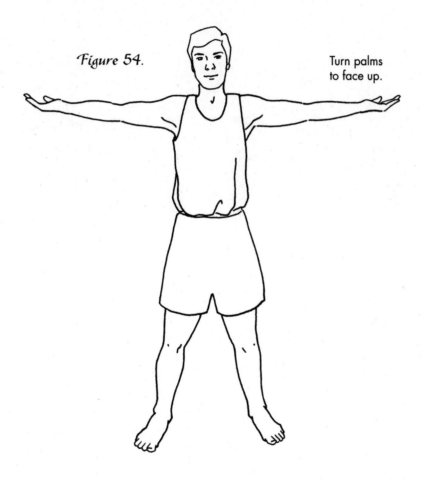

Figure 54.

Turn palms to face up.

Position 4.   Maintain the same general pose as Position 3, only this time you turn your palms so they face away from your sides as much as possible while your fingers are pointing toward the ground (Figure 55).

This position should put tension on your forearms so your chi will begin to collect there. Breathe as slowly as possible for nine breaths. When you have completed the required number of breaths, go to the next position.

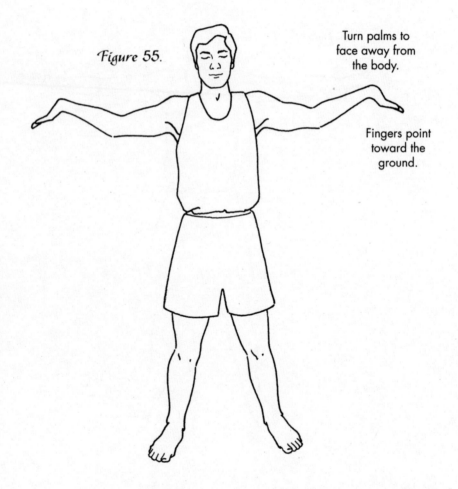

Figure 55.

Turn palms to face away from the body.

Fingers point toward the ground.

Position 5.   Maintain the same general pose as Position 4, only this time you should flair your fingers as wide as possible (Figure 56).

This position should put tension in your hands so your chi will gather there. Breathe as slowly as possible for four breaths. When you have completed the required number of breaths, go to the next position.

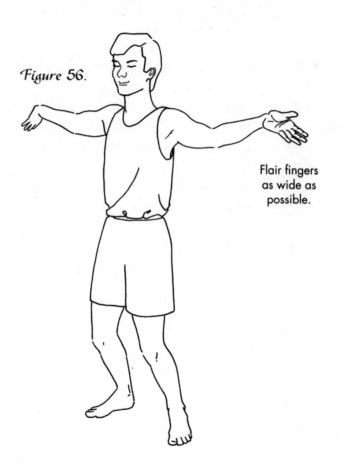

Figure 56.

Flair fingers as wide as possible.

Position 6.   This posture repeats Position 4.

Position 7.   This posture repeats Position 3.

Position 8.   This posture repeats Position 2.

Position 9.   This posture repeats the same general pose as Position 1 (see page 83). Lower your arms to your sides and let them relax as much as possible. Keep your legs slightly bent as you hold this position for twenty-five breaths.

This is a relaxation position, and at this point, you should focus your mind on your shoulders and upper back as the tension slowly disappears. You will probably feel a sense of warmth and possibly fullness progressing down your arms into your hands. When it gets there, your hands will most likely tingle as they fill with chi. When you finish the required number of breaths, you will have completed this series of exercises.

The total time for the exercise will vary depending on how long each of your inhalations and exhalations are, but for most beginners, it will probably take about twenty minutes. As you learn to slow your breathing even more, you can either shorten the number of breaths for any given position, or you could even choose one or two of the positions and try holding this limited number of positions for greater lengths of time.

As you practice this series of positions, try to feel the chi as it moves through your shoulders, arms, and hands. Continue this exercise for at least thirty days.

Moving Forward

After a month of daily training, it is time for you to switch your breathing pattern to Buddhist Breathing. This means you will now be starting basic Nei Dan training along with your Wai Dan exercises. Do the same series of positions you did for "The Beautiful Flower Opens and Closes Her Petals," except this time, as you inhale, let your stomach push out, and as you exhale, let it return back in to its normal position. Be sure to read the section called "Regulating Your Breath" so you have a greater understanding of this breathing method. Use the Buddhist Breathing method for the next thirty days.

At this point, it should be the beginning of your third month of training. Instead of using Buddhist Breathing, you should use Taoist Reverse Breathing. This is described in detail in the section called "Regulating Your Breath." Basically, Taoist Breathing involves pulling in your stomach as your inhale and letting it return out to its natural position as you exhale. This is the exact opposite of Buddhist Breathing. You should use the Taoist Breathing with "The Beautiful Flower Opens and Closes Her Petals" for an additional thirty days.

An additional posture you should use from now on for the rest of your Chi Gung training, as you progress from a beginner to a master, is called "Hugging a Tree." As a beginner, you will use this posture primarily as a Wai Dan pose by using your muscles to generate chi. As you advance and begin to understand the principles of Nei Dan, you can use this pose to combine both Wai Dan and Nei Dan training. You will do that by holding the posture while mentally directing your chi to flow to various spots in your body, such as your hands or your feet.

Hugging a Tree

Step 1.   Stand with your feet about shoulder width apart and have your knees slightly bent. As you advance in your training, you can bend your knees more until eventually your thighs are parallel to the ground. Always remember, though, to never extend your knees beyond the ends of your toes.

Step 2.   Hold your arms about level with your shoulders while having your palms about two feet in front of your chest. This position should look like you are hugging a tree (Figure 57, next page).

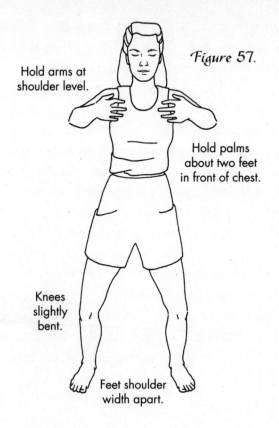

Hold arms at
shoulder level.

Figure 57.

Hold palms
about two feet
in front of chest.

Knees
slightly
bent.

Feet shoulder
width apart.

Step 3.   Use either Buddhist or Taoist Breathing as you breathe in and out through your nose and keep your tongue lightly pressed against the soft palate of your mouth. Remember to breathe as slowly as possible. You should try to increase the length of each of your breaths as often as you can. For example, if this week your normal inhalation and exhalation take ten seconds each, then the next week, try to make them last for eleven seconds each. Eventually, maybe you will be able to make each breath last a minute or longer.

Step 4.   Hold this position for as long as you can. Initially, you might only be able to hold it for a few minutes, but by practicing regularly, you will eventually build up enough strength to hold the position for twenty minutes per day.

After you gotten to the point where you can hold this position for twenty minutes, it will be time to start using Moving Wai Dan training.

How to Do Moving Wai Dan Chi Gung

Moving Wai Dan uses the same principles involved in Still Wai Dan, only with this variation you move your body and appendages in continuous, slow, controlled movements that are coordinated with your breathing.

The reason you began your Chi Gung training with Still Wai Dan is because you need to build up a supply of chi in your body. In addition, daily practice of Still Wai Dan exercises should help you build a basic foundation of muscular strength and coordination. In Moving Wai Dan, you need to move in as relaxed a manner as possible. The concept of relaxed movement is often difficult for beginners to grasp immediately because many approach Chi Gung having spent a good portion of their lives tensing muscles during movement. Also, slow, relaxed movement requires a great deal of concentration, which hopefully was built during Still Wai Dan practice.

The first position is called "Parting the Tall Grass." This exercise builds chi in your arms, shoulders, chest, and upper back. As you practice it, try to sense any warm or tingling feeling in your moving muscles. Be sure to move your arms as slowly as possible while coordinating them with your breathing. As you part the grass, exhale. As you bring your arms back toward your chest, inhale.

Parting the Tall Grass

Step 1.   Stand in a comfortable position with your feet about shoulder width apart and your knees slightly bent.

Step 2.   Slowly raise your left arm until your hand is even with your right shoulder (Figure 58, next page). Let your arm bend at the elbow, while keeping your palm facing away from your body, with your thumb pointing toward the ground. As you raise your arm, inhale using Taoist Reverse Breathing.

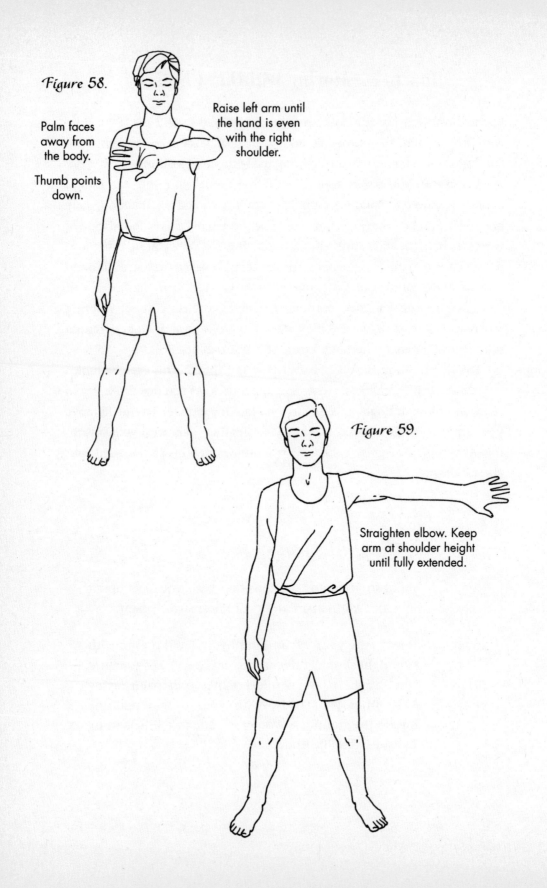

Figure 58.

Palm faces away from the body.

Thumb points down.

Raise left arm until the hand is even with the right shoulder.

Figure 59.

Straighten elbow. Keep arm at shoulder height until fully extended.

Step 3.   Imagine there is a bunch of head-high grass growing in front of you. You slowly push it out of the way by straightening your elbow, keeping your palm facing away from your body and your thumb pointing down. Keep your arm at shoulder height until it is fully extended (Figure 59). As you move your arm across your body, exhale.

Step 4.   Lower your left arm to your side so it hangs in a natural position.

Step 5.   Repeat this exercise with your right arm by raising your right hand to your left shoulder, then moving your arm to the right until it is extended. Then lower it.

Step 6.   Do this exercise twenty-five times with each arm.

Practice "Parting the Tall Grass" every day until you can definitely feel chi moving in your arms. It will probably make your arms feel warm, tingly, or heavy. Try to do this exercise for twenty minutes per session. If you finish the required number of repetitions in less than twenty minutes, then add a few more until the time limit is up. On the other hand, if it takes you more than twenty minutes to finish twenty-five repetitions with each arm, then you can stop for the day. With advanced practice, this exercise should eventually take you one minute to move either your right or left arm through the pattern once. Therefore, at the advanced level, you would do ten repetitions with each arm in twenty minutes.

Once you have felt The Flowing with the first exercise, it is time to move to the next exercise, "The Monkey Walks the Vine." This position will increase your coordination as well as the strength of your arms, shoulders, upper back, lower back, waist, stomach, and legs. It also will massage your internal organs, particularly your liver.

At this point, you might want to practice "Parting The Tall Grass" for sixteen minutes and "The Monkey Walks the Vine" for four minutes. As you gain experience with the new exercise, build up your time practicing it while simultaneously shortening your training time of "Parting the Tall Grass." For example, start out with sixteen minutes and four minutes, then do fourteen minutes and six, followed by twelve minutes and eight. Eventually do "The Monkey Walks the Vine" for the full twenty minutes.

The Monkey Walks the Vine

Step 1.   Stand with your feet about shoulder width apart and raise your arms in an arc over your head with your palms facing in (Figure 60).

Step 2.   Step forward with your right foot, placing it about a foot in front of you as though you were walking on a tightrope suspended hundreds of feet in the air. Each movement of your foot should be slow and deliberate. As you place your foot down, point your foot at about a forty-five-degree angle (Figure 61). Keep your legs slightly bent with each step you take. In addition, let your body naturally sway to the right by bending it at

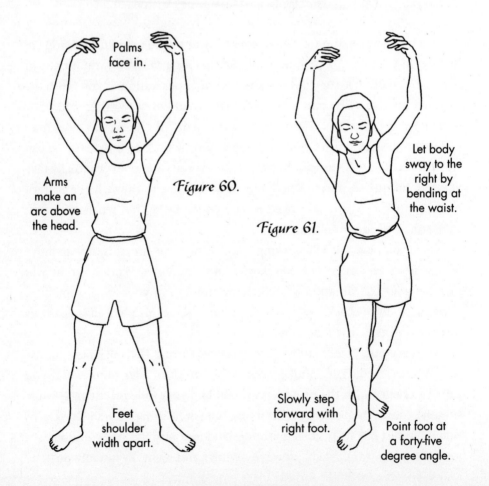

Palms face in.

Arms make an arc above the head.

Figure 60.

Figure 61.

Let body sway to the right by bending at the waist.

Feet shoulder width apart.

Slowly step forward with right foot.

Point foot at a forty-five degree angle.

the waist. As you step forward and sway your body to the right, exhale through your nose as slowly as possible using Taoist Reverse Breathing.

Step 3.   As you straighten your body to prepare to step forward with your left foot, inhale through your nose. Then, as you begin stepping forward with your left foot and your body starts to sway to the left, begin exhaling.

Step 4.   Now step forward with your left foot and place it directly in front of your right foot. Once again, move as slowly as possible. As you step, let your upper body sway to the left.

Step 5.   Continue walking like this for four minutes. If you run out of room, carefully turn yourself around, remembering to position your feet in such a manner that they would remain on the tightrope you are supposed to be walking. Remember to coordinate your breathing with your walking. As you step forward with either foot and your body starts swaying out, exhale. As you straighten your body and prepare for the next step, inhale.

Practice "The Monkey Walks the Vine" until you can eventually do it for twenty minutes.

After you have practiced "The Monkey Walks the Vine" and built up your leg strength, you can move to "The Monkey Picks Fruit." This is an extremely important exercise because it will build your leg strength as well as give you greater flexibility. Both are vital for proper chi flow in your legs.

The Monkey Picks Fruit

For all movements, move as slowly as possible and coordinate your movements with your breathing. As you extend an arm or a leg either up or away from your body, exhale using Taoist Reverse Breathing while also practicing the Three Regulations. As you lower an arm or leg, inhale.

Step 1.   Stand with your feet about shoulder width apart, your knees slightly bent, with your arms hanging loosely at your sides.

Step 2.   Raise your arms high over your head with your palms facing forward as though you were hanging from a branch (Figure 62).

Step 3.   Extend your right leg directly in front of you so your thigh is parallel to the ground (Figure 63).

Raise arms over head.

Palms face forward.

Figure 62.

Figure 63.

Extend right leg directly in front.

Thigh is parallel to ground.

Step 4.   Bend your right knee and bring your foot as close as possible to your left knee. Then lower your left arm until your hand is near your knee, and touch your left palm to the sole of your right foot (Figure 64).

Step 5.   Extend your right leg to the side until it is parallel to the ground (Figure 65).

Figure 64.

Figure 65.

Bend right knee

Touch left hand to sole of right foot.

Bring right foot to left knee.

Extend leg to right side until it is parallel to the ground.

Step 6.   Bend your right knee and bring your foot as close as possible to your left knee. Then lower your left arm until your hand is near your knee, and touch your left palm to the sole of your right foot.

Step 7.   Extend your right leg behind you and reach with your foot as far as you can (Figure 66).

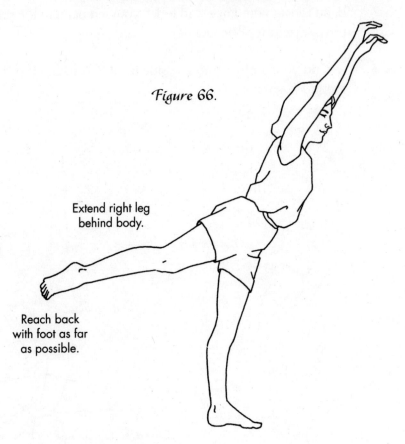

Figure 66.

Extend right leg behind body.

Reach back with foot as far as possible.

Step 8.   Bend your right knee and bring your foot as close as possible to your left knee. Then lower your left arm until your hand is near your knee, and touch your left palm to the sole of your right foot.

Step 9.   Switch legs, then repeat this entire exercise for a total of sixteen times with each leg.

You should practice "The Monkey Picks Fruit" until you can move your legs without any apparent effort and so they can flow as smoothly and softly as your arms. Try to imagine your legs are supported by huge balloons filled with air and the slightest breeze will affect their movement. At the advanced level, you should be able to hold your leg in any of the three extended positions for twenty minutes without having to lower it.

The next exercise is called "Looking at the Sky," and you can begin practicing it whenever you want. "Looking at the Sky" stretches your legs, shoulders, back, arms, and waist. It is a wonderful exercise to do first thing in the morning as you wake up.

Looking at the Sky

You will want to do this exercise very slowly so you don't get dizzy. If you start to feel light-headed, stop the exercise and stand in the step 1 position while focusing on your breathing.

Step 1.   Stand with your feet about a shoulder and a half width apart (Figure 67). Keep your knees slightly bent. Your arms should hang loosely at your sides. Inhale as slowly as possible through your nose.

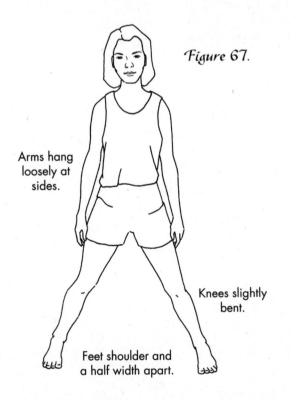

Figure 67.

Arms hang loosely at sides.

Knees slightly bent.

Feet shoulder and a half width apart.

Step 2.   As you exhale using Taoist Reverse Breathing, bend forward at your waist and try to touch your hands lightly
to the ground (Figure 68). If you can, let your hands
sweep between your legs so you are looking upside
down at the sky behind you.

Step 3.   As you inhale, slowly stand back up and swing both of
your arms wide to your sides. Continue your body's
movement by arching your back so your face and chest
point to the sky (Figure 69).

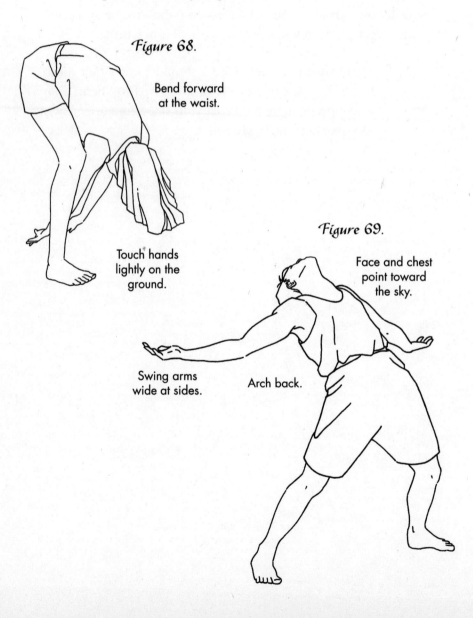

Figure 68.

Bend forward
at the waist.

Figure 69.

Touch hands
lightly on the
ground.

Face and chest
point toward
the sky.

Swing arms
wide at sides.

Arch back.

Step 4.   Inhale and straighten your body back up as you start to pull your arms in toward the center of your body. Then let yourself bend forward at the waist and repeat step 2.

Step 5.   Continue this exercise for sixteen breaths.

"Turning to Look at the Moon" is the next exercise. It involves turning your waist both left and right in order to exercise your waist, lower back, and spine. The twisting elements of this exercise also work your legs, arms, and neck.

Turning to Look at the Moon

Step 1.   Stand with your feet about shoulder width apart. Keep your knees slightly bent. Your arms should hang loosely at your sides. Inhale as slowly as possible through your nose using Buddhist Breathing.

Step 2.   Exhale as you raise your left hand to your right side so it is about a foot in front of your right shoulder (Figure 70, next page). As you raise your hand and arm, slowly pivot your body at the waist so you are turning toward the right.

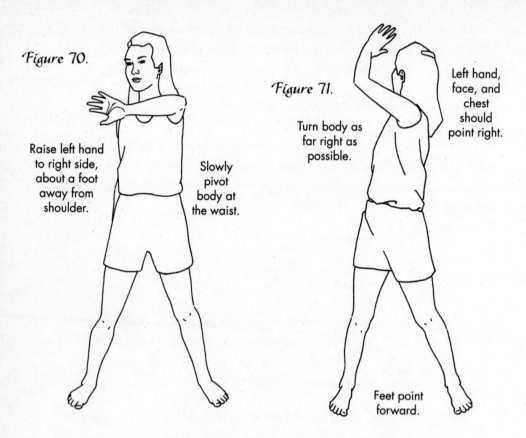

Figure 70.

Raise left hand to right side, about a foot away from shoulder.

Slowly pivot body at the waist.

Figure 71.

Turn body as far right as possible.

Left hand, face, and chest should point right.

Feet point forward.

Step 3.   Continue turning your body until you are looking as far behind you as you can. At this point, your feet and right hand should point in your original direction, and your face, chest, and left hand should point in the opposite direction (Figure 71).

Step 4.   Inhale as you slowly turn your waist and lower your arm, until you face forward once again as in step 1.

Step 5.   Exhale and repeat step 2, only this time raise your right arm and turn your body to your left.

Step 6.   Repeat this exercise twenty-five times.

Practice Moving Wai Dan Chi Gung every day. It will eventually teach you how to sense chi as you move in any kind of position. The ability to sense chi will then enable you to practice Chi Gung no matter where you are with whatever type of physical activity you happen to be doing.

How to Do Nei Dan Chi Gung

Nei Dan is one of the higher levels of Chi Gung practice. It is relatively difficult to understand and requires a lot of dedication to master. Though it can be learned from a book, this training is best undertaken with the aid of a master because he or she can direct the flow of chi for you, and you can better understand what is supposed to happen in any given exercise.

Nei Dan is a static, mental exercise in which you use your mind to direct the chi through your vessels and meridians. Before you undertake this training, you should first learn how to regulate your body, your breath, and your mind. I suggest you read those previous sections and practice them until you have an understanding of the basic principles of relaxation.

There are two different exercises that you will work on mastering when you do Nei Dan. The first one is called the **Small Circulation** or the Microcosmic Cycle, and it involves circulating your chi around your body and head without having it enter your arms and legs. Once you have mastered the Small Circulation, you can start practicing the **Grand Circulation**, also called the Heavenly Cycle. Grand Circulation teaches you to move the chi throughout your entire body along all twelve meridians and in all eight vessels.

Here is how Nei Dan works. The first thing you have to do is relax your mind, body, and breath while also controlling your emotions. In other words, you need to feel as calm, comfortable, and relaxed as possible.

If you are ready to try the exercises, put on some comfortable clothes and find a place where you won't be disturbed. If at all possible, you should do this training outdoors, but base your decision on the weather and your own physical constitution. If you practice indoors, you might want to buy a plant —maybe a small evergreen tree such as a juniper—and place it near your place of exercise. Bonsai trees work great for this (Figure 72, next page). Because plants give off oxygen, the tree will help you with your breathing as well as teach you lessons in the art of stillness. You can watch the tree to give you something to focus on while you train. Once you have found a place to sit,

Figure 72.

face east if you are training in the morning or the afternoon and south if you
are training at night. In the morning, you are aligning yourself with the rising sun as well as the Earth's natural rotation pattern. At night, you are aligning yourself with the Earth's magnetic field.

Try sitting comfortably on the floor with your legs crossed (Figure 73). If
you are a beginner, you may want to either place a folded blanket under the
back half of your buttocks to relieve some of the muscular strain of sitting
upright, or you could support your back against a pillow.

Figure 73.

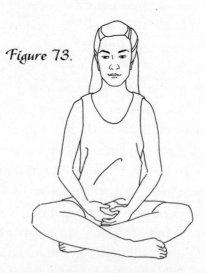

As a warm-up, merely sit still and breathe normally. Allow all of your muscles to relax as much as possible as your thoughts center exclusively on breathing. Let yourself relax deeper and deeper. After about four minutes, it is time to start the first exercise.

At this point, you should change your breathing style to Buddhist Breathing. As you inhale, allow your stomach muscles to expand so your belly pushes out. As you exhale, let your stomach return to its normal position. Continue breathing in this manner for twenty-five minutes. If you feel any tenseness in your chest as you breathe, you are using too much muscular force. If this is the case, relax and try to breathe slower, smoother, and lighter.

You will want to do the warm-up and the Buddhist Breathing exercise at least once, and preferably twice, every day until you feel a sense of warmth build up in your belly. For most people, this will take about 100 days of daily training. Some highly sensitive people will feel this warmth almost immediately and others will require even greater lengths of time. You must base your training on your own results.

You will know the chi has built up in your Dan Tien because of its distinct warm feeling. At this point, it will be time for you to try switching your breathing pattern to the Taoist Reverse Breathing method.

In this exercise, as you inhale, you should use your stomach muscles to pull in your belly—kind of like sucking in your gut. Then, as you exhale, let your stomach muscles relax and your belly should return to its normal position. Make sure you breathe through your nose while keeping your tongue lightly pressed against the roof of your mouth. Also, coordinate your breathing with your stomach movement. This method of breathing will enable you to build up a greater supply of energy than the Buddhist Breathing method. Practice the Taoist Reverse Breathing method until you are comfortable with doing it. Then, it will be time for you to learn how to circulate your chi.

Small Circulation Training

There are three main paths chi can take as it travels through your meridians during both the Small Circulation and Grand Circulation cycles. These are the Fire Path, the Wind Path, and the Water Path. The Fire Path is the first one you will work on developing.

There are twelve meridians and eight vessels in your body. The two vessels you will use for this exercise are the Conception Vessel and the Governing Vessel. The Conception Vessel runs down the front of your body and the Governing Vessel goes up your back (see page 33). The Fire Path leads chi from your Dan Tien, down the front of your body to the Huiyin Cavity, which is located between your legs and just in front of your anus. The path continues to your tailbone and up your spine to your head. It then goes over the top of your head, down your face, and back down the front to your body to its starting place at the Dan Tien. This is the path chi naturally takes, and in a healthy person, it normally completes this cycle once every twelve hours.

The Fire Path

In order to move chi through your Fire Path, you will first have to build up a supply of energy by practicing the previous exercises in this section. Once you have done that, you can begin this training.

The first thing you will want to do is to use Taoist Reverse Breathing. Then, as your mind is focused on your Dan Tien, you will lift up your anus. The way to do this is by imagining that you are trying to stop urinating. When you do that, you will feel a slight muscular contraction near your urinary duct. Because most people seldom practice this exercise, the Huiyin Cavity is probably the hardest spot to get your chi to travel through. As you tighten your muscles to stop the imaginary flow of urine, the muscles around your Huiyin Cavity will relax, which will enable the chi to move through the area.

Next, you need to visualize your chi traveling up your back. At first this will be primarily an exercise in imagination, but if you practice consistently, you will eventually feel a sense of warmth moving up your back. As the chi gets to your upper back, make sure your shoulders and back muscles are as relaxed as possible. Following this, the chi will travel up the back side of your head, and it will either feel like warmth or a tingling sensation. The chi will then continue over the top of your head and flow down your face. This may give you a flushed feeling around your nose and by the time the chi gets near your mouth, your lips may tingle. From here, the chi will flow down your chest and back to your Dan Tien.

When you do this exercise, you will need to coordinate your breathing with your visualization of where the chi is in your body. As you inhale, imagine the chi flowing down the front of your body toward your Huiyin Cavity and as you exhale, imagine it flowing from your Huiyin Cavity up your back as it follows the Governing Vessel.

Continue practicing this exercise using visualization until you can definitely feel the chi moving as a sense of warmth or tingling. When you can feel this sensation travel through both the Conception Vessel and the Governing Vessel, you will have then completed Small Circulation training.

The Wind Path

Once you have completed Small Circulation using the Fire Path, it is time to try it using the Wind Path. Here, you follow the same principles you have been practicing with the Water Path, only this time, instead of running the chi down the front of your body and then up your back, you reverse the procedure. You start by inhaling and having the chi flow up over your head, down your back, and then to your Huiyin Cavity. Then as you exhale, it moves from your Huiyin Cavity, to your Dan Tien, up past your belly and chest, and back to your head. The basic reason for learning to direct your chi in this reverse pattern is so you can make it more yin. In other words, it enables you to learn to balance and harmonize your internal system better.

The Water Path

Keep practicing the Wind Path until you can circulate your chi that way. Then, it is time to start learning about the Water Path. The Water Path is an extremely advanced method of Nei Dan Chi Gung requiring intense practice. This method involves learning to circulate your chi in the same direction it traveled on the Fire Path, but this time, as it travels up your back, it does so from inside of the spinal column instead of merely next to it. In order to do this, you will have to learn to get chi to permeate your bones. These exercises consist of a combination of visualization, muscular tension, massage, and even beating training.

Grand Circulation

When you have learned how to direct your chi along these three paths—Fire, Wind, and Water—you can then learn how to send it out into your limbs. The key here is to use your imagination because where your mind leads, your chi will follow. Learning to move chi throughout your body is called Grand Circulation.

In Grand Circulation training, you start out the same way you did with Small Circulation. Begin using the Fire Path only this time, after the chi reaches your shoulders, concentrate on sending it down into your arms and then to a spot in the center of your palms.

You will probably find that it is easier to move the chi in your arms than your legs. That is because it is harder for most people to learn how to fully relax their leg muscles. The best way to learn to relax any muscle is by tensing it, then letting it relax naturally. Eventually, you will learn what any given muscle feels like when it is relaxed, and you won't have to reach that state by first tightening the fibers. Practice—it will come.

After you have learned Grand Circulation and know how to move your chi throughout your body at will, you should try increasing your centering and balancing skills. The way to do this is by sending your chi into your feet or even deep into the ground. For instance, find the limits of your balance as you lean forward. Now, as you teeter on the brink of falling, send your chi from your arms and body into your feet. You should notice that this will make you feel lighter from the waist up, which will enable you to lean a little farther than you were able to just a moment ago.

Further Chi Training

When you have reached the point where you can do both the Small Circulation and the Grand Circulation, then it will be time to learn how to move your chi anywhere in your body, at will, immediately. This takes lots of practice. Remember, imagination, creativity, sensory awareness, and relaxation are the keys.

Initially, you should move your chi along the body's meridians. You do this by allowing it to travel in more or less straight lines from one point to another. Once you can do that, you can add a little control. For example, after you can do Grand Circulation, try moving the chi to your arm, then spiral it around clockwise as well as counterclockwise. You can also try varying its speed by moving it both quickly and slowly.

Next you might want to try absorbing chi while you exhale. This is probably going to be a difficult exercise, because you normally would absorb chi while inhaling. One of the easiest ways to learn to do this exercise is by first focusing your mind simultaneously on both of your arms. Next, inhale and imagine chi entering your left palm. As you exhale, let it exit your right palm. This will set up a pattern of chi flow. After a few minutes, as you project chi out of your right hand while exhaling, imagine it is also entering your left palm at the same time. It is as though your hands are in a river with one pointing upstream and the other pointing downstream and the water is flowing in one hand and out the other.

The next step is learning to move your chi without breathing. You see, all of these concepts are training tools that build on each other, but as with any skill, you can eventually put away the individual techniques and concentrate on the smooth flow of a finished product.

This is how Chi Gung embraces all other esoteric energy systems. On a basic level, each system seems dramatically different. For example, a Santero mayor from Cuba might make a clay head with cowrie shell eyes, ears, mouth, and nose, and set it on a white handkerchief with a cigar and a jug of rum in order to raise energy. Likewise, a Jivaro shaman from Brazil might dream about finding and relocating a jaguar that has been terrorizing his village. A Hawaiian kahuna might pray while holding a specially carved stick in his hand before tossing it at an enemy. Each system uses different methods of raising energy, then doing something with it. Ultimately, they are all doing the same thing. That is why advanced Chi Gung offers a way to embrace any energy system, and also why Chi Gung offers more of a complete system than most magickal traditions. You see, most systems require some sort of specialized ritualistic tool in order to work. Even Chi Gung does, at a simplistic level. (Essentially, that is what the various breathing patterns help you with.) However, as you advance, you can dispense with the special breathing and focus instead on specifically moving chi.

Warm-Down Exercises

After you have finished your Chi Gung training for any given session, it is important that you do some warm-down exercises. These are intended to help your chi regulate itself in your body, as well as to bring some of the chi you have collected in the various Wai Dan or Nei Dan exercises and spread it to some additional locations.

Eye Palming

Sit down, rub your hands together briskly, then lightly cover your eyes with your palms. As you inhale using Buddhist Breathing, feel the warmth flow into your eyes.

Head Tapping

While using Buddhist Breathing, lightly tap your fingers all over your scalp.

Teeth Clicking

Slowly open and close your mouth as you very lightly click your teeth together twenty-five times. As you do this, keep your mouth as relaxed as possible.

Face and Scalp Rubbing

Gently rub your hands over your face, making sure you massage your nose, cheeks, ears, and all over the top, sides, and back of your head. Do this for about one minute.

Neck Rotations

Slowly rotate your head in circles by gently turning your neck. Do this nine times clockwise and nine times counterclockwise.

Joint Rubbing

Using your palms, gently rub the joints of your wrists, elbows, shoulders, neck, hips, knees, and ankles. Rub each joint nine times.

Palm and Sole Massaging

Take your left index finger and lightly rub the center of your right palm in concentric circles (Figure 74). Then use your right index finger to rub your left palm. Next, rub the center of the soles of your feet with your index fingers (Figure 75). Massage each of your palms and soles nine times.

Kidney Massage

Make your hands into fists and rub the sides of your lower back where your kidneys are located (Figure 76). Do this nine times.

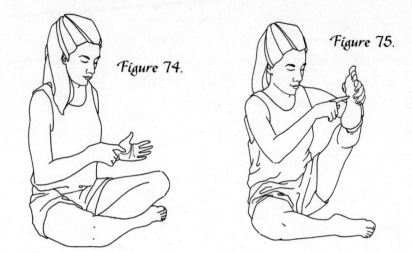

Figure 74.

Figure 75.

Figure 76.

At this point, you should be properly warmed down. Now there is just one more exercise for you to do. While lying on your back (Figure 77), notice any feelings of energy that you have flowing through your body. Don't try to control them or change them in any way, just make yourself aware of The Flowing. After about a minute, slowly stand up. At this point, you are done warming down.

Figure 77.

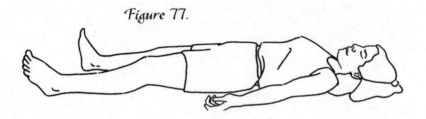

PART
TWO

Physical Training

*P*hysical training involves learning a variety of skills to develop and use your body. At a beginning level, these skills are typically Wai Dan oriented, but as you progress in skill, any of them can be done using the principles of Nei Dan.

Walking Barefoot

We often get so caught up in the artificial lives that we have created for ourselves with modern society, we fail to stay in touch with our biological nature. We live in controlled environments, eat unnatural food, and wear human-made clothes. One way to get back to our roots is by walking barefoot as much as possible. In order to get as much out of this training as you can, you should try walking on carpet, wooden floors, grass, rocks, mud puddles, and even snow. The more surfaces you expose your feet to, the better this exercise will be for you.

The first thing you need to do is spend some time every day walking around barefoot. This will not only increase the tactile sensitivity of your feet, but it will also act as a sort of Wai Dan exercise. Walking barefoot will stimulate the various muscles of your feet because of the greater range of motion it gives you.

Taking off your shoes, even for a few moments, is a great way to build your energy. Picture yourself at work. You are tired, stressed, and fed up with the system. It is break time and you figure that a little energy could do wonders right about now, so you slip off your shoes and socks. You start walking around barefoot for a few minutes. While you relax your mind and temporarily forget your problems, you gather some chi in your feet by the act of moving your soles and toes in a variety of positions. As you practice the Three Regulations, you focus your mind on your relaxing feet. Soon your break is over, only now you are revitalized and ready for anything.

Here is one thing you might want to try. Buy some bamboo and cut it into foot-long sections. Scatter these on the ground, then walk over them, letting them massage your foot muscles with each step. You will probably find that this exercise causes your feet to sweat as they collect chi in order to deal with the strain of this workout.

Once you can feel your soles sweating, you will know you have energized your feet. This sweating sensation is very common no matter where your chi gathers, especially when you are a beginning and intermediate student. When you notice The Flowing in your feet, it is time to try barefoot chi walking. Take off your shoes and socks and go outside for a walk. Sense the ground against your feet and relish the feeling. Let your mind dance with new sensations. As you walk around, keep your mind focused on your soles. Use Taoist Reverse Breathing while inhaling and walking as far as possible, then exhaling and seeing how many steps you can take. This is an extremely refreshing way to relax and gain energy.

After you have learned Grand Circulation you will be able to direct chi to your feet by using your mind. There are spots located in the centers of your soles near the arches of your feet called the Yong Quan. These spots, along with the center of each palm, are the four main areas through which you can send and receive energy with relative ease by using Nei Dan. Of the five chi spots, the soles are the most difficult to access simply because most people are out of touch with their feet and legs due to lack of exercise and flexibility. On the other hand, the soles offer you direct access to Earth chi, which is soothing and healing.

To practice Nei Dan barefoot walking, picture your soles as being able to breathe. Inhale slowly using Taoist Reverse Breathing, imagining energy flowing directly into your soles, then up your legs to your Dan Tien. Now try exhaling and imagining the energy flowing out of your Dan Tien and down your legs. From there the chi goes into your feet and out of your soles into the ground. When you can do this, you will be able to quickly energize yourself no matter where you are.

Not only can walking barefoot help to build your chi using both Wai Dan and Nei Dan exercises, but it can also help to prevent a variety of diseases and disorders. You see, with each step, your feet are being massaged by the ground you tread. The more uneven and rough the ground, the better it is for your feet. As you are probably aware, you have nerves running throughout your body. These nerves intermingle with your meridians in a variety of patterns. Therefore, while your feet are being stimulated by the environment, your chi is being directed throughout your body to at least half of your organs. This method of foot manipulation follows the same principles as foot reflexology. With that method of healing, a therapist is required to manually massage your feet. By walking barefoot, you are massaging your own feet whenever you feel the need.

Swimming Underwater

Swimming underwater is an excellent way to increase your chi. You have to learn to hold your breath. By continually practicing this, you will gradually increase the time you can stay underwater until eventually you might be able to stay under for up to eight minutes. By learning to absorb oxygen and chi from the water, you can stay under longer than that and, by exposing your hand, foot, or any body part for that matter above the water's surface and properly absorbing chi from the air, you could increase the time even more.

The first thing you have to learn is breath control. This means you need to review the Three Regulations and make sure you really understand how to relax your mind, body, and breath. Before plunging beneath the water's surface, slowly and gently inhale through your nose using Buddhist Breathing. Keep your tongue pressed lightly against the roof of your mouth. After you have filled about three-quarters of your lung capacity, lower yourself beneath the water. As soon as you start to feel even slightly uncomfortable, resurface. Don't try too hard. This is a skill that takes quite a while to develop, so you need to be very careful. It is best to do this exercise only when someone is with you who is capable of lending assistance if you need any help.

With practice, you will gradually increase the time you can hold your breath. Eventually, you will hit a plateau where is seems like you just can't progress any further. This is perfectly natural. For many people, this will be around thirty to forty-five seconds. Whether your plateau is longer or shorter than this is not important. You are only working with what you can do. It doesn't matter what anyone else can do. Everyone is unique and has his or her own abilities. There really is no such thing as comparisons simply because there are too many variables.

After you have progressed about as far as you can with this exercise, it is time to start to learn to take chi from the water. First, however, you have to convince yourself that chi can actually travel through water. If your mind believes, your body will believe. Try standing in a pool or lake in shoulder-deep water. Inhale slowly, using Taoist Reverse Breathing and concentrate on sending chi to the palms of your hands and the soles of your feet. If you can't do this using Nei Dan, try this Wai Dan technique. As you stand in the water, submerged to your shoulders, keep your fingers and toes clenched. This will help direct your chi there. If you are properly relaxed, you will probably notice tiny bubbles released from your hands and feet. These bubbles will float up your arms and legs to the water's surface. You might not see them, but they will probably tickle your skin as they rise.

Water also offers a way for you to learn to completely relax your muscles. While in the water, practice the Three Regulations, then really focus on relaxing your shoulders and arms. Next, clench your fingers in order to collect some Chi in your hands. After a few minutes of breathing using Taoist Reverse Breathing, your arms should slowly float to the surface of the water as they fill with chi (provided you have relaxed properly). You can also try this with your legs. Clench your toes to build up chi, then focus your mind on relaxing your hips and legs. If you relax completely, your leg should rise.

Practice being underwater as much as possible, even if it is only in your bathtub. The important thing to remember with this exercise is to relax completely and not try too hard. Progress will probably seem very slow compared with some of the other training techniques. Keep practicing, and you will find that swimming underwater greatly increases your breathing and relaxation skills.

Massaging With Chi

Massage is one of the easiest ways to open your chi channels so that your energy can flow freely. It is also a way for you to help heal yourself, or others.

In addition, massage is something that is rather natural to all of us. Have you ever bumped, banged, or bruised yourself? More than likely the first thing you did in such a situation was to vocally express feelings. The second thing was to grab the sore spot and start rubbing. By crying out, you automatically raised your level of chi. Then, when you rubbed the bruise, you dispersed any stagnant blood and chi, thereby starting the healing process.

Massage can be used for a number of different purposes. It can help to relieve mental and physical tension, distribute stagnant chi, heal broken bones, and aid in the recovery from disease. You can massage yourself and others, as well as plants and animals. When you are massaging, be sure to use a variety of different tools. You might want to try using your fingers, knuckles, palms, sides of your hands, forearms, and feet. Each of these can penetrate the muscles in a unique way, thus changing the massage slightly. It is important for you to experiment with each of these methods in order to determine how they affect you.

Your fingers make excellent massage tools. Because you use them every day, they give you the greatest degree of control. You can rub softly or hard, shallow or deep. Knuckles can be used when you have to apply a lot of pressure deep within a muscle. Often your fingers will not have the strength or endurance for such deep penetration.

The palms are one of the best massage tools because they offer the easiest way to send chi into a muscle. The simplest way to build chi in your palms is by rapidly rubbing them together until they feel warm. You can then massage with your hands until they cool down. You can also increase your chi by tightening your hand muscles or by mentally directing chi to them using Nei Dan.

If you have a spot that needs a relatively long and deep massage, you might try the outside edge of your hand. This gives you a narrow but strong tool for deep penetration. Using your forearms offers a soft rolling motion that is ideal for massaging extremely sore spots.

You can also massage with your feet. They offer advantages similar to those of your palms, because the center of the soles of the feet also act as powerful transmitters of chi. It is a little harder for most people to massage using their feet because most people have not taken the time to build up as much coordination with their legs as they have with their arms. The legs, however, are much stronger than the arms, and therefore you can send the chi deeper into someone's body.

Once you have picked the tool to use during the massage, there is a variety of techniques you can use. Try caressing, chopping, flicking, grabbing, lifting, pressing, pulling, pushing, rubbing, scratching, shaking, slapping, swinging, tapping, and vibrating.

Caressing is a light, graceful dance of your fingers or hands as they glide over the skin. It helps to smoothly move the chi along the meridians.

Chopping uses the sides of the hands to rapidly chop against the muscles. It sends Chi deeply into the body.

Flicking is when you create tension between one of your fingers and your thumb, then allow the finger to snap against the skin. This method raises chi in a small, specific location, generally on an acupressure point along one of your meridians. It also can be used to send chi to the skin in order to improve its tone.

Grabbing involves lightly squeezing the skin and muscle and gently squeezing. A firm steady pressure is used to send chi from your palm into the muscle as you exhale. As you inhale, relax your grip. When you use this method, you generally grab the acupressure points on the body.

Lifting is used to gently loosen large parts of the body such as the legs, arms, and waist. Grab these parts and slowly lift them into the air. This method is usually used before many of the other techniques. This is particularly useful for damaged areas of the body because if coaxes chi into the area.

Pressing usually involves using your hands. You press down into the muscles with a steady, even pressure as you exhale. Pressing is used primarily to penetrate shallow or moderate depths.

Pulling is usually done to the arms and legs in order to straighten the muscles, ligaments, and bones. It involves a steady, even pressure. As the limbs are pulled, they stretch, which helps the chi to flow smoothly.

Pushing involves pressing against a muscle to help move chi along its length. Use the palm of your hand to press into the muscle, then smoothly slide your hand along the grain of the muscle.

Rubbing is the most common technique. You can use any of your massage tools to rub the surface of the skin, but you would generally use your hand. When you rub with your hand, make sure the motion is soft and relaxed. This method does not usually penetrate too deeply, so it is often used for tender areas or sore bruises. It is also a method to lightly direct chi throughout the body. Rub in a circular motion and try to gently move the muscle beneath the skin.

Scratching uses the fingers and fingernails to gently brush the skin. It is generally used on the head to lightly generate chi in the scalp.

Shaking is a slow steady movement of a muscle in order to gently raise the chi.

Slapping uses the hand to slap the skin. This raises the chi to the surface of the skin so it can then be spread by pushing.

Swinging is holding onto an arm or leg or any other appendage and allowing it to slowly move back and forth. This method is used to determine how relaxed a muscle is. If you can push an arm or a leg and it swings freely, then it is relaxed. This is a very gentle way to send chi into the appendages.

Tapping uses your fingers to gently, yet rapidly press on the acupressure points. This is most often used on the top of the head in order to raise your chi and make you more alert.

Vibrating is a quick, back and forth shaking kind of movement. This method is used to quickly generate chi in a muscle.

When you massage with chi, relax yourself first. Focus your mind. Breathe. Let the air sink deep into your belly as you begin to circulate your energy. Imagine your chi flowing into whatever tool you are using for the massage—your hand, foot, arm—and picture it spreading into the massaged area. You will probably feel heat build up and possibly a tingling or tickling sensation. Start in a small, localized spot and gradually move the chi over larger areas. Pull it from the head toward the feet and from the center of the body to the extremities.

You can give yourself a massage or you can massage someone else. The tools and the techniques are the same. It is a little easier to massage someone else or to have someone massage you than it is to massage yourself. That is because if someone is massaging you, you will probably find it is quicker and easier to relax. When you massage yourself, there will be certain areas that are difficult to reach, such as the shoulders, neck, and back, and you can't totally relax because you have to at least use some of your muscles in order to massage yourself. There are, however, areas you can easily massage on yourself, including your feet, legs, hands, arms, stomach, chest, face, and scalp. Massaging these areas offers a viable solution when someone else is not available to do it for you.

Massage is a basic Wai Dan method of self-healing. Once you learn Nei Dan and Grand Circulation, you will be able to massage yourself with chi without actually having to use your muscles as tools. You do this by practicing the Three Regulations, then using Buddhist Breathing. Use your mind to direct your chi wherever you want the massage to occur. Then, picture your chi moving in a variety of patterns as it gently massages your muscles.

The purpose of learning how to massage with chi is to learn to increase the circulation of the chi, blood, and oxygen that is in your body or someone else's, thereby increasing health. Therefore, it is something you should try to do as often as possible.

Whirling

Whirling is a way to learn to focus your mind and coordinate it with your body. Whirling is nothing more than repeatedly turning yourself around in circles (Figure 78). Most of us have done it at one time or another in our lives, most likely when we were children. In fact, children are often better at this skill than adults because they not only have fewer preconceived ideas, but they have a greater tendency to experience the moment. Their minds are focused on what is happening at the time instead of on something else. As adults, we take a greater amount of time to reach this state, and whirling disorients us. After all, when was the last time you dared to ride on the Tilt-A-Whirl or a merry-go-round?

The main reason you get dizzy as you whirl is because you keep your mind too active. In other words, you are thinking about too many things. Even the fear of vomiting can make you dizzy, because your fear will hinder your chi flow. In order to excel at whirling, you need to calm your mind and let yourself move without thinking about it.

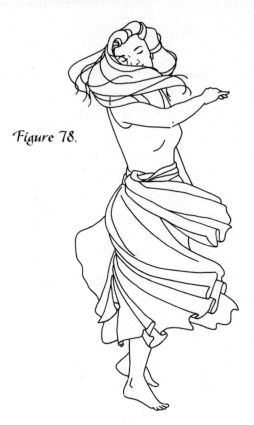

Figure 78.

As a safety precaution, I suggest you don't eat or drink for at least a couple of hours before trying this. Once you start whirling, keep your eyes unfocused. If you watch the world turn around you as you spin, you will probably become dizzy very quickly.

Don't practice whirling too often, and don't do too much at any given time. You will have to be your own judge as to how much you can do. Not only can whirling teach you how to center yourself, but it also helps build your intuition by giving you a sense of how long you can spin at any given time.

The way that whirling opens your mind to new ways of thinking and perception is by offering a method of focusing your mind so you can eliminate excessive mental chatter. If your mind is too active, you will know it right away because you will fall. Only by learning to control your ability to concentrate can you whirl for longer periods of time.

Whirling offers you a way to gain greater control over your mind. This degree of control acts as a stepping stone toward increasing your skills at Nei Dan Chi Gung. It does this by helping you develop concentration and sensory awareness, and by creating a link between physical action and mental control.

Zhan Zhuang

Zhan Zhuang (pronounced *jan jong*) is one of the most demanding forms of exercise you can do. On the surface, it seems so simple. Too simple, in fact. Once you begin practicing, you will learn how challenging it really is. Zhan Zhuang is a way to learn to relax your mind, your muscles, and even your spirit. In addition, it can help you to develop incredible internal strength and power and it can also teach you unlimited lessons about yourself.

By definition, Zhan Zhuang means to stand like a tree. It is both a Wai Dan and a Nei Dan form of exercise. Essentially, you stand still, with your legs slightly bent, and your arms raised like tree branches. Without moving, you hold your position for as long as you can. Initially, you might only be able to hold a position for a minute or two. Eventually, you should strive for remaining in position for twenty minutes. With extensive practice, an hour or two is not unrealistic.

There are numerous postures that are common in this form of energy development but I have found almost any position will work. Ideally, you should start out with your arms hanging naturally by your sides while standing with your feet about shoulder width apart and your knees slightly bent. As you gain experience, you can slowly raise your arms to higher starting positions. With time, you might raise them directly over your head. You can do the same thing with your legs. Start out standing evenly on both legs. Then practice holding one leg slightly above the ground as you maintain your balance on the supporting leg.

Here are some different positions you can try. Pick any one of these positions and hold it as long as possible. Practice a different position each day.

Position 1.   Stand with your feet about shoulder width apart and your knees slightly bent. Let your arms hang naturally at your sides (Figure 79).

Position 2.   Stand with your feet about shoulder width apart and your knees slightly bent. Raise your arms slightly until your hands are about a foot in front of your belly button (Figure 80).

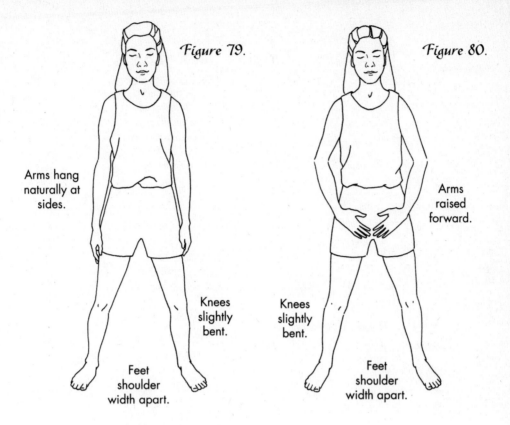

Figure 79.

Arms hang
naturally at
sides.

Knees
slightly
bent.

Feet
shoulder
width apart.

Figure 80.

Arms
raised
forward.

Knees
slightly
bent.

Feet
shoulder
width apart.

Position 3.   Stand with your feet about shoulder width apart and
your knees slightly bent. Raise your arms at your sides
until your hands are about the height of your belly button (Figure 81, next page).

Position 4.   Stand with your feet about shoulder width apart and
your knees slightly bent. Raise your arms in front of
your body with your hands about a foot in front of your
chest as though you were going to catch a basketball.
Your palms should face away from your body (Figure 82,
next page).

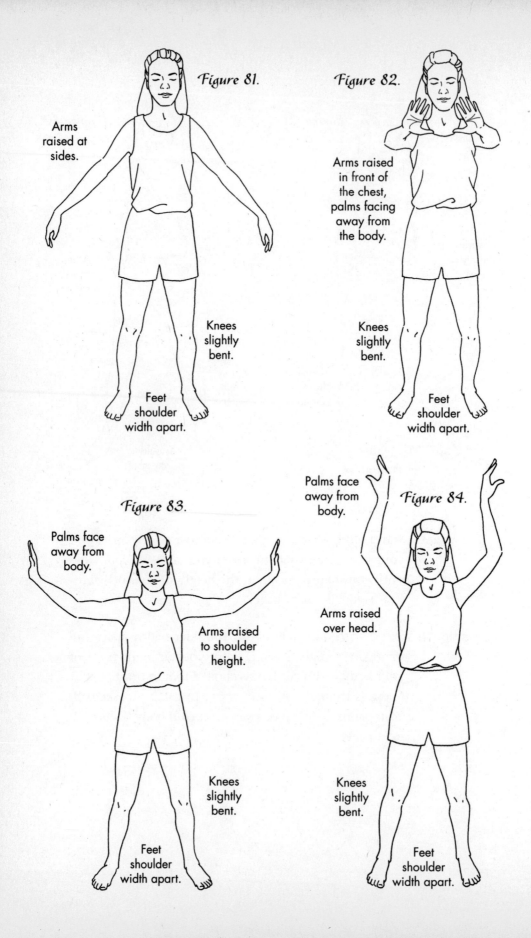

Figure 81.

Arms raised at sides.

Knees slightly bent.

Feet shoulder width apart.

Figure 82.

Arms raised in front of the chest, palms facing away from the body.

Knees slightly bent.

Feet shoulder width apart.

Figure 83.

Palms face away from body.

Arms raised to shoulder height.

Knees slightly bent.

Feet shoulder width apart.

Palms face away from body.

Figure 84.

Arms raised over head.

Knees slightly bent.

Feet shoulder width apart.

Position 5.   Stand with your feet about shoulder width apart and your knees slightly bent. Raise your arms at your sides until they are about shoulder height with your palms facing away from your body (Figure 83).

Position 6.   Stand with your feet about shoulder width apart and your knees slightly bent. Raise your arms over your head, with your elbows slightly bent, and with your palms facing away from your body (Figure 84).

One of the things you will notice as you begin practicing this art is that your muscles will start to shake and maybe even briefly hurt a little. At first, this can feel rather alarming, but it is important for you to try to ignore this discomfort and continue your training without lowering your trembling limbs. Work through the pain and the shaking. Within a few minutes, you will discover that your secondary muscles will kick in and the exercise will seem easier. It is kind of like getting your second wind when you are jogging.

Practice Zhan Zhuang every day. Go ahead and invent your own training variations. For example, while you are driving, you could hold the steering wheel firmly with one hand and let the other one barely rest against it. After twenty minutes, switch arms. Whenever you read a book, you could sit comfortably in a chair and hold your book up with both arms unsupported by arm rests. You might want to try starting with a paperback book first, because they are generally smaller and lighter than most hardcover books. Stick with Zhan Zhuang as a primary training tool for as long as you practice Chi Gung.

Freestyle Tai Chi Chuan

Tai Chi Chuan is a wonderful ancient Chinese art that is thousands of years old. It consists of a series of slow movements that were originally created as a martial art. By practicing in slow motion, the martial artist was able to learn to generate and use chi for combat situations. The movements brought chi to the person's muscles and skin, which increased his or her sensitivity to energy, which then enabled the practitioner to sense what an opponent was going to do before the action occurred.

Very few people today understand Tai Chi Chuan's martial applications; most people practice it as a method of improving their health. The chief way this is done is by learning to build and identify the chi in your body. Once you have built up a supply of energy by practicing the movements, it will start to flow through your body, which will increase your health and fitness.

Freestyle Tai Chi Chuan is essentially your own interpretation of how you need to move based on your own uniqueness. Some people are large, while others are small; some are strong while others are weak. Because of these variables, each of us has our own way of moving. What you have to learn to do is to find out for yourself what is good for you. Therefore, you must experiment.

When you practice Tai Chi Chuan, it is important to move as slowly as possible. You should think of your movements as controlled and purposeful. For example, use your imagination and move as though you were moving through water. In fact, practicing in a swimming pool, lake, or even while seated in a bathtub can be an excellent way for learning some of the movement skills.

As you move, concentrate on feeling The Flowing. Lose yourself in its travels through your body. You will probably get an urge to move your arm here or your leg there. Go with it. That is your body telling you what to do. If you feel slightly apprehensive, try putting on some music that you enjoy.

Here are some movement ideas for beginners.

Tai Chi Chuan Fan Exercise

Get a wooden fan about a foot long. Open the fan and slowly move it through the air. Instead of just fanning with your wrist, the way most people would use a fan, let your entire arm move. Concentrate on the feeling of air resistance as you gently and softly work with the fan. Move your body and arms in as many positions as you can, as slowly and gracefully as possible. Here are some examples of exercises that you could try.

Exercise 1.   Move your arm to shoulder height and extend it in front of your body as far forward as you can reach, then move the fan back toward your body as you let your arm slowly bend at the elbow. Do this ten times with each arm.

Exercise 2.   Raise your arm as high over your head as you can, then lower it so your fan goes below your waist. Do this ten times with each arm.

Exercise 3.   Move the fan in a large circle in front of your body. Reach as high as you can, as far to the side as possible, and also let the fan gently brush the ground. Make ten large circles with each arm moving the fan both clockwise and counterclockwise.

Tai Chi Chuan Ball Exercise

Get some sort of beach ball or child's rubber ball. It should be at least a foot or more in diameter and should be as light as possible. (A basketball would be a little too heavy for most people.) Hold the ball in both hands and gently move it up and down, left and right (Figure 85). Be sure to step in a variety of patterns with your feet so that you can slowly walk in straight lines, circles, and a variety of turning and pivoting positions. As you move, be sure to let your waist move freely and loosely.

Figure 85.

The Crawl

This exercise resembles the swimming stroke called Freestyle or the Crawl, except you do it while you are walking. Step forward with your right foot as you swing your left arm in a large clockwise circle at your side, bringing it up and around from back to front (Figure 86). Then, as you step forward with your left foot, swing your right arm forward at your side in a large counterclockwise direction. Move as slowly as possible and coordinate your arm movements with your legs. As you practice this exercise, establish your own rhythm and walking pattern so the movements become your own interpretation of how you would represent a swimming exercise while walking. Do this exercise for ten minutes.

Figure 86.

These are just a couple of ideas to get you started with Freestyle Tai Chi Chuan. You can get other ideas for movement patterns by watching animals and plants move. Try imitating a monkey or a flamingo. Let your body move like a swaying palm tree. You could even imagine how you would move if you were a rainbow.

Pick one or two exercises to practice, then do them for twenty minutes, at least once a day. Practice Freestyle Tai Chi Chuan on a regular basis. It is a great way to get your energy moving in the morning and a fantastic way to relax at night.

Swimming and Bathing in Cold Water

Cold water can enhance your chi by giving you a way to test your ability to warm yourself. You should try to swim or bathe in cold water as often as you can. Personally, I meditate in it every day.

What constitutes cold water? It is sort of a personal definition. Our average body temperature is 98.6 degrees, so anything cooler than that would feel cool or even cold to our skin. For most people I have talked to, tolerable cold water is around sixty-three degrees. Much colder than that and most people don't want to venture into it.

It is important to be careful when using cold water training. You have to make sure your body, particularly your heart, can stand the strain cold water can place upon it. Before you undertake any type of exercise program, it is always good to talk to your doctor first.

Whether you jump into the water in a single quick plunge or slowly immerse yourself is a personal choice. It depends on how well you deal with system shock. Either way will work. Once you are totally wet, the real training begins.

The first thing you need to do is to practice the Three Regulations. You might find this challenging until you gain some experience with cold water. When most people jump into cold water, they tense their bodies, shut down their minds, and gasp with deep, powerful exhalations. These natural responses by your body are examples of Wai Dan methods you can use to warm yourself. Tensing your body brings chi to your muscles and skin. Thinking about the numbing cold naturally focuses your mind on one thought. Breathing hard actually raises your energy level. You will want to learn to control your mind, body, and breath by will, instead of by natural response. That way, you can have greater control over your body when you need it.

After you have entered the water, breathe as slowly as possible through your nose using Taoist Reverse Breathing and draw the air down to your Dan Tien. Focus on your internal feelings. Concentrate on bringing chi to your skin by tensing your body. Try to ignore the cold and focus your mind on your breathing. This is a training program for your will power. If you get too cold, just get out of the water.

One of the training methods used by a variety of Asian monks is to plunge naked into a hole in a frozen lake. They stay in the water for a few minutes, then, after climbing out, they sit down on the ice and place wet sheets over themselves. Using a combination of Wai Dan and Nei Dan exercises, they test their chi skills by seeing how many sheets they can dry using their own internal energy. This is a very advanced form of self-testing; it is not recommended for anyone below master level skill in Chi Gung. It is also very important when doing this type of thing to make sure other people are with you in case you need any medical assistance.

Take the plunge into cold water as often as you can. Learn to relish its numbing embrace, then, learn to ignore it. When you can enter cold water without noticing, you will have reached quite a high level of Chi Gung.

Snow Baths

Snow bathing is similar to cold water training in its effect on your chi. There are a number of ways you can do this activity.

One way is to walk outside in the snow for short periods of time while barefoot. It is important you don't let your feet freeze, so you will want to limit your time at this activity to a just a few seconds the first few times you try it. As your feet cool down because of the cold, chi is directed up your legs. Therefore, you need to learn to bring it back down to your feet. A basic way to do this is by wiggling your toes and contracting your foot muscles. If you know how to do Grand Circulation, you can also use your mind to send The Flowing to your feet. This advanced skill should enable you to concentrate your chi in your soles so you can keep them warm for as long as you desire.

You might want to try other outdoor activities while wearing your swim suit. The first thing you should do is to walk into your yard while the snow is falling and let it melt on your bare skin. Practice the Three Regulations and Taoist Reverse Breathing and tighten as many muscles in your body as you can. By alternately contracting and relaxing your muscles, you will send chi to your skin, which should warm you up. A similar response occurs if you shiver. See how long you can comfortably stay outside while remaining warm. With practice, you should be able to gradually increase your ability to withstand the cold. Eventually, as you learn Nei Dan skills, you can try sending chi directly to your skin.

Once you have learned how to warm yourself against falling snow, you may want to try making snow angels. Lie on your back and swing your arms and legs in wide arcs through the snow, which should make a pattern that looks like an angel with wings. This exercise is a little more advanced than the previous one because instead of just having a little snow fall against your skin, you are actually pressing most of your body deep into the snow. Naturally, this will make you colder much quicker. As a beginner, use the Wai Dan technique of tightening your muscles to warm yourself. If you are more advanced, send chi through your skin and into the snow.

The Inuit of the Arctic have over twenty different words describing various types of snow, but most of us can think of only a few. Snow is dry, light, slushy, wet, hard, or crunchy. It can be good or bad, depending on your perspective. The point is, the more ways you look at something, the more sensitive you become to it. In other words, you gain a greater understanding of things through familiarity. Because chi training emphasizes increasing your sensitivity, it offers you a new way to expand your horizons. In this case, don't just think of snow as snow. Instead, really look at it. Feel it, smell it, taste it, and even listen to it as it falls. Try to sense its essence. What lessons can snow teach you? For this, you will have to listen to your intuition.

Not only can snow bathing teach you how to warm yourself with energy by using the muscular tension of Wai Dan and the mental projection of Nei Dan, it also opens your body up to new sensory stimulation. The more you gain mastery over your senses, the better you will be able to experience The Flowing.

Belly Dancing

Belly dancing is a wonderful way for both men and women to develop their chi skills. There are many different styles of belly dancing, depending on which country it was developed in and the type of music used.

The first thing you will need to do is find and purchase a style of music you enjoy. You may wish to sample African, Middle Eastern, Spanish, or Polynesian music. Then, you may also want to get a set of brass finger cymbals called zills or you may want a tambourine. In addition, you may want to buy yourself a silk or rayon outfit with a wide, flowing skirt. If you are interested in hula, you might want to buy or make a grass skirt. You also might want a large scarf or veil. Finally, you should consider getting some jewelry, particularly long, dangling jewelry such as earrings, necklaces, bracelets, and belts. These outfits and paraphernalia are not necessary, but they can help to get you into the proper mood, and they also offer greater freedom of movement than more restrictive clothes.

Now I realize some of you may balk at the idea of learning belly dancing, but why limit yourself because of social or sexual stereotypes? Belly dancing is a way for anyone to learn to relax and to let go. This is especially important for everyone today because modern living has made many of us more uptight and less emotionally developed than we could be. Learning belly dancing helps all of us cultivate our feminine sides, which then enables us to better experience the polarities of both yin and yang.

Belly dancing will teach you how to move softly and gracefully. It is a perfect way to master relaxation in movement. In addition, the unusual stomach and hip movements lead to the stimulation of the Dan Tien, which will further increase your energy supply.

Listen to the music. Concentrate. Then slowly let your body flow to the beat as you move as lightly and as relaxed as possible. Let your hips make circles and figure eights. Move them forward, backward, up and down, and side to side. As you move your center, let your legs relax and follow the movement generated with your belly. At the same time, gracefully sway your arms. When you are a beginner, you will probably find you have a lot of muscular tension, but the more you practice, the looser you will become.

After you have practiced a variety of movements and become fairly comfortable with them, you might want to try holding a lightweight veil in your hands. Working with the veil is an excellent way to measure your chi control. Let the veil glide about you as though you were a bull fighter. Slowly flap it, swing it, and twirl it as you follow its movements with your body. Feel how the veil floats through the air. Once you have gained some control over the veil's movements, try sending chi through it. If you are a Chi Gung beginner, you will probably be exclusively using Moving Wai Dan techniques to build up The Flowing. At this level, just imagine your energy is spreading into the gracefully moving veil. If you use Nei Dan and have completed Grand Circulation, then you can focus your mind on deliberately sending chi into the material. Energize it and see if you can make the veil float just a little longer than it normally would. Perhaps this will be only a portion of a second at first, but with persistence it will spread into a second or two and maybe even longer. Keep practicing.

You can also wear a skirt and practice with it in a similar manner as the veil. You will want a skirt that is as wide as possible at the base; that way, it has fuller movement. Try different kinds of material to see what flows the best. Grass skirts are good because in addition to moving naturally, they make a variety of swishing noises that add energy to your dance. As you twirl in circles, let your skirt flow out from you. Then stop as it slowly whips around your legs. Try sending energy into the skirt to make it as light as possible. Let go of your inhibitions by letting yourself have fun and smile.

Belly dancing is not only a great way to exercise, it is also a practical way to develop and test your chi. If you don't want to wear a specific outfit, then don't. It is totally up to you. The important point, though, is to make sure you don't limit yourself merely because of what you think other people will think of you. After all, the only person you can ever really please is yourself.

Mental Training

$\mathcal{M}$ental training involves skills that use your mind. Though some of these skills can be applied to Wai Dan training, they are more specifically geared toward enhancing your Nei Dan training by developing your ability to concentrate and expand your thinking. Many of these skills present new ways of thinking instead of merely offering specific concrete exercises for you to perform.

Record Your Dreams

Almost everybody dreams. Most people dream numerous times each night, but we don't always remember our dreams. We sometimes feel like we go days or weeks without dreaming, but that is not the case. In order to help you remember your dreams, you should write them down.

Our brains need to keep active, so when we dream our minds take us on journeys we might never have otherwise imagined. It is not all just imagination, however.

When we dream, our minds enter another state of awareness. We are in a condition called rapid eye movement or REM. That is one of the physical signs that we are dreaming.

There are lots of different theories on what dreams are or what they mean. Some dreams are forms of escape from the daily pressures of life while others seem prophetic. Some are just really weird.

Because dreams deal with our mental states, they are a form of Nei Dan training. For this form of Chi Gung, I suggest you keep a journal of your dreams. Place a pad of paper and a pen within easy reach of your bed. If you happen to wake during the night and remember a dream, write it down immediately. At first, this may seem rather difficult, but eventually you can make a habit of it.

Later, read what you have written and try to determine how it can apply to your life. Open your mind and you will begin to see patterns.

Another thing you can do is learn to program your dreams, or to change them to other dreams while you are asleep. Start by allowing yourself to become aware of any given dream. Then, as you are dreaming, imagine your dream is a TV program. Simply think about changing the channel. With a little practice this will become easy. Next, you may want to try to program a specific dream. Prior to going to sleep, think about what you want to dream about by using vivid details, then see if it happens.

By tapping into the power of your dreams, you open yourself up to your subconscious mind. This, then, enables you to broaden your awareness, which will help you gain greater Nei Dan skills.

Develop Your Intuition

As you practice Chi Gung, specifically Nei Dan, you will notice that it requires a tremendous amount of imagination, especially when you are a beginning and intermediate student. So many of the chi feelings you will experience are so subtle that it is easy to miss them. You will find yourself wondering whether you sensed something. That is your intuition talking to you. You have to learn to listen to your gut feelings. If you think you sensed something, you probably did. You have to learn to trust your intuition. As you gain experience, you will find your feelings are becoming right more frequently.

Developing intuition is a skill you can work on throughout the day. For example, should you have cereal or eggs for breakfast? Should you go out to lunch with an office colleague? Should you walk through the park alone tonight? As you can see, some of these things seem trivial and others could have dire consequences. The point is that you can practice constantly. Keep a journal of any intuitive feelings you have, and record the results of what happened. As you gain a greater understanding of The Flowing, you will be surprised to see how skilled at this you can become. It is a "Catch-22" kind of thing. Getting better at Chi Gung will increase your intuition, and increasing your intuition will make your Chi Gung stronger.

An immediate example of a way to practice your intuition might come from reading this book right now. What section or chapter are you going to read next? Where does your intuition lead you?

Discover Multiple Solutions to Problems

Chi Gung training can help you solve virtually any type of problem by teaching you how to think more quickly and with greater clarity. This type of thinking then enables you to discover multiple solutions to problems instead of looking at merely one side of a situation or at only one answer.

By learning to breathe properly you are able to have more oxygen available for the best possible functioning of your brain. Essentially, the more oxygen you breathe, and the better you utilize that oxygen, the better you are able to think with clarity. This in turn enables you to find more solutions to your daily problems and tasks.

Many people are interested in intelligence and their intelligence quotient (IQ). They frequently wonder what their own IQ is and how, or even if, it can be increased. If it can, they often wonder what new ideas or skills they would be able to perform.

Well, by increasing your oxygen efficiency and chi flow, you can indeed increase your intelligence, and in many cases, it can be a substantial leap. You will then be able to find more ways to do almost any task you set your mind to accomplish.

As a beginner, one of the ways to begin achieving this is by learning to look at problems from someone else's point of view. For example, let's say your child failed a math test. Instead of immediately becoming upset, take a moment, breathe deeply and relax all your muscles, then practice Buddhist Breathing and the Three Regulations until you feel you have become relaxed and able to concentrate clearly. Next, look your child directly in the eyes. For this, you will want to relax your vision so you use peripheral vision instead. You can do this by directing your awareness to objects that are at the extreme left and right of your forward vision instead of on the child directly in front of you. Because you are focusing on your peripheral vision, instead of your central vision where you normally get visual clarity from, your child's face should appear somewhat blurry to you. Inhale through your nose while moving your chi completely through your body for one full cycle. Now, try to imagine why your child might have had this particular problem. Perhaps your child didn't study adequately, or maybe he or she didn't feel well. Possibly the material was inappropriately presented by the teacher, or maybe the material was just too advanced. Perhaps the book is not complete. Your child might have been under stress from some social situation between peers.

Let your mind freely flow from thought to thought as you embrace each new idea as it comes. Then, ask your child why the problem may have occurred and listen carefully to the answer. It is very important you listen not only to the actual words spoken, but also to any hidden meaning behind the words. In addition, you should carefully watch your child's non-verbal communication. For example, does your child lean toward you as he or she talks, or appear to almost hide? Does he or she make eye contact or look away?

If you really want this to work, you have to learn to empathize. You will find that empathizing with someone is a much better way to deal with a problem than just jumping directly into it. It gives you the opportunity to find multiple answers and then the chance to choose the best one. In addition, you need to let your thoughts and emotions freely explore the problem. Only after you have really tried to understand your child's point of view will you be able to come up with an accurate and appropriate solution.

In order to become a good problem solver, you need to be able to see the many sides of any given problem. When you find yourself faced with challenging situations, take a moment or two, relax your mind, body, and emotions, breathe, and try to remove yourself from the situation as much as possible. By following these steps, you have the potential of becoming more objective, and therefore a much better problem solver.

Think Positively

In order for you to progress in the art of Chi Gung, it is necessary for you to believe your training can work. One of the ways you can do this is by learning to think positively.

Chi is energy. It is our vitality, our very life. We can live for a month without food, for a few days without water, but only for a few moments without oxygen and energy. It is important, therefore, to absorb the best possible chi energy you can, and that basically means positive energy. Think about this idea for a moment. How do you feel when you are happy, in love, or fulfilled? At times like these, your mind is relaxed, you think clearly, and you more than likely feel great physically.

Now think about how you feel when you are angry, hurt, or scared. You will probably find that your mind shuts down, your body tenses up, and you cease to function at your best. One of the sad things about life today is that many people often feel they are indeed at their best when they feel bad.

For example, do you find yourself motivated by stress? Perhaps you are the type of person who thinks peak efficiency comes from working under extreme pressure. Interestingly enough, that is not the natural way of things. Instead, it is a result of modern living. Just because that is the way life is today, does it indeed make it the best way? No, of course not. If you happened to answer "yes" to the previous question, then perhaps you are looking at the world from a rather narrow point of view, and maybe you should consider expanding your horizons a little. Sure, we can adapt to lots of situations. That is one of the strong points of the human race. But how does that affect us in the long run? Well, it gives us heart disease, strokes, and high blood pressure, as well as a slew of other diseases.

So, is it better to live under excessive stress, thriving on negativity, or is it better to learn to relax and live a positive life? Ultimately, that is a choice only you can make for yourself. Just be sure you are indeed making the choice, not letting society do it for you.

One more thought. Negative thinking may apparently get you a lot of material things in our modern world, and you may even delude yourself into innumerable rationalizations that negative thinking makes you happy. But, frankly, isn't positive thinking a lot more fun?

Master Skills Using Visualization

No matter what task you find yourself facing, the best way to master it is by visualizing how to do it. This particular skill has been used quite successfully recently in the Olympic Games. For example, Picabo Street, the 1994 silver medalist in skiing; Danny Everett, the 1988 gold medalist in the 400-meter sprint; and Janet Evans, the 1988 and 1992 gold medalist in swimming, all have enhanced their athletic performance with visualization skills.

Things are not always as simple as they seem, though. There is more to visualization than just picturing yourself doing something new. You need to practice just as hard as if you were really doing it.

Try visualizing a simple skill first. Imagine yourself drinking a glass of water while sitting in your favorite chair. All you have to do is to picture yourself reaching out for a glass and picking it up. Really try to sense your arm moving even though it actually isn't. Imagine the muscles slowly contracting and stretching. Try to sense the weight of your arm in the air. Now, as you bring the glass to your mouth, imagine the taste of the water as you drink it.

After you can do this exercise, try doing it with chi. In order to do this exercise, you will have to had at least some experience with Wai Dan so you know what chi feels like. As you imagine moving your arm, picture the feeling of energy flowing along your arm. This exercise requires you to really focus your mind. In a sense, you have to actually live The Flowing. Relax your breathing as you inhale and exhale exclusively through your nose.

Next, you might want to try picturing yourself doing more advanced exercises. Pick a skill you are familiar with and trying to improve. If you are a skier, pick skiing, and if you are a swimmer, choose swimming. No matter what skill you practice, you can improve your abilities through visualization.

For this next exercise, you should have some experience with Nei Dan and Grand Circulation. Let's say you are a mountain climber and you want to improve your skills by visualization training. Picture a mountain in extreme detail. Now try to see yourself climbing one of its slopes. Imagine every muscle you would have to move as you climb one step at a time. As you are safely sitting in a comfortable chair at home, try to really sense what it would feel like to hang thousands of feet in the air by nothing more than a couple tiny finger and toe holds. Visualize how your weight would feel taxing your muscles. As you think about reaching out your arm for a new hold, actually try to feel your arm moving. Don't literally move it; instead, use your mind, and use it with as much detail as possible. Sense how high you are and how the altitude makes your breathing slightly more difficult.

By practicing visualization on a daily basis, you will eventually get very good at it. Suddenly, you will find that you will be able to do almost anything better and more efficiently than you have ever done it before. You will think better, move better, and your chi flow will be better, all of which should make almost all aspects of your life more harmonious with how you would like things to happen.

Emotional Training

*E*motional training teaches you how to control your feelings. It primarily aids in the development of your Nei Dan skills. It is, however, applicable to Wai Dan training, especially at a beginner's level, because your emotions are distinctly linked to your physical body.

Cultivate Patience

Chi Gung develops patience, and patience develops chi. In order to get in tune with your body at its subtlest levels, you need to become patient. One of the things you will quickly realize as you train in Chi Gung is that chi development takes a tremendous amount of time and effort. To reach some of the more advanced levels of experiences in Chi Gung may require years or even a lifetime of training. I have practiced a wide variety of Chi Gung skills for about thirty years and still find new ways of experiencing chi daily.

By focusing on your breathing, you are bringing your awareness to your innermost senses, which requires both will power and patience. When you begin your training, most of it will be mental effort, consisting of creativity and imagination. It is very important you stick with it by practicing every day, throughout the day. You can practice, for instance, while you wait in lines or any time you can let your attention drift from your current activity and focus inward. Obviously, you have to be careful while driving, operating machinery, or doing any potentially dangerous activity, but as long as you use common sense you should be okay.

You will soon discover that your Chi Gung training has made you a more patient and tolerant person. Instead of seeing traffic jams or long grocery lines as inconveniences, you will see these as perfect opportunities to train. Instead of becoming stressed, you will learn how to relax your mind, body, and emotions. You will probably also find yourself taking a greater interest in nature and therefore want to spend more time outside. Once there, you may surprise yourself by finding enjoyment in watching a tree grow or observing the stars traveling the night sky. All of these things, and many more, are examples of a greater awareness of internal arts and increased patience. In whatever you do in life, learn to take your time and let things happen. Most of all, learn to enjoy the moment.

Patience Through Copying

One of the best ways to develop patience is by copying something. For example, pick up a book—any book—and start writing it word for word and line by line. Copying may seem like the act of a student, but it is really the art of the master. At advanced levels, copying requires tremendous attention to detail.

After you have tried copying a book or two, try copying a painting or a drawing. Pick an artist you really like and try to create exactly what he or she has made. With practice, you will get better and better, but you will never totally succeed. Why? Well, let's use the example of Japanese calligraphy called *Shodo*. When you first start this skill you might have difficulty getting the right amount of ink on your brush. Too much and you will drip it on your paper. Too little and your brush will dry out before you finish your stroke. Once you have figured out how much ink to use, then you need to be careful not to make a mistake. One wrong line and you ruin the entire project, because you can't erase. You must commit yourself to each movement of the brush. If you really concentrate on what you are doing, and you care about doing the best job you can, then it is as though life and death reside in each sweep of your arm. Beyond this level of training, you need to learn to concentrate and send chi into the brush. To adequately determine how your chi is flowing into your brush, you would need to use a microscope to look in detail at any given line you have drawn. When you first start out, you will probably notice that the bristles of your brush separate from each other, but as your chi skills increase, you will find the bristles can be made to stick closer and closer together until it eventually looks like they are all touching each other. So you see, no matter how much your work resembles someone else's, it will never be quite the same. That is why copying is such an excellent way of cultivating patience.

Take your time while achieving your Chi Gung goals. If you do, you persevere. All of your goals can be reached if you are patient.

Explore Your Sexuality

Even though many people are becoming more tolerant of "alternative lifestyles," a lot of us still get hung up on sexual labels such as "he," "she," "gay," or "straight." As you gain experience with Chi Gung and open your mind to new possibilities, you will probably find that labels, regardless of what they are, unnecessarily restrict your growth. In order to reach your maximum potential physically, intellectually, and spiritually, you need to experience as much as possible. One of the ways you can do this is by exploring your own sexuality more openly.

For example, in today's society, women are allowed to wear men's clothes but men aren't allowed to dress in women's clothes. If they do, they are labeled transvestites, transsexuals, or homosexuals. But think about it for a second. What difference does it really make what we wear or how we act as long as it doesn't hurt anyone else?

By denying ourselves access to our alternative feminine or masculine sides, we are hindering our own development and consequently limiting our chi growth. For example, as a male, you might strive to fit into the mold of what a man is supposed to be according to society. You could drink beer, fix cars, watch football, hunt, excel at your job, or smoke cigars, but what do you really get out of all of this sexually stereotypical behavior? Has it indeed made you more of a man? No. Instead, it has merely made you look like you fit into our society's definition of the proper male role.

What if instead of exclusively following sexual stereotypical behavior, you also openly expressed your alternative sexual side? For example, if you are a man, you might realize that you like growing flowers, cooking exotic dishes, or sewing. If you are a woman, you might like racing motorcycles, wrestling, or belching at baseball games. Do any of these activities really label you in any way? No, not really, other than revealing you have a variety of interests and are therefore a well-rounded person.

By openly expressing yourself, you have freed your mind, body, and spirit. Instead of placing limitations on what you can or can't do, or like or not like, you have allowed yourself to pursue your interests wherever they may take you. That way, you have opened and relaxed your mind, body, and emotions, so that your internal energy can flow much more freely. Thus, you have expanded the possibilities of what you can achieve and experience. This in turn enables you to achieve and experience even more.

Whenever we feel uncomfortable doing something, we tense our bodies and minds. Then, even if we try whatever it was that made us uneasy to begin with, we discover we have a difficult time with it because of our tenseness. In effect, we have stifled our own ability. That is why it is important to learn to open ourselves up to things we have never even considered before. Try new foods, visit new places, and do things you never would have considered doing before. Don't let your sexuality stifle your enjoyment or participation in any activity.

Learn to embrace both your masculine and feminine sides. After all, they are indeed present in all of us. Did you know, for instance, that all babies are initially created as female and it is only after a period of time in the womb when hormones kick in and make some of us males? Therefore, don't let your genitalia determine what you can or can't like.

By allowing yourself to freely experience things that stereotypically would interest only one of the sexes, you will find a whole new you. Life will never seem boring again, because any topic, idea, or activity may contain exactly what you might subconsciously need or desire for personal growth.

Instead of adopting a right or left approach to life or taking a black and white viewpoint, try experimenting with the middle ground.

Develop Your Self-Confidence

In order to excel at Chi Gung, you need to have the self-confidence to believe in what you are doing. A lot of the techniques are rather esoteric in nature and you need to trust that they will work. By believing in yourself, you will gain even greater skills, and by attaining these skills, you will have even more to believe in.

So which comes first, the belief or the skills? As you may have guessed by now, your faith must come first. The reason is simple. To do anything in life, you have to believe you can do it. If you never thought about it, then you couldn't do it, because you would never even know the task existed. Remember, though, just because you believe in something, it is not necessarily going to happen. You need to combine belief with effort in order to accomplish anything.

One of the things you need to do is to trust your senses. Don't let other people tell you what you can or can't experience. You are the sole judge of all that happens to you. Therefore, broaden your opportunities to include anything you desire. Believe in yourself, and your self-confidence will help everything flow into the proper place at the right time.

Form Friendships Based on the Person

When we are young, our friends are often apparently thrust upon us by fate. Because we often have no form of long-distance transportation as kids, our friends often are within walking or biking distance. As we get older, we may form a variety of friends, but we still tend to base them on location. Our friends live near us, work with us, go to school with us, or do the same activities we do.

Do we choose friends wisely? Naturally, we all like to think we do, but how many of your friends are negative people? Do they whine and complain? Some of them do, I suspect. Have you ever stopped to think about how this can affect you? Other people's negative thoughts and actions examples of negative chi.

People who are angry, whiny, depressed, snooty, arrogant, manipulative, or mean are actually more of a hindrance to you than you would think. Their chi oozes out of their very being and saturates all it encounters, including you. I have known people with extremely negative chi. When they enter a room, the air grows thick and heavy. Suddenly, everyone feels the doom and gloom. Try to avoid these types of people. If you must deal with them, focus on positive thoughts to counteract their negativity. On the other hand, I have known people who radiated positive chi. They beam and glow. Wherever they go, they lift people's spirits.

Now you are probably wondering how you can go about choosing good friends. Your Chi Gung training can help you. As a beginner in the art of Chi Gung, you will find yourself working on a greater sense of self-awareness. You do this by practicing the Three Regulations and also by concentrating on your development of chi. When you meet people, try to relax your body, breathing, and mind. That way, you will be in a better position to understand more about the new person you just met based on your increased receptivity to his or her chi. This sensitivity will help you sense any tension or stress the other person may have. (As you gain experience in Chi Gung, you will be able to know more about a person in a faster rate of time.) Once you have developed the ability to sense another person's chi, you will know instantly who someone is, what they are like, and if the two of you will become friends. In the meantime, though, trust your first impressions; they are usually right, provided you have an open mind.

Expose Yourself to as Much as Possible

If you really want to broaden your chi skills, or any skill for that matter, it is necessary for you to open your mind and expose yourself to as much as possible. As we wander through life, we too often stick with known and comfortable things. We often eat the same foods, drive the same cars, and go to the same vacation spots, year after year.

In the case of studying energy systems, it is easy to study just one type. After all, you may ask yourself, "Why would I need to study some apparently weird, foreign energy system? I know what I like and what I need." Well, no matter what mystical or esoteric art you specialize in, after you gain enough experience, you will begin to see the relationships between all disciplines. However, you will need this maturity of experience in order to open yourself to your greatest learning potential.

You will want to open your mind to trying new things is because that enables you to really learn. The chief thing opening your mind will do is teach you how to make unusual analogies, which then can substantially increase your intelligence. As your intelligence rises, you will see new opportunities to expand your Chi Gung skills. In addition, by opening your mind to as much as possible, you will begin to accept everyone and everything for who and what they are. This, you will find, is the beginning of real spiritual growth. And once you experience a leap in spiritual growth, your chi skills will have even more opportunities for development.

So you see, everything is connected to everything else. In other words, we are all one. By choosing not to accept something, we are, in a sense, turning our backs on ourselves. Instead of following such a destructive pattern, open your heart. Allow yourself to see the magick in everything, everywhere and learn to embrace all. When you can do this, you will be more willing to expose yourself to new experiences, which, in turn, will further increase your chi.

Spend Time With Children

Kids are natural powerhouses of chi. They can play all day; they eat whatever they want, then burn it off; and they are into everything. If you have kids of your own or have done a lot of babysitting, then you know how exhausted you can feel after trying to keep up with them. However, there is a way to harness some of their youthful energy.

When kids play, they fill the air around them with powerful energy. The simple act of being around kids bombards you with their chi. Try to absorb some of their excess energy from the air around you. Stay as calm as possible, relax, breathe, and imagine their energy flowing into you. If you do it right, you can have just as much energy as they have. Absorbing children's energy a great way to slow the aging process.

Watch kids play and see if you can imitate what they do. Start exploring different things. Open your mind so everything seems new and exciting. Don't be afraid of looking foolish, and forget about the stereotype of acting like an adult. Remember, everyone and everything can teach us something. So spend time with children and learn from them. Allow yourself to find the child hidden within you. When you do, the world will become your playground.

Once you realize this, you will probably discover you have greatly enhanced your Chi Gung skills, because by imitating children's perception of the world, you can learn to eliminate a lot of your own prejudices and tensions. This will enable your chi to flow better, which can make you a happier, healthier adult.

You should spend time with children. Not only do they need you, you will probably find that you need them, too.

Health
Training

*H*ealth training is primarily based on specific activities you can follow to increase your chi and therefore improve your health.

Follow a Proper Diet

What you eat definitely has an effect on your chi because your body automatically absorbs any food's energy. However, not all foods are created equal. Some food offers substantially higher levels of The Flowing. You have probably noticed that some foods can make you sluggish, while others seem to pep you up and give you lots of extra energy. Because your chi makes up who you are, what you eat is indeed what you are. Of course, each of us has our own dietary needs based on numerous factors such as age, sex, weight, physical condition, activity level, and even mental and emotional states, but there are a few guidelines you can try

First of all, you should eat a low-fat diet. Eat plenty of complex carbohydrates, fruits, and vegetables. You don't have to become a vegetarian, but the less meat you eat, the greater your chi will feel. Have you ever noticed that when you eat meat you are more aggressive? If you must eat meat, try to eat naturally killed animals as opposed to slaughtered ones. The reason for this is simple. When animals are killed in a slaughter house, they are often extremely stressed prior to their death because they detect fear and suffering from all of the other animals. This negative energy carries directly into their meat. (While it is true that animals killed by predators often die violently, they are, in a certain sense, dying semi-naturally. After all, when one animal kills and eats another, that certainly seems violent to us, even though it is natural.) Therefore, if you must eat meat, try to obtain it yourself and kill the animal as naturally and quickly as possible. Then when you eat it, its chi will be better for you.

Another thing you can do is to try eating a greater number of smaller meals spread throughout the day, rather than one or two large meals. Eat to live; don't live to eat. If you can, eat foods that are fresh and natural rather than preserved. Try to avoid as many additives as possible, particularly sugar, artificial sweeteners, artificial preservatives, and flavor enhancers such as MSG (monosodium glutamate) and salt.

As you progress in Chi Gung, you will begin to learn how to take energy from the environment, which means you will need even less food. There is an ancient Taoist saying that says it is possible to live on sunshine. As you can imagine, that is going to be far beyond most people's skill level, but it is not as unbelievable as it seems. When you eat food, you convert the food into energy for physical use. By taking chi directly from the environment, you eliminate one of the eating and energy-conversion steps of the food chain and instead, go directly to energy utilization.

Losing Weight

By following the proper food intake, you will have a greater chance of maintaining your ideal weight and health levels. Your ideal weight is based on your height and body build. Any medical doctor can tell you how to find it exactly. Maintaining your ideal weight is important because it increases your health, gives you more energy, and enables you to but also do a greater variety of activities. It also enhances your Chi Gung abilities, because the less fat you have on your body, the greater chi flow you will experience.

You can increase your intelligence by losing weight. Fat requires a tremendous amount of blood, oxygen, and chi to flow through it. Without the fat, all of these energy aids can freely flow to your brain, nourishing it, and therefore increasing your intelligence, manifested by clearer thinking, quicker reactions, and a better ability to concentrate. With increased intelligence, you have the potential to do your job better, improve your social relationships, and even find interest in new pursuits. Losing weight can also increase your sensory awareness because your chi flows easier and more efficiently when it doesn't get bogged down in excess fat. This means everything you sense and feel will become more intense.

People often battle their weight, sometimes for a lifetime, and they seldom win. This doesn't have to be the case. So how can you lose those extra pounds? After all, you are hungry.

The answer is simple—breathe. By taking in chi, you are energizing yourself. Instead of grabbing a candy bar for energy, absorb chi from the sun, moon, forests, or seas. As you progress in your Chi Gung training, you can alter your metabolism and consequently need less and less food in order to maintain your strength and endurance. By eating less, you gain more access to your chi, and having more chi will enable you to eat less. (However, even though you are eating less, you still have to follow a proper diet.)

Next time you are hungry for a snack, try filling up on chi. After all, the energy you get from food is just one source of energy.

Exercise

When we think of exercise, we probably all think of something different because there are so many different kinds available. From a health standpoint, it doesn't matter too much what type you choose to do for yourself, as long as you do something.

Some people want exhausting physical workouts, such as a complete weight lifting program, while others want something less strenuous, such as walking. Regardless of what you choose to do, you can enhance it with Chi Gung. For example, while you are walking, you could do chi breathing. Not only will this make your walk more relaxing and healthy for you, it also enables you to increase the intensity of your walk at will.

Try the exercise on the following page.

Supporting the Sky

Step 1.   Stand with your weight supported evenly on both feet with your knees slightly bent. Your back should be straight, but not stiff. Hold your head erect, as if it were supported from the ceiling by a string. Keep your neck loose and relaxed.

Step 2.   Raise your arms over your head with your elbows slightly bent. Have your palms facing straight up toward the sky (Figure 87).

Step 3.   Try to relax your muscles as much as possible as you hold this position. Use Taoist Reverse Breathing.

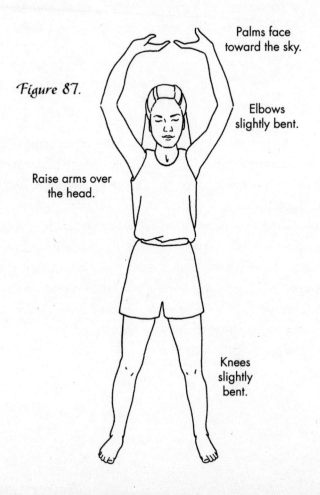

Figure 87.

Palms face toward the sky.

Elbows slightly bent.

Raise arms over the head.

Knees slightly bent.

Step 4.   Hold this position for up to twenty minutes without moving anything other than your stomach muscles as you breathe. This posture may be difficult, so be prepared. Your muscles will probably shake and you will more than likely sweat profusely, but don't quit or move until the time limit ends.

When you are done, compare that exercise with almost any exercise program you have ever followed. I'll bet this was at least as strenuous as a majority of them. If it wasn't, then good for you, because you are in great shape. If that is the case, try the same exercise only this time hold a five-pound weight in each hand; if that is not enough, use ten pounds or squat deeper until your thighs are parallel to the floor.

The point of this exercise is to show you that merely standing still can create incredible physical exertion. Incidentally, the exercise you just did is an example of Zhan Zhuang. It can produce tremendous results in strength, endurance, coordination, mental control, and will power. I suggest that if you are really serious about sports, no matter what other sport or exercise program you follow, you include a twenty-minute, daily dose of Zhan Zhuang as a supplemental training exercise.

In your personal exercise program, try doing whatever sport or exercises you do, but learn how to add The Flowing to it. You can do this by following the Three Regulations as well as adding the principles of Wai Dan and Nei Dan. You will probably find that chi helps you exercise with more energy, for greater lengths of time, at higher intensity levels, while utilizing greater coordination, and thus performing at peak efficiency like you have never reached before.

Here are some ways you can add Chi Gung training to a variety of different sports.

Baseball—Throw the ball or swing the bat while exhaling chi for added power. Use chi to help you sense where to hit the ball in relation to the fielder's lack of attention. If you pitch, use chi to increase your throwing stamina and intensity. As an outfielder, get a quicker sense of where the ball will land.

Basketball—Use chi to sense the locations of players you can't see. Shoot the ball with chi for greater control and accuracy. Sense your teammates thoughts through chi. Increase stamina by using breathing techniques to help absorb extra energy and chi.

Climbing—Take energy from the rocks you scale for greater strength and endurance. Develop a sense of which path will lead you to where you need to go. Increase flexibility by sending chi into your muscles.

Equestrian Sports—Increase your sensitivity to your horse with chi and also use chi to help you communicate with your animal. Gain more coordination by becoming attuned to your body's energy.

Fencing—Send chi into your sword for increased sensitivity. Use relaxation and increased flexibility to dramatically increase your speed. Learn to predict your opponent's moves before they occur.

Fishing—Locate fish with chi. Realizing that we are all one, keep only those fish you truly need. Honor those fish you have caught and thank them for their sacrifice.

Football—Use chi to predict your opponents' plays. Gain greater endurance, strength, and coordination. Alter the flight of the ball while it is in the air.

Golf—Swing your club with chi using relaxation for increased power. Gain greater confidence in your ability to choose the right club.

Gymnastics—Send chi throughout your body for greater body awareness, strength, coordination, and balance.

Hiking—Absorb energy from the environment. Share energy with plants and animals. Locate animals using chi.

Hockey—Locate unseen opponents with chi and increase the strength, speed, and accuracy of your shots. Predict your opponent's moves.

Martial Arts—Generate more speed, power, and endurance with chi. Focus on sensing your opponent's moves before they happen.

Running—Gain greater endurance. Increase speed and flexibility.

Swimming—Absorb chi from the water for endurance and speed. Learn to breathe more efficiently.

Tennis—Develop the ability to anticipate your opponent's shots. Hit with more power, speed, and precision.

All sports and exercise programs carry a risk of injury. If you get injured, you can use chi to help heal yourself by using the Three Regulations and a combination of Wai Dan and Nei Dan exercises to help your chi flow properly. Proper chi flow helps your body to heal much faster and better.

No matter what sport you do, Chi Gung can help you get better at it. So go ahead and play sports of all types and see if you can come up with new ways to incorporate Chi Gung principles in your workouts. Regardless of whether you are an amateur or professional athlete looking for an edge, you can use Chi Gung to dramatically increase your performance.

Stretch

It is extremely important to stretch all of your major joints and muscles daily if you want to excel at Chi Gung, as well as to maintain excellent health throughout your life. There are numerous ways to stretch. Some are safe while others are quite dangerous.

Let's start with the dangerous way. A lot of you will remember when you were in school and your gym teacher had you bounce as you stretched. Don't do it. Bouncing is an excellent way to tear your ligaments and muscles. Another fallacy is the idea of no pain, no gain. This is a misunderstanding and a misuse of a valuable biological principle. Our bodies experience pain to tell us something isn't quite right. When it signals to us that it hurts, we should stop doing the damaging activity. Many of us choose to ignore our bodies and think pain indicates growth and increased skill, when in fact it means decay and an eventual decrease of skill.

Instead of hurting yourself, it is better to stretch slowly and gradually so that your body can actually grow into each new position you attempt. Muscles need to be relaxed to properly stretch. By relaxing them using Chi Gung, you can safely increase your flexibility. When muscles are tense, they inhibit chi flow. They also hinder our athletic potential and our health. By being supple, you can actually experience innumerable benefits. Relaxed muscles will enable your blood to circulate more freely through your body. This can increase your intelligence, make your hair and skin healthier, improve your breathing, and warm your extremities.

Here are a few of the muscle groups you should stretch. Remember when you are stretching to stop as soon as you feel any pain. Stretch slowly and smoothly, and hold each stretch for a minimum of thirty seconds. Use

Buddhist Breathing as you stretch your muscles. Exhale as you stretch and imagine chi flowing directly into your muscle fibers. As you inhale, let up on the stretch a little.

Stretches

Neck	Turn your head side to side, forward, and backward, then rotate it in all directions.
Shoulders	Roll your shoulders in forward and backward circles. Shrug them up and push them down.
Biceps	Slowly extend your arm (Figure 88).
Triceps	Raise your arm straight over your head, then let it bend at the elbow (Figure 89).
Wrists	Rotate your wrists in all directions.
Hands	Open your fingers as wide as possible. Move them in all directions.
Upper Back	Roll your shoulder blades forward and backward.
Lower Back	Slowly twist your spine from side to side. Bend forward and backward at the waist.
Hips	Raise and lower your legs using your hips. Swing your legs forward and backward from the hips.
Quadriceps	Stand on one leg as you bend your other leg at the knee while bringing your foot as close to your butt as possible (Figure 90). Use a wall for support if you need it.
Hamstrings	Bend forward at the waist and try to touch your toes.
Calves	Sit on the floor and bring your toes as close to your shins as possible (Figure 91).

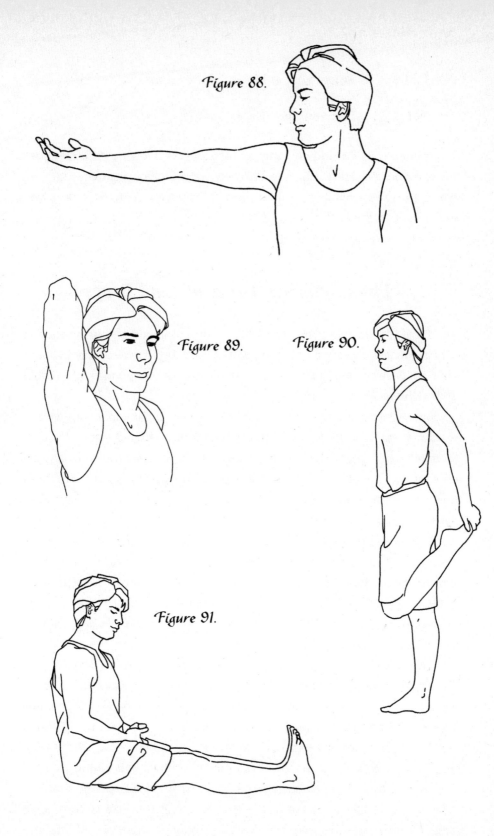

Figure 88.

Figure 89.

Figure 90.

Figure 91.

Ankles   Rotate your ankles in all directions.

Feet   Flex your feet. Flare your toes.

Stretching is a wonderful way to increase The Flowing. Stretching will increase your flexibility, which will allow more chi to flow through your body, which in turn increases your awareness and therefore enhances all of your metaphysical abilities.

Limit Smoking, Drinking, and Drugs

The art of Chi Gung is concerned with the development of your senses. Sensory awareness, therefore, is the key to your training. Therefore, it is vital for your chi development and health that you stop smoking, drinking alcohol, and taking recreational drugs.

Some drugs can artificially elevate your senses. In fact, many indigenous shamanic cultures use a variety of drugs to induce altered states. They use them relatively safely, because they approach this practice with a totally different intent than the recreational drug user. When real shamans uses drugs, they do it with control and purpose; they use drugs to induce specific alternative states of mind, so they can gain knowledge and skills for healing others. The recreational drug user, on the other hand, is merely interested in getting high, either for the sake of getting high or as an escape from the pressures of reality. In either case, drugs are an excuse and a cop-out. The abuse of drugs demands a high price, not only financially, but also from a health viewpoint. So why bother, especially when you can achieve better results practicing Chi Gung?

Both smoking and drinking are very common with many people today, but people often don't realize the limitations they then place upon themselves and the slaves they allow themselves to become to their vices. Smoking not only destroys your lungs, it causes numerous diseases that can kill you. It makes it difficult for you to think and move the way you should be able to, and makes it difficult to breathe at full capacity, which will inhibit your chi progress. Granted, there are some traditions, specifically Native American traditions (the Lakota, for example), where smoking the pipe is considered sacred. In instances like that, they are actually honoring what they do and truly believe in its holy power. Thus, they don't carry it to an extreme or do it casually. Remember, intent is extremely important.

Drinking alcohol is similar. Some systems, such as Santeria, use rum, but once again, they are using it in a special sacred manner and not just out of habit. When used improperly, drinking has devastating results. It deadens your senses, destroys your liver, and slowly kills you.

Life is about living, so why not live it to its fullest? Some will argue that drinking, smoking, and drug use indeed does let them live life to its fullest. These people often point out that if they couldn't do these things, they are depriving themselves of life's experiences. But how much experience is actually gained from these destructive pastimes? Once you have tried them, what new sensations will you gain? Instead, why not open yourself up to an unlimited and even unimaginable amount of sensory stimulation. With Chi Gung practice, you can gain new ideas, sensations, and experiences daily for the rest of your life.

For example, you will gain heightened senses, and the longer you practice, the more intense they will become. You will notice everything seems clearer to you, and you will feel fully alive. Sure, you could drink, smoke, take drugs, and do Chi Gung. On the surface, this might seem like the best of both worlds, but it is not. These vices actually limit your ability to experience chi and its flow. So even though you could practice bad habits, you would not be able to achieve the level of esoteric skill you otherwise could attain.

Therefore, if life for you centers on sensory fulfillment, or if you indeed want the greatest possible opportunities, then I suggest you quit your vices. If you are one of those few who use drugs, smoke, or drink in a controlled manner for spiritual reasons, always remember the importance of practicing moderation and intent.

Activity Training

You can apply the principles of Chi Gung to any area of interest you happen to have. The purpose of activity training is to help you figure out how Chi Gung training can be incorporated into any enjoyable pastime. This chapter offers wide variety of fun, playful activities that almost anyone can attempt.

Play Musical Instruments

It is never too late in life to learn how to play a musical instrument. It doesn't matter if you have never played one before or if you feel that you have no musical talent. There are literally thousands of different instruments that exist in the world, and everyone can learn to play at least one.

What actually is playing and how good do you have to become? Playing merely refers to learning to use the instrument to make sound. You don't have to play any particular types of songs, and it doesn't really matter how good you are. As long as you play, that is what is important. The reason I say this is because the simple act of playing an instrument can bring you enjoyment, which means your chi has been raised.

Most people who learn to play instruments actually want to learn how to play songs, and they measure their success at this skill by evaluating how good they sound. The problem with this is you can never really fairly compare yourself with others because we all have unique gifts and experiences. So try to stay out of this trap.

It doesn't really matter which instrument you choose. In fact, you might want to get a few different ones. Personally, I play Celtic lap harp, banjo, guitar, didjeridoo, jaw harp, shoulder jug, Appalachian dulcimer, bodhran, Congo drum, tambourine, penny whistle, fiddle, rattle, singing sword, and the balafon. All instruments require some sort of body movement, whether you pluck or strike something with your hand or foot or blow with your mouth or nose. Regardless of the muscles you must move to play the instrument, you must learn to really concentrate on what they feel like as you contract them. Try playing your instrument as slowly as possible. For example, if you are playing a flute, make each finger movement last a full second, then two seconds. Keep practicing until you can make a single motion of your finger last thirty seconds or more. By slowing your muscular movements, you gain more control over them, resulting in more precision and more chi development.

As you play your instrument, don't focus on playing any particular song; instead, just play any sounds that seem pleasing to you. This way, you will begin to work chi into your music. Next, concentrate on your muscles by directing The Flowing into them as you play your particular instrument. Use Taoist Reverse Breathing and relax by practicing the Three Regulations. Pick up your instrument, such as a flute or a guitar, and hold it as lightly as you can. Imagine your arms being as light as feathers while using extremely slow muscular movements. This Moving Wai Dan concept will help chi to gather in your arms and hands. After about twenty minutes, you should have built up an adequate supply. Over time, some of your energy will naturally begin to flow directly into your instrument and collect there, and you should eventually be able to sense this any time you pick it up. If you can get enough of The Flowing into your instrument, it should feel warm to your touch.

A few people become master musicians; they seem to be able to play almost anything. However, there is a level that far exceeds even the master level—the bardic level. Being a bard involves an extremely high level of Chi Gung skill. As a bard, it is possible to learn to use your instrument to affect other people's chi as well as the chi in nature. At this level you can send energy or take it from anything with your instrument. In order to reach this level of playing, you need to master Grand Circulation and the projection of chi using Environmental Breathing. If you know how to send chi through your music, for instance, it is possible that by playing a single note you can alter another person's opinion or action in almost any situation. You can also learn to use music to communicate with animals and plants, and you can even use it to heal yourself or others.

Because everything in the universe is based on the principle of vibration, learning music is a wonderful way to tap into magickal energy. Use your intuition to pick out an instrument that appeals to you, then learn how to play it. Focus particularly on the basics. Master them. Once you have, it is time to learn how to send chi as you play.

If you know Grand Circulation and Nei Dan, then you can also mentally project chi into your hands and your instrument. You do this by directing your chi into your hands, then out beyond your body and into the instrument itself. One way to do this is by becoming more aware of how the instrument feels. How heavy is it? Can you feel its weight shift as you play? You should learn to hold it so lightly that if a fly landed on your instrument, you would feel the added weight. In order to learn this type of sensitivity, you can try tying a single feather to a string and tying that to the instrument. As you play, feel the movement of the feather. When you can sense the added weight and movement, use a smaller feather. Keep reducing the size until you eventually just have a string hanging from your instrument, then start shortening the string. By using this type of sensitivity training method, you will learn to become aware of the instrument and its relative position in space, which will then enable you to begin to think of it as an extension of your own body. When you can do this you will be able to send chi into it.

The next step is to learn to send chi through your instrument and out into the world. The most obvious way is through the music itself. You do this by trying to play with emotion. Really feel the power of the music you are playing and project it for all to hear. After you can do this, there is a deeper level of sending chi. Picture your chi extending through the instrument and riding the sound waves of your music. Visualize sending it to specific targets, such as a plant or a pet. As you do this, watch for any noticeable reactions.

The next thing to learn is how to absorb chi while you play. Think of your instrument as some sort of vacuum that sucks chi from objects. The way to do this is to focus on your music while you inhale. Picture in your mind the chi actually coming toward you. Really try to sense this. The more you can focus on your breathing, especially inhaling, the easier this will be for you.

After you have learned how to send and receive chi while playing music, it is time to learn how to read the musical signature of objects. Pick an object—a cypress tree, for example—and try to imagine what kind of music it reminds you of. You are really going to have to trust your intuition here. Don't think specifically about anything; instead, just relax, breathe, and listen to the tree. Watch how it moves in the wind. Notice its various colors. Look at how tall it has grown. Smell it. With practice, you will eventually get some ideas of what this particular tree represents musically. Then, play a few notes. Let the music flow from you wherever it wants to go. When you become better at this skill, you will be able to walk into a building and know how to musically represent the feeling of it.

At the highest level of musical chi training, you can learn the music of people. Because we consist of a series of vibrational patterns and we were all born at different times, we each have a series of notes that represent who and what we are. To discover these musical patterns, you need to really study people. Find out as much as you can about them. When you become really good at this skill, you will be able to glance at people and know in an instant their personal musical songs. Then, you will be able to play for them and heal them, or help them change their behavior, because people will naturally respond to the individual tune they represent.

Don't be afraid of learning new skills. Even though you may never have played an instrument before, there is no reason you can't start today.

Listen to Music

Ultimately, Chi Gung is the study of energy, and all energy is made up of vibrations. One of the easiest and most fun ways to teach yourself about vibrations is by listening to music.

Music consists of sound waves traveling through the air and entering your body. This occurs primarily through your ears, but it also happens through your skin. So, it is possible to sense music even if you can't hear. But what kind of music should you listen to? What is good music? Well, that is a relative question when it comes to personal choice; after all, some people like rock, some like jazz, and some like country.

When it comes down to listening to the ideal music for Chi Gung practice, you should seriously consider music from southern India, especially solos played on the vina. A vina is a type of sitar; it resembles a guitar with an extra sound box. It is a multi-stringed instrument that is plucked with the fingers. Personally, I prefer the sarasvati vina, which is a version of the vina traditionally played by Indian women. The sarasvati vina has the ability to not only produce both sharp and flat notes like the vina, but it also can make a huge variety of micro-tones based on the structure and location of its extra strings.

Buying some sort of stereo system is a good investment in your own health and longevity. You can get records, CDs, cassettes, it really doesn't matter, but you might want to purchase something beyond merely a radio. Then you will have the ability to play whatever type of music you enjoy, whenever you want it. (Personally, I suggest getting a CD player if you can, simply because CDs are more durable than cassettes or records.)

Listening to music helps your Chi Gung practice in a number of ways. The most obvious one is that it helps you relax, which is directly tied to the Three Regulations. That is why slower-paced music is better for your health. By relaxing to whatever music you are listening to, your breathing slows down, your muscles relax, and your mind focuses on what you are hearing.

In addition, you can use music as a way to develop your sense of touch. Listen to a song and feel its beat penetrate your body. This will be a little easier if you start with something with a quick energetic tempo, such as a rock song. Pick one that really makes you want to move. Notice that as you listen you will probably start to get more physically involved. Perhaps you tap your feet, snap your fingers, or even writhe around almost uncontrollably. The song's chi is energizing you. In other words, you are absorbing The Flowing. This is what it is like when you learn to use Nei Dan and absorb chi from anything, such as plants, animals, or rocks. Granted, the intensity level might be different, but the feeling of personal involvement is the same. To train yourself to absorb chi, listen to music and notice how if affects you and how it seems to penetrate your body.

Extend your palms or the soles of your feet towards the musical source. As you inhale, you will notice a greater sense of music entering your body. The more you practice this, the easier it will become for you.

When you choose your musical selection, it is better to avoid violent lyrics or disharmonious rhythms, because they have a tendency to break down your body and disrupt your chi flow. Instead, pick music that lifts your spirits. Listen to this music as often as you can. You'll find it helps your Chi Gung training, which in turn will help you to lead a healthier, more enjoyable life.

Color, Draw, and Paint

Coloring, drawing, and painting can do a lot to enhance your chi. First of all, moving your arm and hand muscles in precise patterns as you perform your art work is a form of Wai Dan. Second, you have to focus your mind and pay attention to what you are doing. You must keep your hand and arm movements steady, and in order to do that you have to keep your mind steady. This is a valuable Chi Gung skill because mental focus is needed to accurately sense chi.

A lot of Chi Gung exercises require a strong imagination, particularly when you are a beginner. Drawing is an excellent way of tapping into the right hemisphere of your brain and developing imagination and creativity skills. Look at any object and then try to draw it from memory. Picture the details. If you are drawing a tree, for example, really try to draw what you have seen based on your own artistic interpretation. What does the tree really look like to you? Can you capture its essence?

Another benefit of drawing, coloring, or painting is they can be very relaxing. They are ways to lose yourself in the moment and to let yourself have a little fun. To become good at Chi Gung, you have to know how to relax. Stiff muscles, a closed mind, and a beaten spirit dramatically hinder chi flow. Practicing alternative skills, such as learning to make some form of art, can help you to get in touch with the pleasurable side of your sensory awareness. You literally teach yourself how to relax in a fun manner.

You can learn to send chi through your pencil or brush to put some of your own energy and life force in your work. (By the way, for all of you artists out there, this will help your work become more absorbing to those who view it.) The way you do this is by breathing properly and focusing your mind on your hand as it lightly grips your brush. Imagine that chi is flowing through your arm, into your hand, then directly into your pencil or brush. From there, it flows into the paper, thereby making your drawing magical and alive.

When you are first starting with this technique, you will use Wai Dan methods for generating chi. Don't rest your arm on a table or chair. Instead, hold your arm freely in the air. Review how you held your arms for the exercise called "Hugging a Tree" in the Still Wai Dan section of this book (see pages 89 through 90). Now, sit comfortably in a chair, pick up your pencil or brush, and hold your arms like that (Figure 92). Practice the Three Regulations. Then slowly lower your arm just enough so the only contact your arm has with the table is through the pencil or brush itself. In this way, chi will

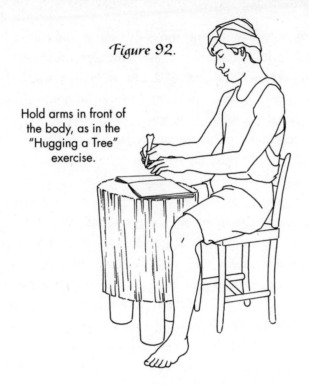

Figure 92.

Hold arms in front of
the body, as in the
"Hugging a Tree"
exercise.

build up in your shoulders and arms. If you are a beginner, your arms might shake, but with experience, this shaking will disappear. When you are at the point in your training where your arms no longer tremble, start to color, draw, or paint using strokes that are as light and controlled as you can make them. With enough practice, your chi will begin to flow into your pencil or brush and when that fills up with energy it will flow into the paper.

At an advanced level of Chi Gung you can trade in your ink, graphite, and paint and learn to express yourself with chi. Once you know Grand Circulation and chi projection, you can send chi into the environment. When you can do that, go outside and notice how your energy changes the world around you. Use The Flowing to heal and make the Earth a better place.

Play Games

As we grow older and allegedly mature, we often stop playing. That is probably because most people feel that playing is something that children do. But playing is for adults, too. You see, playing games is a wonderful way to stay young. It can help to keep your mind and body healthy and alert, and it is a great way to interact with other people while doing something fun.

How does this relate to Chi Gung? Well, Chi Gung is the study of energy, and playing is one type of energy expression. Think about how active kids are. They are constantly exploring, playing, learning, and trying new things. As adults, we often lose that degree of spontaneity, because we allow ourselves to become bogged down under the daily pressures of life. We also don't want to look immature in front of our peers, of course.

Well, it is time to change all of that. This stuffy adult stereotype you work so hard at perfecting actually stifles your ability to do the very things you are trying to accomplish with Chi Gung. If we could learn to relax and lighten up, we would be more energetic, fresher, more alert, and more creative. We would do better at our jobs and probably even have better social lives. By playing games, it is possible to regain these lost attributes. Go ahead and try it. I'll bet the skills you learn while playing will teach you new ways of solving problems and more efficient ways of getting things done.

Don't wait for a two-week vacation to loosen up. Start playing now. Daily or on weekends, it is your choice. The important thing is that you start playing again. Go to toy stores and explore all the marvelous wonders that are available. You will be surprised at how toys and games have changed over the years. Let your imagination run free, and you will have a chance to tap into an almost unlimited supply of energy.

Collect Things Based on Intuition

As kids, many of us had collections based on personal interest and fun. Some collected bugs. Others were interested in toy cars, rocks, or even words.

As we matured, many of us lost our interest in collections. Maybe that is because we often find ourselves too busy working, socializing, or just existing. When we do maintain collections as adults, they are often based on monetary gains in the form of investments. One way to help your chi development is to start collecting for fun again. You can collect anything—stamps, coins, or even memories. The important thing is you allow your mind to relax and learn to follow your gut instinct or intuition.

I like collecting almost everything—rocks, books, pens, toys (especially Barbie™ dolls)—it doesn't really matter. What matters is that I base my collections on feelings. For instance, as I browse through bookstores I relax my mind and just follow the aisles based on their energy. I might end up any-where in the store, such as the cooking, sports, gardening, or geography sec-tions. Any section could call me. Then, once I'm in a particular area looking at the various topics, I once again relax and let my chi flow from book to book. Eventually, I find a title that just feels right. Once I do, I then proceed to find the exact book based on that title. There might be twenty books with the same title, but one of them will feel right, and that is the one I will buy.

How does this work? Well, any object is capable of holding the energy of anyone who touches it. Therefore, in the example of the bookstore, some books may be filled with chi from depressed people, joyous people, or even psychopaths. Thus, each book can indeed feel different if you learn to attune yourself to energy flows.

That is the idea behind lucky objects such as a rabbit's foot or four-leaf clover. They have chi that lots of energy sensitive people have felt at one time or another, then the stories of these objects got passed from person to person until that particular object became lucky.

In India, people who are highly skilled in their version of Chi Gung often give small gifts to everyone they meet. These gifts are simple items such as stones, seeds, or pieces of cloth, but they are much more than what they appear. They carry the chi of the person giving the gift. In essence, these gift givers are giving a piece of themselves—their own vitality and life. The same applies to gifts you give or receive for your own collections.

Start collections of all types. Pick your items carefully and spend time looking at them and touching them. When you hold one of the items you have collected, stand in the "Hugging a Tree" posture so you can build up your chi and send some of it into the object. This will make the item even more special to you. Once you learn Nei Dan, you can also mentally send your chi into your collections. As your interests and needs change, give your old collections to others so they can enjoy them. By giving your once cher-ished collections away, you will be sharing your energy with others.

Fly Kites

Flying kites is an excellent way to practice Chi Gung and energy transference. I first began seriously flying kites when I was about ten years old, and I have flown them ever since. Kites have come a long way from the old paper, pine, single string models I flew as a kid. Now there are stunt kites, fighter kites, and acrobatic designs you probably wouldn't even dream existed.

Personally, for chi training, I suggest you start with a stunt kite. Most hobby stores have them, or you could make one yourself. These kites have two strings and two handles. By pulling on one handle, the kite will turn left; pull the other, and it will turn right.

The first thing you need to do is learn how to fly your kite. Get used to the way it handles under a variety of wind conditions. Then start practicing making it do loops and various patterns. Once you can do this, it is time to start your chi training with your kite.

As you fly your kite, relax. Breathe using Buddhist Breathing. Feel the chi that rides the wind. You can do this by really paying attention to how your kite tugs against the wind. Notice how your muscles tense as the kite strains against you. As you feel this energy, focus on inhaling so you can absorb it into your arms. After you have flown the kite for about twenty minutes, you should have built up quite a bit of energy in your arms and shoulders. At this point, switch your respiration to Taoist Reverse Breathing, and focus your mind on your hands. After a few minutes they should start to warm up. Next, as you exhale, imagine your energy flowing from your hands and up the kite string into the kite itself. Then as you inhale, focus on feeling the kite's movements as it dances in the air. Without moving your hands to change the kite's flight, try thinking about just one of your hands the next time you exhale. Because you have already built up chi, some of your excess energy should collect in that hand. Then, as you exhale, imagine the energy flowing to just one side of the kite, making the kite turn, climb, or dive.

Another skill you can work on is trying to predict how the wind will blow. Sometimes it will gust and at other times it will almost seem to stop. It might change directions in seconds. As you fly your kite, try to anticipate these changes and make the appropriate maneuvers with your kite to keep it in the air. For this exercise, you will have to really practice the Three Regulations and trust your intuition. Initially, you may sense the wind change just as it occurs, but with practice, you will detect it a moment or two sooner.

Once you have learned Nei Dan, you may also want to try taking chi from the air. Use your kite as a tool to help you sense how the wind moves. Inhale using Buddhist Breathing and really concentrate on the minute movements of the kite. Notice each time it dips or bounces even slightly. Inhale and imagine this energy coming into your hands. Once you can feel them warming up, circulate the energy up your arms and down into your Dan

Tien. From there, move it throughout your body and relish the magickal touch of the wind's chi.

Whenever the wind begins to blow, listen to it beckon you, and take your kite out to practice The Flowing. Not only is this a fun way to practice Chi Gung, it is also a neat excuse to go outside to play.

Train With Martial Arts Weapons

Weapons training may sound a little scary to beginners, but don't let it worry you. For one thing, you can pick whatever weapon you want to use so you don't have to learn by using an apparently dangerous one. For instance, a stick isn't as scary as a sword, and a rope isn't as scary as a stick.

You will be using the weapon with extremely slow motion because you are using it as a training tool, not an actual weapon. I'll give you an example. Though a Tai Chi long sword could be used as a deadly weapon, most people who practice with it learn to use it with slow, graceful movements that resemble dance. In fact, watching an expert practice is very relaxing because the movements look so soft and beautiful.

Weapons training teaches you to learn to send your chi through inanimate objects. Because I am also a practitioner of Tanzanian Drunken Chimpanzee Style Kung Fu, I happen to like using those weapons unique to that martial arts style, but you can use any weapon as your training tool for increasing your chi skills. Personally, I use a fourteen-foot-long "monkey rope," a six-foot bamboo staff, a wooden fan, a three-foot diameter willow loop, and a few exotic items such as coconuts, palm leaves, and dirt.

The idea behind weapons training with chi is to learn to use your weapon as an actual extension of your own body. For that, you need softness, precision, and awareness.

The first thing you need is a weapon. Picking one you feel naturally attracted to will be an exercise of your developing intuition. You might pick a sword, knife, stick, staff, rope, or any other kind of weapon. If you look into the Chinese martial arts, you will find there are hundreds of different kinds of weapons available. Because you have probably never used one before, I suggest you start with a bamboo stick. Pick one about two feet long. In fact, if the idea of a weapon concerns you, then you might want to get a wooden flute. Essentially, it is the same thing as a stick.

Once you have picked a weapon, you need to become comfortable with it. Weapons training offers you an excellent way to develop your concentration because if your attention wanes, you could hurt yourself, even if you are practicing slowly. Always treat any weapon with the respect it deserves and you should be fine.

Hold your weapon and become familiar with it. If you have any apprehension about the one you have chosen, perhaps because you are afraid you might get hurt, then put that weapon aside for now and choose another one that doesn't seem as scary. Forget about training using fast movements. Your main purpose in practicing with the weapon is to use it as a Chi Gung training aid for moving meditation. After all, how many sword battles do people really have today?

Practice the Three Regulations, then pick up your weapon and use Buddhist Breathing. Very slowly, begin moving your weapon around you. Imagine you are facing someone who is going to attack you. The attack, though, is happening in extremely slow motion, as in a dream. Concentrate on what you are doing. Move slowly and smoothly. Swing your weapon in as many different directions as you can as you step from one position to another. Dodge, duck, and parry. Really use your imagination as you move. After about twenty minutes you should have built up quite a bit of energy, and you will probably be hot and sweaty.

The slower you move, the greater benefit you will get out of this exercise, because slow movements will enable you to feel your energy flow through your body. As you practice, let your body move the way it wants to by concentrating on what it specifically feels like for each of your muscles to move. Try to think of your weapon as an extension of yourself. That is one of the reasons the monkey rope is my favorite weapon: it can move in any direction with flexibility and precision. With chi flowing through it, the rope feels alive. Here is how you can make and use a monkey rope.

Get a rope about fourteen feet long and one-quarter inch in diameter. If possible, get a braided cotton rope, because it lasts a long time and it moves well. Tie a large knot in one end to make it somewhat heavy. Coil the rope in a loop about a foot in diameter and hold it in one hand. In your other hand, hold the end that has the knot in it. Practice twirling the knotted end. Stretch the rope tightly between your hands and notice how you could use it to block another weapon. You can also learn to swing your rope and cast the knotted end so it ensnares a target such as a tree. You can do this by swinging the knotted end to build up momentum, then casting it toward a tree while you hold the other end of the rope with your opposite hand. Once the rope encircles the target, pull it tight and the rope should hold onto the tree. From a self-defense standpoint, what you are doing is learning to cast the rope around someone's legs. After it encircles his or her legs, you pull the rope tight; the person can't walk and more than likely will trip.

As you practice with whatever weapon you happen to choose, pay particular attention to how it feels in your hands. You want to get to the point where you can know where any spot on your weapon is, even if you were blindfolded. In fact, blindfold training is an excellent way to advance your weapons skills. Blow up a balloon and tie it to your weapon. Now blindfold yourself and see if you can feel the added weight of the balloon. As you move your weapon, notice how the balloon slightly changes the weapon's balance. This type of training will increase the sensitivity of your muscles, which will in turn enable you to sense chi better.

I suggest you practice outside as often as you can. Sometimes I work out along rivers, sometimes in forests or meadows, but mostly in swamps. You don't have to have this type of environment, though. Maybe you have a park, a beach, or a backyard. The idea is that you should train in as natural an environment as you can. That way, not only do you have room to move, you can also absorb chi from your surroundings Another way you can learn sensitivity is by training with falling leaves. As they fall, intercept them with your weapon and see if you can actually feel when your weapon has touched them. As you get better at this, try to keep your weapon pressed lightly against the falling leaf as it continues its journey to the ground.

Go Fly Fishing

My dad taught me how to fly fish when I was about three years old. We lived on a small lake in southern Michigan, and I spent many happy summer days casting dry flies after bluegill, bass, and once, even a huge tiger muskellunge. Over the years, I practiced my casting form until one day it seemed as though the line was alive with energy. Not only could I control where it would go, but I could actually feel it, too. If you want to really get into fly fishing I suggest getting a book on it or watching a video, but I will point out a few of the basics for you here.

Because your main interest in fly fishing will be to enhance your Chi Gung practice, you should get the lightest pole, reel, and line you can. Personally, I use a setup called a super-lightweight model.

Hold your pole by the handle in one hand. Pull out about twelve feet of line and hold it looped loosely in your opposite hand. Now start counting about once every second, "One-one thousand, two-one thousand, three-one thousand, and cast." Because you start with your pole in front of you, you count "one" as you slowly move the pole behind you and let out a little line with your opposite hand. As you say "one thousand" you swing the pole forward, letting out just a little more line. By the time you get to the final words "and cast" you should have out about thirty feet of line. Also, when you say "cast," you cast the line forward into the water. Your line should swing in a large figure-eight pattern over your head on each forward and backward swing. The only time it should touch either the ground or the water is the point at which you finally cast it forward. (If you like movies and you want to see what fly fishing really looks like, rent a copy of *A River Runs Through It* [1992, Columbia Pictures]. This is an incredible movie with some of the best fly fishing demonstrations ever filmed.)

At this point, you need to go out and practice mastering the technique of fly fishing. For now, don't worry about catching fish. I frequently go fly fishing with a dry fly without a hook so I can't catch fish. This also helps when you are learning to cast because then your line has less chance of getting caught on any trees, bushes, or weeds behind you.

Once you have the hang of properly releasing the line and making a good cast, you can start to apply some Chi Gung principles. Use the Three Regulations to relax yourself. Concentrate on your breathing and use Buddhist Breathing as you first learn this skill. At this point, you are trying for smoothness. Learn to synchronize your breathing with your arm movements. Inhale as your arm moves behind you and exhale as you swing the pole forward.

The action of moving your arms acts as Wai Dan training and will energize your shoulders rather quickly. After about twenty minutes, you should have built up enough chi that it will start to move into your fishing pole. Try concentrating your mind on the movement of the dry fly attached to the end of the line, and your chi should project out to it. If you are relaxed enough and you have built up enough chi, this should make your bait irresistible to most fish.

Another way to use chi while fishing is to locate the fish with it. After all, you wouldn't have too much luck just randomly whipping the water with your bait. As you are fishing, relax and try to sense where fish might be swimming or resting. This is an exercise in trusting your intuition. Use Buddhist Breathing and focus your mind on your Dan Tien. With practice, you can get very good at locating fish this way. My dad was a master at locating fish. He introduced me to fly fishing when I was three years old, and over the years, we did a lot of fishing together, each of us constantly honing our skills. Using chi, it is possible to go to any river, lake, or ocean and catch fish even when nobody else has any strikes. For example, one summer we kept a record of our musky fishing. According to the Department of Natural Resources, the average fishing hours per musky was about one fish for every sixty hours of fishing time. We were catching one musky every two hours. (For you die-hards out there, we obviously weren't fly fishing for muskies, though I did have a heck of a fight with one once on a hand-tied dry fly. I use this example because it shows just what chi can help you learn to do.) In case you are wondering, we set almost all the fish free.

Going fly fishing is not only a great way to practice Chi Gung, but it is also a way for you to get away from the daily grind. Not only can you practice finding fish using The Flowing and perfect sending chi along your fishing line, you can also get some good solid experience in the gentle and lost art of reposing.

Carry a Chi Bag

A chi bag is a small bag, about two inches square, generally made of leather or other natural material such as cotton or wool. It is used to carry a variety of items that are special to you. These items are things that have the types of chi that you are interested in using frequently. It is important to realize that each chi bag is unique to each individual. For example, I carry what I feel will aid me at any given time, whereas you would carry those items that are important to you.

Native Americans from many tribes called these types of bags "spirit bags" or "medicine pouches." They often carried items such as bones, feathers, beads, coins, or pieces of plants in their bags. They felt these items gave them special powers and abilities, as well as acting as an extension and amplification of the wearer's inner self. You should collect similar types of items you feel naturally drawn to.

When you make a chi bag, you can use almost anything, but you might as well make it out of a material that has at least one kind of chi you are interested in using as a power source. Personally, I prefer a leather chi bag with long fringe. The leather is made out of deerskin, which gives me the chi from a deer. The fringe is about three inches long, and its purpose is to help to direct energy into the bag by its movement. The moving fringe also helps generate additional energy. The bag itself is about two inches square. In this way, it is small enough to wear around my neck or fit into a pocket. I always wear mine in open view, attached to a leather cord. When you make your bag, be sure to include some method of keeping it closed so your special chi keepsakes won't fall out. I use a long, beaded leather thong, and I bind the thong with a specially tied square knot.

In addition to carrying a variety of items inside the bag, you can also attach things to the bag itself. Mine has a braided loop of wolf hair and an assortment of pink beads. I would like to tell you what's inside my bag but that would give away some of my special energy, so you will have to come up with your own ideas for your own bag.

In order to learn to absorb the chi from your bag, you will need to learn Nei Dan Chi Gung. Specifically, you will have to learn Grand Circulation. Even if you have not got that far in your training, and you might not have developed your senses enough to feel its energy, the chi in your bag will still help you. What you need to do is to rapidly open and close your hand until it gets warm. Then, pick up the chi bag and hold it in your hand. As your chi starts to circulate through your body, it will draw some of the chi from the bag with it.

After you make your bag and fill it with items of your choice, carry it with you or wear it wherever you go. That way, you always have access to the chi it contains. As a secondary benefit, you will probably find that a chi bag also happens to be an interesting conversation starter.

Limit Television Watching

Watching TV is a lot of fun, and it is a great way to relax if done properly. You can also learn a lot, even from sitcoms. However, if you are serious about learning Chi Gung, I suggest you limit your viewing hours to a reasonable amount. If you actively watch TV by using it to learn about other cultures, how to do things, or about social relationship skills, then by all means, continue watching.

Try not to sit passively in front of your screen, merely watching idly. You could argue that it is a way to relax, but is it? If you are just sitting there watching without thinking, not even really remembering what the show was about when it ends, then what have you gained? Not much. A lot of people watch TV just to do something. They say they're bored and there's nothing else to do. How uncreative! Sad, too. There's really no reason to ever be bored. You have the ability to think about anything at anytime. There are no limitations. So why restrict yourself?

If you are going to watch TV, why not turn it into a Chi Gung training lesson? First, use the Three Regulations to relax yourself, then practice Buddhist Breathing. Next, pick a show that interests you and start watching. Instead of watching passively, though, really try to imagine the show happening. Picture yourself as an outside observer in the show. Try to anticipate what will happen, who will talk, and what they will say. Think about how you would solve the dilemmas presented. By doing this, you are cultivating your intuition and imagination. When you get really good at sensing the chi of a show, it is possible to predict how the actors and actresses will respond in given situations. For instance, say one of them misses a line. If you are really in tune with the energy of the show, then that person's mistake will seem obvious.

From now on, try adding Chi Gung training to your TV viewing time. You might want to limit your viewing hours, particularly as you get better at Chi Gung and therefore are more sensitive to energy. All electrical appliances give off energy that can hinder your sensory awareness and development over time. So even though you can use TV viewing as a training tool when you do watch it, limit its use if you can.

Play Video Games

Playing video games may at first seem like a rather obscure form of Chi Gung training, but it works. Granted, you shouldn't play them obsessively, because just like an electrical appliance, they can have a negative effect on your chi flow. Paradoxically through, they offer many benefits. What I mean by video games are some of the high-technology games that are available today for computers or TV game sets such as Nintendo™. Playing them can help your

Chi Gung by giving you ways to practice the Three Regulations while you are under pressure. In addition it gives you ways to learn to think and respond faster in emergencies.

As you play some of these frantic games, you will often find yourself becoming more and more stressed as the pressures of the game get to you. To play well, however, you need to relax and keep yourself calm, and the best way to do this is by using Buddhist Breathing. When you feel your pulse rising to match the pressures of the game, concentrate on increasing the length of your inhalations.

Because most video games force you to think fast as you play some of the higher levels, they improve the neural transmitters in your brain. The games force you to think and respond at your maximum capability. This skill transfers to Chi Gung in situations when you need to send or receive chi quickly. For example, if you need a burst of energy in a crisis situation, this type of training prepares you to think with the speed and clarity you will need. At an advanced level of Chi Gung, for example, if you saw someone who was unaware and about to get hit by a car, you could send chi toward the person to get him or her to look in the right direction and spring out of the way. (To do this you would have to know Nei Dan Grand Circulation and Chi Projection.)

Another way video games can help you is simply by the variety of colors they use. At a beginner's level, you could just take note of the different colors as you play. Because red generates energy in people, you might try focusing your attention on anything red that you happen to see on the screen if you needed to play quicker. After you learn how to absorb chi, you could increase the length of your inhalations and focus your mind on absorbing any color. If you want to stay calm under pressure, you might try blue, and if you find your arm or hand muscles cramping from the strain of the game, you could absorb green.

If you are going to use video games to increase your chi, it is best if you avoid the violent types of games, because the negativity they spew overshadows any positive chi.

Take some time out from your day periodically to play video games. It is a fun form of entertainment that also happens to increase your Chi Gung skills, and therefore your health.

Vacation in High-Energy Locations

In the past, people were more in tune with the environment than we are today. We often feel that today we have important things to do, but in our rush to get things done, we too often forget to sense our surroundings. When people think of vacations, they think of getting away from it all while pursuing their favorite activities, such as skiing, hiking, or going to the beach. However, you can also use your vacation to help you gain more chi, if you vacation at high-energy power spots.

On your next vacation, explore sacred or mysterious spots—churches, famous ruins, or mountains (such as the Himalayas), forests (such as Sherwood), or rivers (such as the Ganges). Throughout history, certain areas have been considered special in one way or another to various peoples. In England there is Stonehenge. In the United States there are the Anasazi ruins in Mesa Verde, Colorado. Other places include the Holy Land in the Middle East, Mayan ruins in Mexico, Inca ruins in Peru, and the Great Pyramids in Egypt.

It is extremely important when you go to a sacred area that you respect the significance of the location. If you can't or won't do this, then you shouldn't go. Also, you shouldn't disturb anything while you are there. For example, in Hawaii, it is considered extremely unlucky to take lava rocks. Many people who have attempted to take it have lost thousands of dollars or suffered other calamities before finally mailing the lava back to the island in an act of desperation.

Every place has its own energy level. Some of it is just naturally stronger than in other areas. Usually, energy spots occur wherever there is a major break from one type of environment to another. For example, a single mountain on a vast plain would be high in chi. Other spots might be a waterfall, such as Niagara Falls, or where two large bodies of water meet such as the Atlantic Ocean and the Gulf of Mexico at Key West, Florida. By visiting high-energy places, you will have a greater chance of sensing what energy actually feels like. This will aid you later when you are in more subtle areas like a meadow or a grove of trees.

Your chi vacation doesn't have to be to someplace exotic. Instead, try to find places that are meaningful to you, places that you feel naturally drawn to visit. In fact, it is better to start this way because then you will find out if this is the type of vacation you are interested in pursuing. It is much cheaper and easier to visit someplace local as opposed to flying halfway around the world only to find out you have no ability to detect energy there, or if you can, that it doesn't mean anything to you.

Once you've picked a spot where you want to try experiencing environmental energy, the first thing you have to do is practice the Three Regulations in order to calm your mind, body, and breath. The best way to experience The Flowing is to find a comfortable place, then sit on the ground. Close your eyes and breathe as slowly as possible through your nose using Buddhist Breathing. With other Chi Gung exercises, you focus on what is happening inside of your body. Here, you are trying to sense the chi in the land and air around you. As you breathe, focus your mind on your skin, especially as you inhale.

It may be difficult at first for you to differentiate between your own chi and the chi that comes from your surroundings. What you need to do is try the above exercise in a variety of locations. Pay special attention to any sensations you feel. Some locations might make you feel relaxed and soothed by giving you a feeling similar to a warm massage. Other spots could send chills through your body, making you feel tense or scared. Just as places can have positive chi, others can have negative chi. These negative places are best avoided.

Instead of going to the same vacation spots year after year, why not try something new next time? Let your intuition and imagination tell you where to go and visit high energy places. As you become more sensitive to The Flowing, you will find each location has a slightly different feel to it. In fact, it is possible to classify these power places by the type of chi they emit. The world has many mysterious places awaiting those brave enough to explore their hidden secrets.

Live or Vacation in High Altitudes

The higher in altitude you go, the greater your chi will flow. It is more difficult to breathe as you go higher, so you have to learn to use oxygen, and therefore chi, more efficiently. Living or vacationing in the mountains forces you to breathe properly.

Not too long ago I lived in Colorado at an altitude around 9,200 feet. Whenever I got the chance, I practiced The Flowing in the mountains that surrounded me, particularly Pike's Peak, which is 14,110 feet above sea level. It was amazing how much even the 5,000-foot change in altitude made in relation to what chi felt like and how it responded. The higher I went, the more I sensed the chi, and the easier it was to manipulate and detect at greater distances.

The first thing you will notice at high altitudes is that even the simplest of physical activities can tax your breathing. You are going to need some time to adjust if you intend to work out like you did in the lowlands. Take it easy at first as you ascend mountains, and be careful what you do. For example, if you are accustomed to rock climbing at 1,000 feet altitude and you try it in the high mountains, you won't have your same strength or endurance. It could be dangerous, so use common sense.

When you are in the mountains, you will probably be able to hear, see, smell, and sense energy better than in other places. This is not only because of the height, but also because there usually is less pollution, population, and problems. The lack of pollution enables you to experience your environment in a more natural state. Likewise, with less people around, there is less sensory interference by such things as traffic, lights, and noise. Finally, people who live or vacation in mountains often are more relaxed and more willing to shelve their problems because of the slower pace of living, the vast expanses of nature, and their willingness to accept a little less materialism at the cost of living or visiting semi-inaccessible places. Mountain people are often happy people, which means they have an abundance of positive chi.

If you ever get the chance, go to the mountains to vacation or better yet, to live. You will find it greatly enhances your chi.

Enhance the Energy of Your House

The Chinese call the study of environmental energy *feng shui*. Experts in this art learn how to determine the energy of geographical locations as well as humanmade structures such as homes.

Your home is where you spend a large amount of your time and it reflects who you are. Your energy permeates its very walls. How often, for example, have you entered a room somewhere, perhaps at work, and immediately felt tension? Or maybe you can remember how good it felt at times to visit a friend's home.

Our home indeed becomes an expression of who we are. When my partner and I bought our first new home, it definitely was a reflection of who we are. It was a rustic-styled Swiss chalet on about three acres of land. There was a creek, a grove of trees, a swamp, a pond, and a huge gently rolling hill with solid boulders. Each of these features added chi to the property.

The house sat on a large hill, which means it had a focal point for energy. (The top floor in an apartment would be similar focal point.) In front of the house was a series of ponds fed by a fresh-running mountain stream. The running water also carried a good supply of energy. The yard was landscaped with trees, shrubs, flowers, rustic wooden fences, rock piles, and even a bridge. All of these things gathered The Flowing. The road and driveway formed a long lazy *U* shape, which helped the energy collect at the house instead of continuing unnecessarily down the road. Plus, the shape of the house was a Swiss chalet style with a high pointed roof that drew energy from the sky. The siding on the house was wood, which added tree chi.

In addition to the chi that was on the outside of the house and in the yard, there were things we had inside our home to increase the energy. All of the doors and cabinets are solid wood, and there was also a hardwood floor and wood walls. All of this exposed woodwork helped energy flow easily from room to room. There was also a woodburning stove in the living room. This room was a great place for energy exchange, because as the wood burns, energy is produced. (A fireplace works the same way. Fireplaces are also good spots to gather the family while relaxing and sharing good times. Their very usage adds positive chi.)

The walls of our house were adorned with a variety of multi-colored pictures, decorations, and knick-knacks. Each of these separate items shared their own energy of color, shape, and memories. We hung mirrors on as many walls as possible to help reflect chi throughout the house. This was particularly important in areas that didn't get as much sunlight or activity.

In the bedrooms, the beds all lay east to west, with the heads of the beds to the west. This position increased The Flowing as well as helped us develop our own creativity as we slept.

Whether you live in a house, an apartment, or a condo, you can do things to increase the energy in your home. Decorate it. Add color, sound, smells, and a variety of textures. Grow as many plants as you can; they will add both oxygen and chi to each room. Try to buy natural furniture, such as wood, instead of plastic. Change your living space from a place where you survive to a magickal home that energizes you, so you can live a long, healthy, adventurous life.

Work With Candles

Candles are wonderful tools that can be used in lots of different ways to increase your chi skills. You can use them as a way to measure your chi flow, to learn to focus your mind, and to sensitize yourself to fire chi.

As a beginner, there is an easy way to practice Wai Dan and to test your chi development. Place a candle in a sturdy candle holder and light it. (First make sure you have removed all flammable objects from the area so that if the candle tips over, nothing will burn. It is extremely important to always respect fire.) Once you have the candle burning, fully extend your arm until your palm is an inch or so away from the flame. Don't burn yourself. Withdraw your hand, then quickly thrust it toward the candle, making certain you don't accidentally collide with it. As soon as your arm fully extends, retract it. If you do it correctly, this movement will extinguish the flame. The movement is sort of like the snapping of a whip, only your arm is the whip, and your hand acts as the whip's tip. Keep practicing until you can extinguish the flame. If you want this technique to work, you need to keep your arm as relaxed as possible. If you use too much muscular force, the flame won't extinguish. This exercise will reveal how well you have learned to relax your body.

Once you can consistently put out the candle, move back an inch or two. Keep practicing and keep moving back. As you progress, you may be able to extinguish the candle from about twelve feet or more away.

When you can do that, you will probably have learned Grand Circulation. This is a requirement for the next exercise called "Stationary Candle Extinguishing Training." Start with your palm about an inch from the flame. Inhale slowly using Taoist Reverse Breathing. Draw chi into your body and down to your Dan Tien. Then quickly move the chi through your body and to your palm using only your mind. You can do this by focusing your mind on your palm. Imagine your chi surging from your hand and shooting toward the flame. It will probably take awhile, but you should eventually be able to make the flame flicker. With more training, it is possible to actually put it out. When you can extinguish a flame at one inch, back up and try again. Candle extinguishing training is an easy way of actually measuring your Chi Gung abilities. Use it frequently and chart your progress.

Another thing you can do with candles is use them to increase your attention span. Light a candle and watch the fire. Don't stare too intently; you want to allow yourself to blink naturally, but try to keep your mind riveted to the dancing flame. How long can you watch it before your mind wanders? Every

time you practice this, try to increase the length of your concentrated awareness. When you do this exercise, use Buddhist Breathing and practice the
Three Regulations. This exercise can teach you to relax your eyes, which can
help to eliminate headaches and stress.

You can also use candle work to improve your eyesight and lower the pre-
scription of your lenses if you wear glasses or contacts. The way to do this
involves a variety of exercises. The first one requires you to let your eyes follow the dancing flame. Do this about five minutes a day. It will build up the
strength of your eye muscles. You can work on your near- and far-distance
visual focusing skills by alternately looking at the candle flame, then something that is as far away as possible. Do this thirty-six times. I practice these
exercises regularly and have completely eliminated my need to wear correc-
tive lenses.

It is also possible for you to dramatically increase your observational skills
by watching a lighted candle. Have you ever noticed that we often have a difficult time differentiating between things that appear alike? For instance, a rose
is a rose, right? In this case, a flame is a flame. Well, try to really get a sense of
your particular candle flame. Personalize it. How tall is it? What colors does it
have? How far out does it appear to shed light? What temperature does it
appear to be? Does it move in any recognizable pattern? No two candle flames
could ever be exactly the same. By learning to focus on the differences, you are
training your mind to look for the tiniest distinctions. This is an invaluable skill
when learning how to categorize the chi of different objects.

The most important method of training with candles is to learn to take
chi from the flame itself. Hold your hand within an inch of the side of the
flame. Do you feel its heat? (Don't hold your hand directly over the top of the
flame or you could burn yourself.) Now use Buddhist Breathing. Inhale slowly
and evenly through your nose. Also imagine inhaling through the palm of
your hand. Does the flame now feel hotter? Practice this until you can notice
a temperature change.

When you can, try moving your hand farther away and do the exercise
again. Try to see how far away you can move and still sense the flame. Next,
try sensing the heat of the flame with your face, specifically, the energy spot
located in your forehead directly above the bridge of your nose. As you practice this skill, notice if the flame gives you any sensation other than heat. One
way to further practice this skill is by having someone light a given number
of candles in a room. Then, while you are blindfolded, try to determine how
many candle flames there are and where they are located.

Candles offer you a variety of ways to train with Chi Gung. If nothing else, they evoke a sense of peace and contentment as they burn in a dark room at night.

Work With Paper

You can use an ordinary sheet of notebook paper as a unique way to measure your Chi Gung skills. Suspend the paper from a thin piece of thread, so the paper can move freely. Make sure you hang it in a place where no air currents will blow it.

Extend both of your arms until your palms are about an inch away from your paper target. Use the Three Regulations to relax your entire body, particularly your extended shoulders, arms, and hands. Breathe slowly and smoothly through your nose using Taoist Reverse Breathing. Without moving, focus your mind on your palms. Maintain this position until your palms begin to feel warm. When they do, focus your mind on the piece of paper. You are using a combination of Wai Dan and Nei Dan for this exercise. Imagine your chi is projecting out from your palms and entering the paper. Then, imagine the paper moving. Practice this exercise about ten minutes a day until you can make the paper swing on the thread by sending chi into it. When you can move the paper, gradually increase the distance between your palms and the paper. Try using a variety of different kinds and sizes of paper.

Another thing you can do with paper is to try to determine what type of tree it came from. Because every tree has its own chi signature, paper does too. Hold a piece of paper lightly in your hand and feel it. Close your eyes and use Buddhist Breathing. Imagine the energy of the paper entering your hands through your palms. Trust your instincts. What does the paper feel like to you? What can you learn from it?

Paper can also be used to develop your sense of differentiating other people's chi. Go to a bookstore and find a section of books that interests you. Then, as you scan the titles with your eyes, let one of your palms glide across the rows of books. When you first try this, you might want to keep your hand within an inch or so of the books. With practice, you can do this from several feet. Use Buddhist Breathing and, while you inhale, try to pick up any interesting or unusual sensations from any of the books. You will eventually be able to determine how many people have touched a given book and what their chi was like. This will give you a sense of who these people were. If you are thinking of buying a book, make sure you get one that seems neutral or has good chi in it. You don't want to bring someone else's negativity into your home.

Chi Gung training with paper also applies to card games. Randomly pick a card from a deck, and without looking at it try to determine what card it is. Use Buddhist Breathing and keep the card face down in the palm of your hand. How does it feel? Because each card has different amounts, kinds, and colors of ink on it, you can try to learn how each individual card feels by its energy. If you are sensitive enough, you will notice that each card will vibrate slightly differently. Keep practicing until you can sense this.

Once you learn the principles of working with paper, you will be able to transfer these same types of exercises to an infinite variety of objects. Try the exercises described above using leaves, grass, feathers, or even dust balls. Working with paper and other light objects is a great way to enhance your sensitivity and also to measure your growing chi skills.

Sensory Training

*S*ensory training involves learning how to develop and hone all of your senses. This chapter begins by introducing Wai Dan principles that a beginner could use. Then, it offers ideas on how to increase your senses even further using Nei Dan training. Sensory training is one of the most important elements of Chi Gung training. The exercises are important because the skills you learn from practicing them directly correlate to all other aspects of Chi Gung training.

Touch

One of the main lessons of Chi Gung is teaching our bodies to become more sensitive. One way to do this is through touch training.

Blindfold yourself or close your eyes and begin feeling a variety of objects—apples, rocks, cats—you can touch anything. By doing this, you will learn to discriminate with your sense of touch. How does an orange feel different from a grapefruit? Don't think about just size and weight, but also texture, shape, and density. Is one more slippery than the other? What about temperature differences?

Try touching as many different objects as you can, as often as you can, and focus on what they really feel like. Blindfold yourself and touch only parts or pieces of objects, and see if you can correctly identify what they belong to. By increasing your touch sensitivity, you will enhance your ability to sense physical changes in your environment. What does wind feel like? What does shade feel like?

Try absorbing chi from the objects you touch. As a beginner, you will have to use Wai Dan to do this. Hold the object in your hands and extend your arms in front of you at about shoulder height. Use Buddhist Breathing and focus your mind on inhaling. Can you detect any energy from the object? Keep practicing until you can. When you do, it will probably feel like a slight vibrational pattern. A rock is a really good object to work with when you do this exercise, because rocks have lots of vibrational chi. Try to determine if different items appear to give off different energy sensations.

After you have begun to learn what a variety of objects' energy feels like while actually touching them, it is time for you to try feeling their chi from a distance. Relax using the Three Regulations and breathe using Taoist Reverse Breathing. Concentrate on both the object and the palms of you hands. Point your palms at the object from a distance of an inch. Imagine you feel The Flowing as the object's energy directly contacts your skin. When you can clearly sense the chi, try the exercise from an even greater distance. With years of practice, it is possible to correctly identify the chi of anything from any distance.

For example, what does a mule deer's energy feel like from 200 yards away? Try it and see. In case you are wondering, mule deer chi often manifests itself as a spiral of energy in your ear closest to the animal. If I'm walking in the woods and I feel a slight clockwise-spiraling sensation in my right ear, I know a mule deer is on my right side somewhere in the distance. Depending on the intensity of the sensation, I can determine how far away the animal is, if more than one is present, and what sex it is.

Everything has its own chi pattern, which is identifiable once you learn how to interpret the similarities and differences. Then all you have to do is categorize the different sensations. The more you practice touching objects and sensing their chi, the more sensitive you will become to energy patterns. Once you gain proficiency at this, you will be able to identify objects you can't see, or determine people's moods and thoughts. Touch training is the basis for all advanced Chi Gung skills. You should practice this skill every day as often as you can.

Smell

Did you know that once you have smelled something, you will probably be able to correctly identify that particular scent for the rest of your life? Your other senses are not nearly as reliable as far as your memory is concerned, but we seldom pay attention to this powerful sense. It seems a lot easier and more convenient to look, listen, touch, or even taste.

Everything consists of vibrations of one sort or another. Even smells give off vibratory patterns, though that is not the way we usually think of odors. With proper training, however, you can learn to alter sensory input so that you can see or hear smells instead of merely using your nose.

To develop this kind of scent sensitivity, the first step is to practice the Three Regulations while using Buddhist Breathing. Next, you should start paying attention to the way things smell. For example, what does an orange smell like? How does a California orange smell different than a Florida orange? What about other different kinds of oranges?

Discriminate smells. Try to determine their subtle differences. One way to do this is to smell two things at the same time, one in each nostril. Another skill you can practice is determining how far away you can smell something. Start with something that has a rather strong smell. Have a friend gather a variety of items that each have a unique and commonly identifiable smell. Then, tell your friend to place one of the items on a table the length of a room away from you as you blindfold yourself. Slowly walk toward the table and stop when you can identify the smell of the object. With practice, you should be able to correctly name lots of different scents from greater distances.

One of the things you will discover as you practice Chi Gung is that your sense of smell increases, primarily because you spend so much time and energy focusing on your breathing. To make this skill even stronger, try absorbing chi through your nose as you smell something. To do this, first practice the Three Regulations, then breathe using Buddhist Breathing. Imagine that whatever you are smelling is sending its energy directly to you. Focus your mind on your nose as you inhale as slowly as possible.

Cultivate your sense of smell. Fine tune it to the point where you can discriminate between the odor of any two given objects. As you practice this, pay particular attention to any chi sensations you might have. That way, you can eventually learn to blend your senses. For example, what does red smell like? You will have to fully develop your senses in order to differentiate something like this, and you can do that by practicing developing your sense of smell for at least a few minutes every day.

Hearing

As our second most advanced sense, hearing is extremely important for chi development. Through the use of hearing, we learn to interpret the vibrations in the air, which are called sound waves. Sound has a tremendous impact on us. How many times have you noticed that when a song you really liked played on the radio, it lifted you out of the doldrums, raised your spirit, and within moments, had you feeling energetic, alive, and fully aware? Perhaps an emotional song ripped at your soul and you felt as though all of your energy drained from your body.

With many of the Chi Gung training exercises, you are trying to focus on one thing at a time. Hearing is a little different because it is sometimes harder to completely focus your listening skills on just one noise. In the beginning, it often seems like hearing training is overwhelming, because you can actually hear so many different things at once. This makes it difficult to concentrate on a certain task. However, because hearing is actually one skill, when you initially practice this, just focus on your hearing. As you progress, you can add other sensory awareness skills simultaneously. Eventually, you will want to focus on breathing, feeling, seeing, and hearing, all at the same time.

It is possible to develop your hearing to the extent that you can hear echoes bounce off of a six-inch curb as you walk along the street, or identify trees and plants by the sound of wind blowing through them. The key to developing hearing is to learn to pay attention to the sounds around you.

The first thing you need to do is practice the Three Regulations, then use Buddhist Breathing as you start really listening. You may listen all the time, but for most of us, listening is done passively. We don't really focus on most of the things we hear. As you are reading this, how many of you have actively noticed the various sounds that are accessible to you right now? Perhaps someone is talking somewhere in your house, or maybe the TV is on. Can you hear the wind blow outside? Is your refrigerator humming? Is there any activity going on near you? If there is another person near you, can you hear the sound of their clothes as they move? What about footsteps? Can you hear your own breathing? How about your heartbeat?

By actively listening, we become more in tune with the world around us. This allows us to experience more, which then enables us to live fuller lives.

One of the interesting things about hearing training is it teaches us to identify sound waves. Because everything in the universe consists of moving particles of energy, it is possible to eventually train yourself to hear things like colors, shapes, and sizes. First, however, you need to develop your hearing skills a little more.

The best way to do this is to blindfold yourself. You will probably find that when you can't see, your hearing suddenly seems more acute. It hasn't really changed, you are just paying more attention to it. While you are blindfolded, listen to a TV and see if you can still follow along with what is happening on a given show. This may take a little practice because you will have to remember more than you do by merely passively watching. Once you can do this, try listening to people around you. Eventually you will learn to identify them by their footsteps, breathing, voice, and even the rustling of their clothes.

When you can identify people by the way they sound, try it with animals. How does a dog sound different from a cat when it walks? Do they sound different when they drink or eat? Do they sound like they breathe differently? Once you have established the differences between dogs and cats or any other two animals, you might want to try listening to two animals of the same species, such as two dogs. The next thing you should do is go to a zoo and listen to all of the animals there. Try to identify any kind of noise they make, whether it is vocal or merely from the wind blowing in their fur. By the time you can tell which animals are making certain noises, you can work with plants. Listen to the wind as it rustles the trees. How does a juniper's sound compare with a maple's?

Continue to practice discriminating between sounds. Listen to everything. Try finding sounds that are similar but actually come from very different sources, such as the similarities between the sounds of a pencil eraser rubbing paper and a steam locomotive.

By developing your hearing, you are teaching yourself to become more aware of your senses. The finer the distinctions you learn to make, the greater you will benefit. One of the things you can do to learn to hear even better is to absorb chi in your ears. Practice the Three Regulations, then use Buddhist Breathing as you inhale as slowly as possible. Imagine chi entering your ears. Then as you exhale, picture your energy flowing out of your ears. When you become proficient at manipulating your chi, you will probably notice that sending chi in and out of your ears is a great way to cool off on a hot day or to warm up on a cold day.

Taste

Chi can affect all people differently. It can register with any of your senses. Some feel it, others taste it. Regardless of how you happen to sense chi, it is a good idea to increase your sense of taste. By learning to discriminate tastes, you are indirectly learning to develop all of your senses, because at a fundamental level, they are all linked. To progress in Chi Gung, you need to develop your senses as much as possible, including your sense of taste.

The next time you are hungry, instead of thinking of just eating something, take the time to really taste it. How does an orange taste different from a tangerine? How are nectarines similar in flavor? How many different kinds of apples can you identify by taste? (If you said more than twenty, you are doing great.) Experiment with sweet, sour, salty, and bitter foods. Compare textures, as well as the length of time a given flavor lasts.

After you get used to trying different foods, try increasing your sense of taste using chi. As a beginner, the easiest way to do this is to open your mouth as wide as you can for a couple of minutes as you practice the Three Regulations and Buddhist Breathing. This Wai Dan exercise will send chi to your mouth. After about five minutes, close your mouth and notice if you feel any tingling or warmth. Then pick up something and eat it as slowly as possible. Take small bites and chew each bite as much as you can. As you chew, imagine that the chi from the food is entering your meridians through your mouth. After you swallow, slowly inhale and see if you can sense the food as it goes down your throat to your stomach.

Eat as many different foods as you can so that you can fully develop your sense of taste. One great way to get some ideas is by buying a variety of ethnic cookbooks. Challenge your taste buds. At least once a day, eat something you have never tried before. It doesn't have to be a major food item; it could just be a sample of an herb or spice. By developing your sense of taste, you will learn how to discriminate between different sensations such as flavor, texture, temperature, and consistency. This skill will help you learn to categorize chi.

Sight

How well can you see? Can you see 20/20? Do you know what those numbers mean? They refer to your capability of detecting something at twenty feet that the average person is also capable of seeing at twenty feet. But what is average? It is hard to say. After all, how many people were used in the sample study of determining average? Who knows? Does it really matter? Should you be content if your vision is 20/20? No, not when you can do something to make it even better.

Did you know, for example, that it is possible to see as well as 20/1? This means that what most people could discern at one foot, you could clearly see at twenty feet. Try this as an experiment. Hold a book about one foot away from you and read it. Now prop the book open and walk back twenty feet. Can you read it? Don't be discouraged if you can't, because there are many ways to improve your vision.

The most common way is by doing eye exercises. Naturally, there are countless variations you can do. You can roll your eyes in circles (be sure to go in both directions). You can also look up and down, left and right; don't forget to move your eyes at oblique angles. Other things to try are to focus your eyes on two different objects at once, or try to read a book as it turns on a stereo turntable. One of the best exercises involves holding one of your fingers about six inches in front of your eyes. Focus on the finger for a few seconds, then look at something on the horizon.

You can also learn to send chi to your eyes to energize them. One way of doing this is to lightly cup your palms over each eye. Slowly tighten and relax your hand muscles thirty-six times in order to build chi in them using Wai Dan. As you do that, use the Three Regulations and Taoist Reverse Breathing. To try a Nei Dan exercise, concentrate your mind on your palms and imagine the chi collecting there. Then, as you exhale, picture it smoothly entering your eyes. With either exercise, you will probably feel your palms heat up and perhaps sweat, which tells you chi is collecting and starting to transfer into your eyes. Whenever your eyes feel tired, do either of these exercises for about five minutes. Learning to send chi to your eyes is a great way to refresh yourself at the office. Whenever your eyes feel strained, give them some chi. Your eyes will become healthier, your vision will improve, and you will feel more alert.

If you have achieved Grand Circulation and Environmental Breathing, you can try looking at an object such as a tree and imagining its energy flowing toward you, directly into your eyes. Try to picture your eyes absorbing this chi. It is kind of like thinking you can inhale with your eyes. Inhale through your eyes, move the energy throughout your body, then imagine exhaling the energy back out through your eyes.

By improving your vision, you will be able to see things with greater clarity. This means you can share chi with an even greater variety of objects. For example, imagine you are hiking through the Rocky Mountains. Maybe right now you can't see a Rocky Mountain big horn sheep standing on a bluff a mile away, but by improving your vision, you just might. Then you could share chi with it. If you couldn't see it, you might have missed that particular opportunity of energy bonding.

Seeing the "Unseeable"

In addition to learning to see with greater clarity, you can also learn to relax your sight and see things you normally wouldn't notice. For example, with a little practice, you can learn to see auras. Auras are fields of energy that surround our bodies.

The way to see them is to look indirectly at objects. Try this. Look at someone for a moment. Now start paying attention to your peripheral vision. While keeping your eyes on your target, simultaneously try to see how far you can see to your sides. This is called soft focus. When you become good at this, you can learn to see a little more than 180 degrees. As you center your attention on your side vision, keep your mind aware of the person in front of you and use soft focus to look a few inches around his or her head. When you do it right, you will see hazy light, somewhat resembling a halo. More than likely, it will hint at some color. The more you relax by practicing the Three Regulations, the better you will be able to see this. Once you can do it with people, try seeing animal and plant auras. Then start categorizing the different auras you see. Notice what color aggressive people appear to be. How do happy, energetic people look different? When you can see auras, you will learn to identify how people feel, what type of personality they have, and even what they might do in any given situation.

Sight is your most developed sense, and it is important to continue to develop it to its highest potential. Keep practicing, relax, and look around you as often as possible, particularly concentrating on your distance vision. This will improve your eyesight and increase your opportunities for chi development.

Colors

We often have a tendency to think of color as just something that we can perceive with our eyes, but that is not the case. Color is made up of light, and light consists of vibrations. Thus, colors are actually made of vibrations, just like sound. With proper training, it is possible to actually touch or hear color.

There is a commonly held belief that blind people can feel color. Speaking as a professional orientation and mobility instructor, I have found very few instances of this ability without the person in question receiving training specifically geared toward developing this skill. When people lose their sight, or any other sense for that matter, their residual senses often are developed to a higher degree out of necessity. Generally, though, there is a limit to the heightened sensory sensitivity, but this doesn't have to be the case. Through a specific program of training, it is possible to learn to hear or feel color, or at least to become attuned to some of its hidden powers.

What you need to do is collect a variety of colored pieces of cloth, paper, or some similar substance. Then practice the Three Regulations as you breathe using Buddhist Breathing. Focus your attention on the color. Look at it. Try to sense it. Imagine that as you inhale you can actually inhale the specific color you are looking at. How does it smell to you?

Red is a strengthening and active color that feels energetic, warm, and alive. It gives lots of energy that can make you feel more alert and peppy.

Pink is a soft color that relaxes the mind and body. It feels slightly warm and gently pulsating. It makes you feel intuitive and reflective.

Orange is a powerful color that cleanses the body. It feels moderately warm and makes you feel loose. It also makes you feel like your energy is surging.

Yellow is a reflective color. It promotes tranquillity. It feels slightly warm, full, and stimulating. It makes you feel light and tingly.

Green is a mild and healing color. It is the color of plants and life. It has a neutral temperature, and it makes you feel peaceful yet aware.

Blue is a strong but soothing color. It usually feels cool and soothing, and makes you feel calm.

Violet has the properties of all the other colors. It feels rapid.

Try touching the different colors with the palm of your hand. Once again, imagine you are breathing through your palm, inhaling the color directly into your skin. Can you feel it? Do any of the colors feel different from the others?

Blindfold yourself and place the various colors in a box or hat, then reach in and randomly draw one out. Listen to it, feel it, smell it. You might even try tasting it. Can you determine what color you chose? As you become more in tune with your senses through Chi Gung training, this will get easier. Try again with another color.

Experiment wearing different colors. Try new ones you have never chosen before. See if any particular color makes you feel more energetic. Don't worry about what society has to say about what colors are "in," or which ones are geared toward men or women. Wear whatever feels right to you. You might also try exposing yourself to more color on a daily basis. Add some color to your house or car by buying new items such as blankets, knick-knacks, or pictures.

Whenever you see a color that is new to you, spend a few moments really looking at it. Close your eyes and see if you can remember what it looked like. Touch it if you can and see if you feel any new sensations.

You can also try listening to color, which is a very advanced skill. Relax your mind, body, and breath, then use Buddhist Breathing as you point your ear at a particular color. Imagine that chi from the color is entering your ear. (As a Wai Dan aid, you could try wiggling your ears to build up a supply of chi there. Learn this by holding one of your ears with your hand and moving your fingers to make the ear wiggle. Eventually, you will learn to sense which muscles are moving and be able to contract your ear muscles through conscious effort.) As the chi from the color enters your ear, pay attention to any subtle noises you detect. They are so soft that you will have to listen between heartbeats to detect them. Once you identify them, you will notice that they differ from each other in the speed at which they vibrate. Red is very fast and high, while blue is very slow and low. The other colors fall in between these. Let yourself freely explore the world of color, and you will open yourself up to a wonderful experience that can truly enhance your awareness of life.

Proper Clothing

The reason beginners don't have to worry about clothing is because they are basically trying to learn to identify what chi is. As you gain experience, you will want clothes that do not hinder any of your movements or your chi flow.

When you practice Chi Gung, you should wear loose-fitting clothes that are not too tight in the waist. The reason you want your clothes loose is so your chi can flow freely along your body without running into areas where you have developed muscular tension. For instance, if you are wearing a shirt that is a little small, it could constrict your shoulders, arms, or chest. This would then cause you to tense your muscles in these regions, which in turn would inhibit chi.

In addition to clothes that fit properly, you should also wear natural materials such as cotton, leather, or wool. Try to avoid humanmade material. Natural material not only has an excellent supply of chi that you can absorb, but it also breathes better, which means you will have a greater chance of absorbing chi from the environment without your clothes blocking it.

In many different martial arts, the practitioners wear belts or sashes tied tightly around their bellies. One of the things this is intended to do is to keep the inner organs in the proper place. It also serves to support the lower back. Because the knot of the belt or sash is usually tied below the navel, the material also serves as a reminder of where your Dan Tien is located and therefore where you should try to focus your mind. Those are a lot of valid points for wearing a piece of material tied around your waist, but if you are serious about learning Chi Gung, don't wear a belt. You want your stomach muscles to be able to move freely. A tight belt may build up chi in a person's Dan Tien, but learning to collect chi without the aid of a belt or sash not only makes your mind stronger, it is a more natural form of chi.

You should consider the color of the clothes you wear. Each color has a different kind of chi. Color, after all, is vibrating energy made of different wavelengths of light. Each color has its own vibration pattern and frequency. Find out which color is best for you.

One final thing you might consider is limiting your Chi Gung exercise clothes to just a few outfits. If you make it a point to practice in particular clothes, then they will collect your chi over time. Eventually, the clothes you wear will gain tremendous quantities of The Flowing, and they will be able to help energize you.

Choose your clothes carefully. There is much more to consider than just the label or design. Don't let anyone tell you what you should wear. No matter what you choose to cover yourself with, if it is right for you, then feel free to wear it.

Human Speech

"It's not what you say, it's how you say it." Anybody can say anything at any time, but it is difficult to hide your true emotions and feelings in your voice. One fun way to practice Chi Gung is by listening to people as they talk, therefore, you should study voices. For example, when people are happy, their voices often sound fuller and alive. When they are tense, you can hear the strain in their vocal cords.

By teaching yourself to focus on how people talk, you can learn to predict what they might do in any given situation, or if you are being told the truth. You will notice, for instance, that when people lie their voices change pitch slightly and the rhythm of their speech changes.

In addition to learning about others through their voices, you can also learn a lot about yourself by focusing on your own voice. You can learn to help make yourself less susceptible to illness by monitoring how you sound. Notice how your voice changes when you are upset. Feel the tension in your throat, which, as you can imagine, restricts chi flow to your head, and even limits your thinking abilities. By learning to control your voice, you can increase your intelligence, gain greater health, and boost your energy level. When you feel your voice getting tense, relax your mind, body, and breath. This slows down the internal functioning of your system and helps to eliminate the stress from your voice.

By learning how to reduce tension in your voice, you are indirectly learning how to change what you sound like. More than likely, your voice and accent sound somewhat similar to your parents. However, don't feel like your natural accent is the only one you can ever have. Go ahead and try different accents, play around with them, and see which ones you feel best fit your personality. Change your voice in volume, pitch, and cadence. Experiment. Just because you talk a certain way now doesn't mean you have to sound like that forever.

Let's look at singers as another example. They spend a lot of time culti-vating their voices. Interestingly enough, they often have high levels of per-sonal magnetism. Think for a moment how popular some singers are. For those that achieve superstar status, it seems like everything they wish for hap-pens for them. Well, here's the secret. The voice is a magickal tool. When you learn to use it properly, others will sense your energy. A way to increase your chi is to sing every day. It doesn't matter what you sound like now—you are not trying to become a professional singer. Just sing for yourself and to your-self. Studying the voice is a great way to learn to project chi because your voice is a form of energy, too.

Nonverbal Communication

We often have a tendency to think that what a person says comes to us only in words, but there is a world of information that is shared without a single sound. Animals, for example, talk to each other using nonverbal communi-cation. Consider dogs. When a dog is happy, it pulls its ears back, wags its tail, and stands in a relaxed posture. When it is afraid, it drops its ears, tucks its tail between its legs, and often slightly drops to the ground. When it is mad, it raises the hair on its neck, flexes its muscles, and bares its teeth.

People do similar things. When people are interested in you, they often lean forward as you talk. When they feel uneasy, they fold their arms across their chest. When they lie, they avert their glance or maintain eye contact for too long. When they are happy and full of energy, their eyes twinkle.

By learning nonverbal communication, you can often tell what message a person, animal, or even a plant is really conveying. This can help you deal better with any social situation.

What you need to do is study as much nonverbal communication as you can. Watch someone's behavior and see how it correlates with whatever emo-tion he or she seems to be experiencing at the time. With practice, you will gain a sense of potential problems before they occur. Say you are talking to someone and you venture into a taboo topic. As you present your viewpoint, you notice the person is starting to get uncomfortable. Perhaps he or she is squirming, failing to make eye contact, or beginning to move away from you. Rather than continuing and therefore starting an argument, by being aware of the person's behavior, and therefore possibly their feelings, you tactfully switch the conversation to something else and avoid the fight.

Initially, you will probably find yourself looking for noticeable external signs, such as posture, movement, and unusual sounds. Eventually, you will be able to sense someone's chi and know how their energy is fluctuating in any given situation. The better you get at this, the more subtle the chi flow you will be able to detect.

To sense someone's chi, first practice the Three Regulations until you are as relaxed as possible, which will enable you to open your mind to as many forms of sensory stimulation as possible. You will also want to use Buddhist Breathing. Watch the other person's entire body as you wait for any gut response or intuition you might receive. As soon as you get some sort of feeling, notice if it seems right for the situation. You might find that as you say something, you get a sense of well-being just before the other person smiles. Keep practicing this, and you will increase the length of time between when you predict something and the actual event. Next, you will find yourself having anticipatory conversations in your head before you say anything, conversations that go something like, "If I say something, then they'll respond this way. Then I'll say something else which will increase or decrease their emotional response even more," and so on. Once you recognize this technique, you will be able to avoid verbal conflicts before they occur.

Smiling and Laughing

Laughter is indeed one of the best medicines. A smile a day helps you to live a long, healthy life. When people are mad, upset, sad, or putting on a macho or tough act, they really are not doing themselves any good. All of these things cause tension.

How often on TV or in the movies do you see the main character acting tough and keeping everything inside? Villains are often pictured the same way. The interesting thing is that people watch this stuff and copy it. So you get a bunch of people strutting around, trying to portray what they think is a tough or strong image, when in fact it is a weak one.

Just as it is easier to grimace than smile, it is easier to act tough than to feel soft. During the martial arts training process, hardness often seems to win. However, the reality is that softness beats hardness in the martial arts.

When you are relaxed, you can think better and faster, and therefore respond quicker. Stick with The Flowing, and you will have the potential to excel in any conflict.

Laughing and smiling can also benefit you in a variety of ways. They can help you to heal yourself when you are sick, and they can raise your energy and your spirit. When you laugh, you send vibrations throughout your body that invigorate you. Also, smiling releases a series of biochemicals that influence some of your vital organs.

In addition, it is hard to be tense and uptight when you are laughing, which makes laughter a great form of stress relief and relaxation. Laughing also makes your stomach muscles move, which in turn stimulates your Dan Tien, forming more chi, which then makes you feel even better.

Your life is what you make of it, so why not enjoy yourself? It is a lot more fun. If you want to develop a sense of humor so you can smile and laugh more, take the time to read funny books, watch comedies, listen to jokes, and surround yourself with fun-loving friends.

Nature
Training

Nature training encourages you to go outdoors and experience life to its fullest. The skills you will develop will help you explore the extremely subtle aspects of chi identification and manipulation that are necessary to effectively interact with your environment and all that is in it.

Take Care of Plants

Plants are one of the best sources of chi because they are some of the longest living life forms on Earth. You should learn as much about them as possible. Learn how they grow and move. Study how long they live. Take the time to discover what types of energy they contain. If you have a yard, you might want to plant a variety of trees, bushes, and flowers. In order for them to grow best, it is a good idea to use plants that grow naturally in your particular climate.

Once you have a few plants, it is time to learn how to care for them. Obviously, they need water and sunlight, but there is a lot more to growing healthy plants than that.

One of the easier things you can do for them is to play a variety of music to them on a regular basis. I know you have your own musical tastes, but when you are working with plants, try to stick with classical composers such as Mozart. Heavy metal and hard rock can actually kill plants. (Perhaps our green friends can teach us a lesson or two, if we're willing to listen.)

The next thing you will want to learn is how to give chi to a plant. Practice the Three Regulations and Buddhist Breathing. Don't use Taoist Reverse Breathing because you will build up too much energy for most plants to safely handle. Hold your arms in the air in front of you and point your palms at the plant. After you feel your palms getting warm from doing this Wai Dan exercise, move them all around the plant and gently touch its leaves and stem. As you exhale, imagine your chi flowing down your arms, out your palms, and into the plant. It is important that you don't overwhelm the plant with too much energy or you could kill it. It is best to limit your chi work with plants to not more than a minute or so a day per plant. If you can, work with plants as the sun is rising in the morning, that way they can use your energy as they prepare for a new day.

By carefully observing your plants, you can learn about their needs. If they become dry and brown, they need water. If they turn gray and rot, they probably need less moisture. Physical signs such as these are indeed a form of communication. By practicing the Three Regulations, you will find you are more sensitive to your plants' needs. As you learn to increase your communication skills with plants, you are not listening for words, but learning to develop your intuition. To do this, you need to use all of your senses. Your mind must be relaxed and your spirit should transmit love and kindness. Watch the plant and see if you get any intuitive thoughts. Trusting your instincts is vital to the plant's well-being.

After you start giving chi to your plants, don't be surprised if you find yourself wanting to heal any sick plants you find. If through your chi training you have become sensitive enough, you will sense plants that need help. Often while I'm driving my Jeep, I'll sense a plant or a tree that is sick or diseased, so I'll stop my car and work with the plant for a few moments. If it is not possible to stop, I'll project a dose of chi at the plant as I drive past.

By sharing your Flowing with plants, you will find that they will help you too. If you need a quick shot of energy, find a tree that seems to beckon you and go up and hug it for a few minutes. Then sit with your back against its trunk while you focus on Buddhist Breathing. Relax and feel the rhythm of the tree as it gently sways with the breeze. Concentrate on allowing its energy to enter your body as you slowly inhale. Keep your thoughts relaxed and open and see if the tree sends you any intuitive messages or lessons. Maybe it will teach you about patience, adapting to circumstances, or communicating with nature.

Our very existence depends on our brothers and sisters from the plant kingdom. They give us oxygen, food, shade, and love. All they ask in return is for you to share your chi with them. Many people today want to save certain highly visible animals, such as dolphins, whales, or wolves. That is a wonderful, noble cause, but don't forget about plants. They need respect and care, too.

Connect With Rocks and Minerals

People in almost all cultures throughout history have felt that various rocks and minerals held special powers. These powers do indeed exist, and if you want a little more of an edge in your chi skills, I suggest you start working with earth elements.

Do you remember picking up rocks when you were young? At the time, you might not have known what attracted you to a particular stone. Perhaps it was color, shape, size, or maybe it was just an intuitive thing. You found yourself drawn to it, so you grabbed it and carried it around in one of your worn and overloaded pockets. Over the years, I have picked up a number of stones and metals. Each, at its time, seemed to call to me. Usually I was wandering aimlessly, enjoying the day when suddenly I'd have a feeling of being watched. I'd look, and there would be that special stone.

If you have never felt a stone's energy, you might want to try this. Pick up a small rock in one hand, sit down, and relax. Practice the Three Regulations and use Buddhist Breathing. Breathe deeply, slowly, and evenly. Hold the stone lightly in the center of your open palm. Focus your mind on the stone. Feel its shape, weight, temperature, and texture. Relax. In a few moments, you should start to feel a vibration in your hand—a pulsation actually. That is the energy moving from the rock to you.

You may think all you are feeling is your own pulse, but that is not so. If you have reached the level of Chi Gung training where you can detect your pulse within your body without having to press on a blood vessel or artery with one of your fingers, then you will know that the vibration of the stone and your own pulse are indeed two different beats.

If you don't feel the sensation with your chosen stone, try another one. Eventually, you should be able to sense this energy. With time and sufficient practice, you should be able to feel the beat of a stone or a piece of metal, or a living plant or animal, at quite a distance.

Carry rocks with you wherever you go. That way, when you feel like you need some grounding or perhaps a bit of energy, you can take some chi from the rock. Do this by holding the rock in your hand and extending your arm out at about shoulder height. This Wai Dan technique will build chi in your arm and hand. Focus your mind on the rock as you inhale and some of its energy will flow into your hand. I have given numerous stones to people when I have taken them on extreme nature hikes, and they have all found that by holding the rocks in their hands these stones gave them added energy, warmth, and insights.

Take Care of Pets

When we are young, we frequently have a variety of animals as pets. As we get older, we often don't take the time to share in an animal's life anymore. We should.

Taking care of animals is a fantastic way to increase your chi. Pets can lift your spirit, act as companions, and even become excellent friends. Because they are dependent on us, they require a commitment of time, energy, and responsibility. Each of these commitments can help our physical, intellectual, and emotional health. Besides, pets can be a tremendous amount of fun.

When choosing a pet, you need to consider where you live, how much money the pet will require for food and care during its lifetime, and how much energy you want to devote to your new pet. You also need to determine what kind of animal you want and where you want to get it from. I know that many people prefer purebred animals, but why not give common pets a try? Go to the local pound or Humane Society and pick out an animal. All of them crave the love and attention of a new owner. All of these animals are individuals and special in their own way. So go ahead, give them a chance. They can bring you happiness, devotion, and a special bonding that only an animal can give.

Any animal can bring chi into your home. Each species has its own personal kind. Once you have a new pet, spend time with it. Learn how to extend chi from your hands and give it to your new pet whenever you can. As a Chi Gung beginner, the easiest way to do this is to hold both of your arms in the air in a similar manner to the exercise called "Hugging a Tree." Then, very slowly, reach out and massage your pet. By holding your arms up while moving slowly, this Wai Dan position will increase the chi in your arms and hands so it can flow into your animal. By giving your pet chi, you can help it to have a long, healthy life. It can do the same thing for you.

By diligently practicing Chi Gung, you should eventually be able to attune to your pet's thoughts. In other words, it is possible to learn to talk to animals. You may be wondering how they can talk to you. Do they use language? Yes, sort of. They don't use language like the one you are probably used to. Instead of words and sentences, animals speak by using mental intuition, movement, and sound. They send pictures or thoughts into your mind. For example, I once found a baby fox in the mountains in Colorado. Its mother had been scared away by intense traffic while she was moving her litter to a new home and she dropped the kit in the middle of a busy road. After three hours she had not returned to her offspring. So I wandered up to the baby fox and asked her where she lived. I relaxed and focused on my breathing. Suddenly, I got a clear picture in my mind of a den about 200 yards away from where I was. Picking up the baby animal, I carried her to where I sensed the den was and, sure enough, I found it. Fifteen minutes after dropping her off, her mother came to the old den, picked her up once again, and moved her to their new home.

To start talking to animals, you have to become more observant. Take a look at your pet and watch it intently. Study it. Learn how it moves. What does it do if it needs nourishment or love? Eventually, you will begin to realize what your pet is saying. A dog might cock back his ears or wag his tail when he is happy. A cat might purr when she is content. A fish might rise to the surface of the water when he is hungry. All of these cases are examples of communication.

With time and effort, you can get very good at meeting any needs your pet has, but there is a lot more that they can say. Of course, there are also ways to tune in to their messages.

Keep your body relaxed, your mind uncluttered, and your emotions calm. Breathe slowly through your nose. Practice the Three Regulations and Buddhist Breathing. With each breath imagine thoughts coming from your animal. Open yourself to the possibility. If you get an insight, follow it up to see if you're right. The more you practice, the better you will get.

Animals can teach us many lessons. They can teach us about love, compassion, gentleness, respect, fairness, and righteousness. Learn to enjoy animals of all kinds. As you encounter various animals, be open to what they may have to say. Perhaps they need your help. Maybe they are telling you where something is that you need to find or know, or maybe they are just telling you it is a great day and it is good to be alive. There are so many animals out there that need loving homes; so go ahead, open your heart and adopt a pet. You will be glad you did, because you will make a new friend.

Identify Different Animal Chi

Every living thing is unique. Each creature has its own special type of energy, and all types feel different. Once you have learned to categorize this chi, you can correctly identify a variety of animals simply by how they feel to you.

One of the best ways to do this is to start out with a pet if you have one. A younger brother or sister would also do—after all, people are animals too. (I would suggest using older siblings, but they might not be as tolerant of your unusual training.)

The first thing you need to do is relax and practice the Three Regulations. Breathe as slowly as possible using Buddhist Breathing. Once you are fully relaxed, raise your arm so your palm is pointed at your pet. As you inhale, imagine the animal's energy is transferring from itself to you. Think of it as breathing through your palm. Relax your arm and shoulder as much as possible. Take your time.

With enough practice, you will eventually feel a sensation such as heat, tingling, or pressure in your arm. That is the animal's chi. Pay attention to the feeling and see if you get the same response every time you work with the same animal. When you have developed an awareness of the consistency of the energy, then it is time to try working with other animals.

The best place to do this is at a zoo, which is a great place for Chi Gung practice. Most zoos have a wide variety of animals on display and you can take your time strolling from exhibit to exhibit as you share chi with each species. Learn what each animal feels like. Some will feel like a twirling sensation moving up your arm. Others seem to have a tapping energy. Some surge, others ooze. Each animal is different. As you gain skill, you will no longer need to point your palm at an animal to sense its energy. You will find you can detect it anywhere in your body. In fact, one of the ways to tell what different animals feel like is to sense where the chi of certain animals reacts in various parts of your body.

After you learn to identify animals strictly by their energy, you can learn to discriminate between individual animals of the same species. Think about some of your friends for a moment. Some are full of energy—they are alive and happy all the time. Others are thoughtful or withdrawn. It is the same with animals.

Once you have learned to identify animal chi, you will be surprised how many different creatures are around you all the time. Think for a moment about the last time you took a walk in the woods, in a park, or along the edge of a misty bayou. How many animals did you see? You might not have seen them, but they were there, and they saw you. So why not learn to turn the tables a bit? When you are highly sensitive to their energy, you will be able to feel them even before they sense you. Then nature walks will take on a whole new meaning. Not only will you know what is out there, you will know how many of them are there, and how far away they are.

Once you learn how to give and take chi, it is your responsibility as a steward of animals to give them chi whenever they need it, especially if you have borrowed some of theirs. I propose a new sport called "chi tag." All you need to do is go into the wild and gather animals' chi, before they collect yours. It is a lot more fun than hunting with a weapon, because you are helping the animal by giving it energy just as it is helping you by giving you some.

Track Animals

I have spent the last twenty-five years learning how to track animals and people based on their footprints and any marks they leave on the ground. Tracking is an archaic art in our world of modern technology, but as we become more removed from nature, this skill becomes more important, especially for people who like exploring the wilderness. Learning to track is an excellent way to test your Chi Gung skills. If you are to succeed at this skill, you need to develop intuition, concentration, and attention to detail.

Lots of people get lost in the woods each year, but few of them know much about basic survival skills. This creates a very real danger. When people are lost, they rely on our police forces and natural resources specialists to find them. These people use all of the latest high technology equipment, but sometimes it just doesn't produce the results that are needed. That is when it is time to return to the basics and call upon the services of a tracker. Chi Gung training can teach you how to track with incredible efficiency and accuracy.

To learn to track, you first need to learn about the different tracks various animals leave, then you need to learn about their movement patterns. What do tracks look like when an animal is running instead of walking? How do the tracks differ when the animal is tired or hurt? You also have to understand how weather affects the tracks. Wind can blow dirt over them, rain can wash them out, and the sun can dry them to dust.

I suggest starting by tracking dogs or cats. If you have a pet, go into your yard and see if you can follow where it walked. If you don't have access to animal tracks, try making a tracking dummy. Take a two-by-four board, about a foot long, and pound a series of nails into it so they stick out of all sides. Then attach about a ten-foot rope to the board and have a friend drag it around the ground. Now all you have to do is follow the trail. Encourage your friend to be as tricky as possible by dragging the dummy through water, over rocks, and around trees.

After you have learned to track based on what you can see, you then need to develop your intuition. Have your friend move a tracking dummy around your yard while periodically lifting it off the ground so it leaves no tracks for several feet. This will help you to learn to predict where the tracks might have gone.

Once you learn Environmental Breathing and Chi Projection, you can start to learn identify animal chi. If you want more information on this, read the next section called "Identify Different Animal Chi."

Learn About Weather and Climate

You can learn many energy lessons from watching the weather. Have you ever looked at clouds? What about when a new front moves in? How about the first drops of rain—or the last? By watching weather patterns you can learn patience. How long does it take for the sun to set? Have you ever watched the moon rise, travel the night sky, and eventually disappear at dawn? These lessons in patience transfer directly to Chi Gung training, because that is precisely one of the main skills you have to hone. To feel energy travel through your body, you need to put in a lot of work. Learning to control that energy requires extreme patience.

You can also learn to take chi from the sky when you need a quick boost of energy. Go outside and stand in a relaxed position with your arms outstretched at shoulder height and your palms facing the sun. Use the Three Regulations to relax yourself and breathe deeply, slowly, and softly using Buddhist Breathing. Feel the sun as it strikes your palms. As you inhale, imagine the sunlight absorbing directly into your skin, and you will quickly feel your palms become warm. While still inhaling, try to picture the sun's energy moving through your hands and up your arms. Can you feel it? If not, keep trying. It will eventually come.

Try to spend as much training time outdoors as possible. Train in rain, snow, and summer heat. Practice at the beach, in the mountains, and in parks. Don't always train at the same time. Sometimes, go outside as the sun rises, sometimes as it sets. Train at midnight and noon. If your schedule permits, you should try staying out all night on occasion—it is a phenomenal experience. Personally, I train throughout the day and night, but one of my favorite times is between 2 A.M. and 5 A.M., a time when the world seems quiet, and energy moves freely. I often find myself getting so filled with chi during my three-hour nightly sessions that I can perceive extremely small sensations, such as the vibrations of my cat walking across the carpeted floor twenty feet from me, or my partner's pulse as she lies on the opposite side of the bed.

If you truly want to learn about the deeper intricacies of The Flowing, then you must learn firsthand about the weather.

Lie on the Ground and Watch the Sky

I have many memories as a child of lying on my back in a field of grass while watching the sky. Those seemed like such special, magickal times, when nothing mattered. It was a time when anything seemed possible and all of life was simple, fun, and relaxing. Well, those days are not behind us. We can still experience them, and gain a lot in the process.

You may be wondering how merely relaxing could help you to achieve anything. After all, you need to pay the bills, fix dinner, and do a million things. But take a moment and consider this idea. When you allow yourself to become stressed, your blood vessels constrict, you breathe harder, and your muscles tighten almost to the point of bursting. Though you may not know this, you no longer are capable of functioning at peak efficiency.

Though it seems like you can accomplish more if you push and strive and drive yourself mercilessly, that just isn't so. It is a myth created in ignorance and greed by our employers, teachers, and other authority figures. It is time to take a stand. Prove to yourself and others that you can indeed achieve your best results by learning to relax—and, of course, by absorbing chi.

By lying on your back on the ground while watching the sky, you are absorbing chi from both the earth and sky, you are relaxing your mind and body, and you are opening yourself up to new ways of looking at life. Find a spot that seems to call to you, then lie down and practice the Three Regulations. Use Buddhist Breathing and feel your weight sink into the ground as your body relaxes. Then don't try to do anything other than to just open up your senses. Listen, smell, feel, and look.

The art of reposing is both an ancient and lost discipline that needs to be revived. Take the time to practice this skill. If you think you don't have those precious moments in life to look after yourself and your own well-being, then ask yourself if you really know the inner secrets of time. If you are not really sure what this means, then take a few minutes each day to lie on the ground and watch the sky.

PART
THREE

Advanced Chi Gung

After you have learned the fundamentals of Chi Gung by practicing the basics, you may be interested in learning about the more advanced levels of training Chi Gung offers. To master the material in this chapter, you will have to know how to discharge chi from your body and project it into other objects. Therefore, one of the basic requirements for this material is at least knowing how to do Grand Circulation. There are, however, a variety of exercises you can begin practicing as a beginner that will help you to start building a foundation for attaining these skills once you have completed Grand Circulation.

Slowing Down Aging

One of the great side benefits of Chi Gung is that it slows down the aging process. With proper training, you can learn to reduce wrinkles and hair loss, gain flexibility and strength, and obtain more energy and clearer thoughts.

Conquering Wrinkles

In order to reduce wrinkling you need to send chi directly to the skin. First, practice the Three Regulations, then add Buddhist Breathing. Remember to breathe as slowly possible through your nose. Breathe for a few minutes, until you feel yourself relaxing. Next, focus your mind as intently as possible on the areas of your skin that are wrinkled, most likely the areas around your face, neck, and hands. Pick one of them to work on first.

Let's say you chose your face. Tighten your face muscles by making as many different facial expressions as you can. By doing this for a few minutes, you will begin to send chi to the skin on your face. After you have practiced general Buddhist Breathing, focus your mind on your exhalations while imagining your chi flowing directly to the skin on your face. At first, just try to picture it flowing around in a broad pattern. Inhale and exhale slowly. Now slower, and slower. Feel the warmth of your chi as it spreads across your forehead, your temples, your cheeks, your nose, and your chin. If there is one area that has more wrinkles than another, feel free to concentrate your efforts there. Relax. Allow yourself to smile. Just breathe and become aware of your senses.

Another way to get chi to your face is to rapidly rub your hands together. Do this thirty-six times, then gently hold your palms against your face.

Battling Baldness

Hair loss is another common problem as people age. One of the main reasons people lose hair is because their pores become blocked with oils, dry skin, and dirt. In addition, they often have poor blood circulation in their scalp. Where circulation is poor, there is limited chi flow. What you need to do is relax, breathe slowly and deeply, and focus on your thinning hair spots as clearly as possible. Where are they exactly? Focus your mind on sending chi to these areas. Let it flow smoothly. Spiral it. Surge it. Pulse it. Relax your scalp as much as possible.

If you have trouble sending chi to where you need it to go, try using your hands to massage your head. Gently place the palms of your hands on your thinning hair. This time, instead of focusing your mind on your head, send the chi into and through your hands. Picture your energy flowing out of the center of your palms. Keep your arms as relaxed as possible. Practice this exercise about five minutes per day, and you should start seeing results.

Enhancing Flexibility

As we age we often loose flexibility in our muscles. Usually, this is because we don't use them as often as we did when we were younger. Because proper chi flow requires loose, relaxed muscles, it is vital to stretch all of your major muscle groups as often as possible. As you stretch, concentrate on sending chi into the muscle tissue itself. Stretch to your comfortable limit, inhale using Taoist Reverse Breathing, focus your mind on any tight areas, then exhale and stretch a little bit farther. Now hold this position for a minute. Each time you exhale through your nose, stretch just a little farther. Be sure to stretch all of your major muscle groups including your legs, hips, waist, shoulders, arms, and neck. Stretching regularly will bring a new spring to your step. You should stretch at least twenty minutes per day.

Gaining Strength

Another area that might interest you is strength training, because as we age we often lose our muscle tone. Most people think strength training involves lifting heavy weights, but that doesn't have to be the case. A different approach to gaining strength involves moving all of your muscles as slowly as possible as you exercise.

When you lift weights, you probably have a tendency to move quickly and jerk your muscles. It is easy to keep a heavy weight moving once you get it started, because the laws of physics say that objects in motion tend to stay in motion. If you move quickly, it is easy to let gravity and inertia move your muscles for you. This technique has a tendency to develop the muscles at their ends where they attach to bones and ligaments.

By moving at a snail's pace, each muscle fiber is worked to its maximum capacity. You will find that when you practice strength training using extremely slow motion, your muscles have a tendency to move in spurts, because the muscle hasn't learned to move smoothly. With continued practice, the entire muscle will develop, and you will acquire graceful movements that look similar to moving underwater. The slower you move, the better this type of exercise is for you. As you move your muscles, imagine that your individual limbs weigh hundreds of pounds. Let your chi flow. Try to picture what it would feel like to support that kind of weight. The better you can imagine this, the better workout you will have.

Now I know many of you will say you don't have time to exercise. Well, by using these principles, you can turn any activity into an intense strength training session. For example, use these concepts while eating, changing the TV channel with a remote control, driving your car, shopping, or even standing in a line.

Recapturing Energy

Chi Gung breathing supplies energy. The more you practice, the more energy you can get. At first you will want to simply practice breathing slowly and evenly, then you will need to learn how to store your new energy in your Dan Tien. You do this by focusing your mind about an inch and a half below your navel and keeping your attention riveted there every time you want to store more energy.

As you need your supply, you can access it in one of two ways. With Wai Dan, you can tighten a specific muscle group and gather chi in that muscle, or you can use Nei Dan and move the chi throughout your body by thinking of specific areas such as your hands or feet and using your mind to flow it there. Wherever your mind goes, your chi will go.

Staying Sharp, Getting Smarter

Finally, Chi Gung will help your brain. As we age we often find ourselves forgetting things, but that can be remedied. The reason we start to forget is we don't often breathe as deeply as when we were younger, and therefore our brain doesn't get the oxygen supply it did at one time. To rejuvenate your brain, all you have to do is send chi to your head and to let the oxygen, blood, and chi circulate around. Breathe slowly and deeply using Buddhist Breathing. As you exhale, imagine your energy going to your head. Try to feel it moving inside your brain. Move it from place to place, being sure to cover everything with energy.

In addition to energizing your brain cells, Chi Gung also increases your intelligence by requiring you to utilize more of your brain. You do this by developing your various senses, cultivating your intuition, and opening your mind to new possibilities. Just the act of learning anything new helps increase your intelligence, because you are practicing a variety of intellectual skills, such as memorization, logic, orientation, awareness, creativity, communication, and perspective.

By following these exercises, as well as the others mentioned in this book, you should be able to dramatically slow down the aging process. You should practice Chi Gung for at least a half-hour every day. The main exercises you should practice are the Three Regulations, Buddhist Breathing, and the Wai Dan exercise called "Hugging a Tree." These will help you build your chi supply, as well as increase its circulation, which will benefit your entire body.

Healing Yourself and Others

With proper training, Chi Gung can teach you to heal a variety of ailments, from curing headaches and arthritis to helping stop cancer. For thousands of years, highly trained Chi Gung specialists have used their training to cure people in China. Today, they are beginning to be accepted by Western countries, particularly in relation to acupuncture, which is an external form of manipulating chi.

There are some exercises, such as the Still Wai Dan exercise called "Hugging a Tree," that you can practice as a beginner in order to help you to achieve overall health. However, in order for you to deliberately send chi to specific areas of your body, you will have to have completed both Small Circulation and Grand Circulation training.

To begin to learn to heal yourself of even simple disorders, the first thing you need to do is practice Chi Gung breathing. Breathe as slowly and evenly as possible through your nose using the Buddhist Breathing method. By properly following the Three Regulations and Buddhist Breathing, you will begin to improve your overall health, which in turn will help you to eliminate some diseases simply because you will no longer be as susceptible to them.

Once you have learned to build up your supply of chi using Wai Dan exercises, you can send it to some areas of your body by tensing your muscles wherever you feel the chi needs to go. For instance, if you have arthritis in your hands, you can practice the exercise called "Hugging a Tree" to build chi in your shoulders and arms. Then you could open and close your fists or tighten your hand muscles, which sends the accumulated chi to your hands, until you feel a sense of warmth or tingling.

After you have improved your visualization skills by following some of the exercises in the "Mental Training" and "Emotional Training" chapters, you need to learn to accurately visualize illness or injury. Upon completing that, you can send your chi to the damaged area by using your mind (provided you have learned Small Circulation and Grand Circulation).

More than 700 chi cavities can be found on your body, located along your meridians. These cavities coincide with all of the common acupuncture or acupressure points. By learning in which of these cavities to concentrate chi, you can often accelerate your own healing.

Healing the Head

At the center of the top of your head is the Bai Hui Cavity (Figure 93). Directing chi here helps a variety of head-related disorders such as headaches, insomnia, and hypertension.

A beginner could use the simple Wai Dan technique of massaging this chi cavity with one of the fingers. Slowly and gently move your finger in a tiny circle for eight breaths using Buddhist Breathing. At the same time, use the Nei Dan technique of imagining your energy flowing out of the top of your head. You don't want to send too much energy to your head or you could increase your head disorder. Therefore, limit this type of exercise to about five minutes twice a day.

Curing Facial Tics

Sometimes you may experience facial muscle twitching, usually near one of your eyes. By sending chi to the Si Bai Cavity (Figure 94), located about an inch below your eye, you can often stop this irritation. In addition, energizing this area also helps increase eyesight.

Start out using Wai Dan by massaging this spot with one of your index fingers. Simultaneously, imagine energy flowing from your finger into the Si Bai Cavity. Doing this exercise for about one minute should stop most muscle twitches. For improving eyesight, practice this for one minute, three times a day.

Defeating Congestion

When you are sick and have a stuffy nose, try sending chi to the outside edge of your nose near your nostrils (Figure 95). This should clear your breathing quickly. Because you might find it difficult to concentrate on breathing properly with a stuffed nose, beginners should try using a combination of Wai Dan exercises and massage.

One way to do this is to simultaneously rub both sides of your nostrils with your index fingers while lifting your elbows as high as possible. Because this elevates your arms, you will be gathering chi in your shoulders. The massage will concentrate some of your energy in your nose, and by focusing your mind on your stuffed nose after you have lowered your arms, more of your chi will flow there. Do this up to twenty minutes, three times a day.

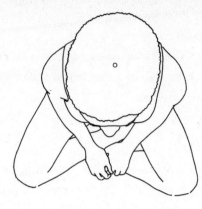

Figure 93.
The Bau Hui Cavity.

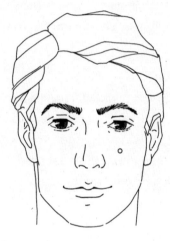

Figure 94.
The Si Bai Cavity.

Figure 95.

Energizing Yourself

If you ever need to increase your energy quickly, you can try massaging the Ren Zhong Cavity. It is located at a spot below the center of both nostrils and above the upper lip (Figure 96).

Clearing Chest Pain

If you find yourself experiencing asthma, coughing, or chest pain, you could send chi to the Shan Zhong Cavity in the center of your chest (Figure 97). As a beginner, very gently massage this spot. You don't want to use too much pressure because you have to be careful not to over-stimulate your heart. Do this about five minutes whenever you have the symptoms. (Warning: If you experience severe or prolonged chest pain, see your physician immediately.)

Relieving Backaches

At one time or another, most of us have had backaches. Usually, they occur in the lower back. By circulating chi in this area, you can quickly diminish the soreness. One way to do this as a beginner is by rubbing your lower back with the palms of your hands as you imagine energy flowing from your palms into your lower back. When you practice this exercise, use Taoist Reverse Breathing. Do this for about ten minutes.

Curing Headaches

Between your thumb and forefinger is a web of skin. Feel there until you find a solid clump that feels like a tendon. That is the He Gu Cavity (Figure 98). Sending chi here relieves most headaches almost immediately. If you don't really know how to send The Flowing yet, you can try squeezing this spot ten times on each hand. It will probably hurt your hand for a moment, but your headache will almost assuredly go away.

Helping Someone Who Faints

If you ever see someone faint, try sending chi into the tips of their fingers. As a beginner, you can massage the outside edges of the tips of the fingers as you imagine chi flowing from your hand into the cavities. Do this exercise for about a minute.

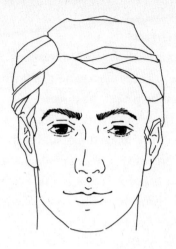

Figure 96.
The Ren Zhong
Cavity.

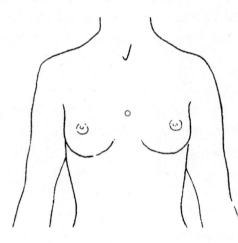

Figure 97.
The Shan Zhong
Cavity.

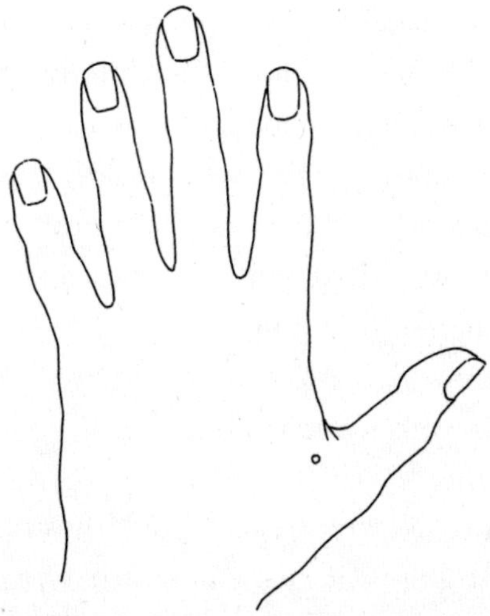

Figure 98.
The He Gu
Cavity.

Working with Arthritis

Arthritis can occur in almost any joint in the body, but it is most often found in the hands and fingers. There are a variety of techniques you can use to alleviate the pain and even help heal the disease.

One of the things you can do as a beginner is gently massage the area, which will bring chi to the damaged spot and help heal it. Another thing you can do is move the joint as slowly as possible in a variety of positions. For example, if your hand is bothering you, one of the things you could do is slowly open and close your fingers as you make fists. You could also move your fingers independently of each other in as many directions as they can move. While you are doing these types of exercises, imagine your own energy flowing to the arthritic area and warming it. Keep doing the exercise until you can definitely feel a sense of warmth building up. Slow movement anti-arthritis exercises should be done for about twenty minutes a day.

Cancer and Chi Gung

Cancer obviously is a tough disease to cure, but Chi Gung actually can help cure it if you start practicing it as soon as possible after diagnosis. Even as a beginner, there are a number of things you can try that can increase your chances of successfully combating this disease.

The first thing to realize is that it is extremely important to keep a positive attitude. In addition, you need to circulate your chi throughout your body as often as possible, particularly in the damaged area. One way a beginner can do this is by practicing the Still Wai Dan exercise called "Hugging a Tree." This exercise will build up your body's supply of chi so it can then flow through your body as needed. It is important for you to absorb as much chi from nature as possible, so you should practice the "Hugging a Tree" exercise outside if you can. Try doing it beneath a pine tree for the best results.

You should also improve your eating habits by eating a strict vegetarian diet with a variety of foods that have the right kinds of chi. Some examples of foods that have properties that can help heal cancer are apples, asparagus, bamboo shoots, bananas, cantaloupes, celery, cucumbers, eggplant, grapefruit, lettuce, mushrooms, oranges, pears, seaweed, soy beans, spinach, tea, tomatoes, watercress, wheat, and wheat germ.

When something is wrong with you physically or mentally, it is extremely important go to a doctor and do what he or she says, but also be open to the idea of trying to build and circulate your own chi. You can do this by practicing Wai Dan exercises if you are a beginner and Nei Dan if you have had a little more experience. By diligently practicing the exercises in this book, you can often speed up the natural healing capabilities of your body. In addition to exercising, though, you must also realize that the most important point of your training is your own belief. You must honestly believe you can help cure yourself or even others, because when you have faith, you can dramatically increase your chi flow, which, cyclically, will increase your healing skills even more.

Moving Objects With Your Mind

Telekinesis is the ability to move something without touching it. Interestingly enough, the way to do this is by not really trying to do it. In fact, the harder you try, the less successful you will be.

Start with trying to direct the movement patterns of living animals. By sending chi into them you can persuade them to move to a new location and mentally direct them to where you want them to go. Incidentally, you must do this with love and compassion. Never hurt them.

To direct an animal's movements, you need to relax, so practice the Three Regulations. Use Taoist Reverse Breathing. Build up a large quantity of chi in your Dan Tien. After you have a good supply, your lower abdomen should feel warm. At this point, lightly hold out one of your arms and point the palm of your hand at the animal. It doesn't matter how far away from you the animal is standing. Imagine sending a flow of chi from the center of your palm into the animal. What you want the animal to do determines where you need to aim. If you want it to start moving, aim at its back end. If you want it to stop, aim immediately in front of it. This exercise combines Wai Dan and Nei Dan. By holding your arm up, you are using Wai Dan, and by visualizing the chi moving to your palm and out toward the animal, you are using Nei Dan.

I'll give you an example of what can be done. Once when visiting a zoo, I decided to energize a Galapagos tortoise, which is a large land tortoise that weighs hundreds of pounds. Normally they spend almost all of their time lying around. As soon as I flowed chi into him, he stood up and vigorously walked about seventy yards until he got under a nice, shady tree.

Animals are extremely sensitive to chi, which is why you should practice with animals until you can direct their movements. You can use this skill to help animals when they are in danger. As you increase your skill in this area, you can learn to direct a dog or cat so it doesn't run into the street, or you can help a deer, rabbit, or a fox to quickly leave a busy highway to avoid being hit by a vehicle.

After you have learned to help animals, you can try to move inanimate objects. This is challenging, but not impossible. Start with something easy to move, such as an air-filled balloon on a slippery surface like a kitchen counter. If you are a beginner, first build chi in your arms and hands by holding them at about shoulder height until they feel warm. Then lightly touch your palm against the balloon. Picture your chi entering the balloon and warming it. When it gets warm enough, the balloon should move. If that doesn't work, try cooling it with chi. The way to do this is to tighten the muscles in your opposite arm to send chi away from your palm that is near the balloon. At the same time, focus your mind on inhaling and sensing chi entering your palm from the balloon.

You can also spiral your chi in large arcs as you aim it at your target. This is a Nei Dan technique and it requires you to have learned Grand Circulation and Environmental Breathing. As you project your chi, picture it spiraling rather than traveling in a straight line. Remember, don't try too hard. If you strain, you limit your own power.

Dreaming Your World

Whatever you dream can happen. Over the years I've dreamed of being a professional writer, owning a Jeep Wrangler, living near a swamp, traveling all over the country, learning martial arts, having a happy relationship, being healthy, keeping my childlike wonder of the world, getting a master's degree in college, playing a variety of musical instruments, and basically living a wonderful, magickal life filled with adventure. All of these things have happened.

Dreams don't have to be restricted to when we are asleep. Daydreams are just as effective because you have more control over them. When you daydream, you can achieve greater success if you also practice the Three Regulations and Buddhist Breathing at the same time you dream. This will help to energize your dreams and give them a greater chance of becoming reality.

Dreams work because they are filled with hope and magickal wonder. The best way to fulfill them is to dream as specifically as possible. Imagine what you want, then picture it actually happening. Of course, you must have the faith that it will work. It could happen, so why doubt?

However, you are going to have to be careful what you dream for. You just may get it in a way you didn't really intend. For example, if you dream of acquiring wealth, it might be at the cost of friendship or loved ones, or if you dream of incredible sex, it could be with a stranger and therefore cost you your marriage.

We must be willing to dream, and when we do, our dreams can indeed became reality.

Predicting the Future

Precognition or seeing into the future, at a basic level, is really nothing more than understanding relationships and patterns. A good way to practice this skill is to begin by concentrating your efforts on people. When you are sensitive to another person's chi, you can accurately predict how they will do in life. By being in touch with someone's inner essence or spirit you can understand where they have been, who they are now, and what they will probably become.

When you are first learning this, you should pay attention to how someone appears physically. How bright are their eyes? Do they have any telling mannerisms? What is their voice like? What type of emotional state do they generally seem to be in? Do they have any unusual odors? Does their skin look pasty or healthy?

By learning what types of people exhibit certain behaviors, you can begin to see patterns. Then what you need to do is sense their chi and determine what it feels like. Do all stressed out, anal retentive, highly aggressive people feel similar to each other? What do spiritual people feel like? How does someone's chi feel when he or she is happy or depressed? As your Chi Gung skills increase, you will be able to determine differences in people's energy. Once you have an idea of what the person is like, you can start to predict some basic ideas about their future. The more you practice, the greater success you will have doing this.

The way to absorb and sense someone's energy to understand them better is by following a set of exercises. First, practice the Three Regulations and

Buddhist Breathing. Next, practice the "Hugging a Tree" exercise. You can modify this by holding one arm up at a time. The way to combine this with sensing energy is to lightly place your hand on someone's shoulder. Talk to them and try to get them as relaxed and calm as possible while you maintain physical contact. Because your hand is barely touching them, your arm will support almost all of its own weight, which will build chi in it. This will sensitize your arm to The Flowing. Once you feel your arm getting warm, start tightening the muscles in your opposite arm in order to send your chi there. This will move the chi from the arm that is touching the person to the opposite arm. As your chi circulates, focus your mind on your palm where it touches the other person and imagine their chi entering it. At the same time, keep your mind open to any ideas or revelations about the other person.

Once you know Grand Circulation, you can try this exercise without actually touching someone. At that point, you imagine their chi flowing into you as you inhale.

These exercises should give you an idea of what type of person you are working with. Once you know this, you will have an idea of what their personality is like, and this is the first step in learning to predict their future. The more you practice, the better you will become.

Predicting on the Larger Scale

After you have gained some skill at predicting what others will do, try it on animals, then try it with plants. After that, try it with the weather. Start out by thoroughly studying your intended target, then once you get to know it well, look for relationships.

For example, let's say it is a nice day where you live. You notice a slight breeze developing. Later you see some clouds forming. The clouds eventually grow and become dark. By understanding weather patterns, you should be able to predict that it will rain soon. Because you saw the sequence from the beginning, you could have known a new front was moving in as soon as the breeze began.

Just as you know that breezes and clouds can lead to rain, understanding the relationships between other, different things can help you predict what will happen in the future. For instance, how can a butterfly's wings beating against the still air ultimately cause a hurricane on the other side of the world? Only after you have begun to understand the total picture will you be able to start to develop a sense for what will happen.

Eventually you will get to the point where you will get feelings about events before they occur. At first, these will probably be small hunches or gut feelings. You may sense them in your head, but not necessarily. (A gut feeling, after all, really takes place in your Dan Tien.) As you start paying attention to your senses, you will notice what you are generally receiving are advanced vibrational patterns of events. These are similar to what happens when a pebble is thrown into a pond. The ripples reach you even though you don't know where the rock is located. If you swam out into the lake, you would eventually encounter the rock.

Another way you can practice predictions is by sitting out in the woods and having a friend start walking toward you from a few hundred yards away. Remain totally quiet, don't move, and abstain from any negative thoughts. Eventually, you may notice birds flying toward you. An animal might run by, then another. Watch carefully, and you will notice the forest in an uproar as your friend approaches. You are learning to determine cause and effect relationships. In this case, your friend in the woods caused the animals to move. If you were in a situation where you didn't arrange for someone to scare the animals, and you saw them moving away from something in the woods, you would be able to determine that whatever was scaring them was probably coming toward you, too. With experience, in a case like this, you would know animals flee from people differently than from another animal that was hunting them. Thus, based on how the animals moved, you would be able to predict that someone was blundering around in the woods and coming toward you. This is a simple example of predicting the future based on observation.

Once you have learned Grand Circulation and Environmental Breathing, you will be able to sense events based on their chi. This will give you an awareness of things that will occur in the immediate future. By practicing this skill regularly, you will be able to sense things further into the future.

Developing this vibrational awareness will dramatically increase your ability to see into the future. It is important to expand your mind to as many new horizons as possible as you train, because then you will be able to see that vibrational relationships can extend over any length of time or distance. The present comes from the past and leads to the future, so one way to learn to predict future events is to study the present and the past. The more information you can get, the better the results will be, so you should use as many sources of knowledge as possible. This means not only utilizing physical information, such as the things you see or hear, but also utilizing apparently intangible information, such as intuition. One way to test intuition is to record any hunches you have and see how many of them turn out to be right over time.

Traveling Through Your Dreams

Astral projection is a technique used by many cultures to gain useful knowledge. Most shamanic traditions make extensive use of it. It is particularly well known among the Australian Aborigines, who call it Dream Time.

By learning to allow your consciousness to leave your body, you can have access to places you otherwise never would have been able to see.

One of the first ways to start to develop this skill is by learning about empathy. Empathy enables you to know and feel what another person is experiencing. In order to become empathic there are a few special qualities you need to develop. First of all, you have to be able to mentally imagine yourself in the other person's position. You need to try to understand what he or she might be feeling and where the person is coming from. One way to do this is by opening yourself up to possibilities and many different experiences. In other words, you have to become open-minded.

You can start to develop this skill by practicing defending points of view you normally wouldn't agree with. For example, let's look at a topic most people have rather firm beliefs about. Should we eat people? Most people would probably say "no," but what circumstances, if any, could warrant cannibalistic behavior? Use your imagination for answers.

Of course, there are a few drawbacks to developing empathy. Other people can often influence you to a certain degree if you let your guard down. Also, when you go to large public places such as football games, you might be easily moved along with the crowd's reactions. In addition, you more than likely will develop strong emotions, which could make you feel hyper-sensitive. Empathy can seem like both a curse and a gift, but in the end, you will probably think it is worth the price.

Once you are empathic, you will be able to feel what another person is feeling. At this point, it is time to try imagining you are actually in someone else's body. Find someone, anyone, and watch that person for a while. Then relax and breathe using Buddhist Breathing. (If you are a beginner and have not yet learned Grand Circulation, you will need to complete that first in order to project your chi, but there are things you can do now even if you don't yet have this technical level of skill.) For now, imagine what it would feel like if you were the other person. Picture yourself entering the other person's body. Feel what it would feel like if you were him or her. If he or she is taller, shorter, heavier, lighter, the opposite sex, older, or younger, imagine what that would feel like. Use your empathy. As that person moves about, try to sense what it would be like if your own muscles were moving exactly the same way. The more you do this, the better you will get at it. After practicing with people, try animals, and then plants. By this time, you should be getting fairly good at sensing what someone or something else is like.

Once you have completed Grand Circulation and learned to project your chi, allow it to enter someone else along with your mind as you imagine that you are that person. Let your chi tell you what he or she is feeling, and experience it yourself.

Setting Your Spirit Loose

Upon learning how to send your chi into someone, you can then start letting your spirit travel a little more freely. You see, when you put your chi and mind into something else, a part of your spirit goes along too.

You don't have to limit yourself to going inside of something. You can just let your spirit explore freely. Start in your own home. It is a good place to start because it is a place that is very familiar to you. Sit in a comfortable chair and relax your mind, your body, and your emotions as you practice Buddhist Breathing. Close your eyes. (Later you won't have to do this, but closing your eyes helps in the beginning because it eliminates outside distractions.) Imagine your spirit leaving your body and exploring your house. Picture in detail what it would be like if you had no body and could float around on the air. Let your mind explore your house room by room. Try to see what is happening in any given room by using your moving chi. Let your spirit float to the ceiling and look down on everything. Then sweep it along the floor, under beds and chairs, and around counters and cupboards. Think of yourself as having no specific shape, but imagine you are fairly small, maybe about the size of a fly.

Explore in detail any particular room, then return your spirit to your body. You can do this by imagining you are flying back through your house to the room where your body is located. Relax while breathing slowly and deeply.

After a few moments, actually get up and walk through your house, particularly to the room you let your spirit explore in detail. When your spirit explored your house, what did you see? When walking the same route your spirit took, notice how accurate you were while in spiritual form. You can start to test your skill at this by trying to locate objects you have lost. Instead of actually looking for them, let your spirit do the search for you, then go and see if you were right. The more you practice this, the better you will become.

Letting Your Spirit Soar

Next, you might want to explore things that are farther away, such as a friend's house or a familiar store. Eventually, you will be able to let your spirit go as far away as you desire to locations that you have never visited. If you can get a friend interested in this type of training, the two of you can learn to have your spirits meet at a given location at a specific time. Try it.

Of course, you might be asking yourself if all of this is logical, fully scientific and all. After all, this is reality, right? Well, is it logical to think that logical thinking is the only real way to discover ideas? What about right-brain thinking? That is certainly not very logical. And how about emotions? Where is the logic there? To say nothing of intuition, inspiration, dreams, and even chi. Has anyone ever measured chi? No, not with complete scientific accuracy according to Western standards, but it exists. So, let go of exclusively left-brain thinking and open your mind to the idea that anything is indeed possible. Just because something hasn't happened doesn't mean it can't, or won't. In fact, maybe it has happened, and we just don't know about it yet.

The important point here is belief. You must believe dream travel is possible. Actually, this concept shouldn't be too hard to accept. If you believe it is impossible, how can you be so sure? Isn't a firm disbeliever just as radical thinking as a firm believer? Experiment for yourself, train hard, and you will discover dream travel does indeed exist and you can learn how to do it.

Withstanding Heat, Cold, and Pain

With Chi Gung training, it is possible to eliminate a lot of the natural discomforts we all face on a daily basis. How many times have you found yourself shivering at a football game, sweating excessively while sitting in a stuffy office, or wincing when receiving a shot?

Pain and discomfort are necessary because they tell our body that something in the environment is stressing us. Without pain and a feeling of discomfort, we could seriously hurt ourselves. For instance, if our bodies couldn't feel the burning effects of fire, we could scorch our hands while cooking over an open flame and end up doing serious damage. It is possible, however, to learn to displace some of the minor inconveniences we experience.

Getting Warm

When you are cold, you can learn to warm up your body. Perhaps you have cold feet or you just got wet in a freezing rain. Your body's natural way to warm you up is by shivering. Most people also lift their shoulders, scrunch their neck, and hug their arms around their bodies.

You can warm yourself even more quickly by consciously tightening as many of your muscles as possible. This is a Wai Dan method that will bring your chi to your muscles and your skin. When you try this, make sure you breathe using Taoist Reverse Breathing and concentrate on exhaling, which should help to energize you more quickly.

The Nei Dan method for warming yourself is by concentrating your mind on your Dan Tien, your center. Inhale slowly through your nose using Taoist Reverse Breathing, keep your tongue lightly pressed against the roof of your mouth, draw in your stomach, and imagine chi collecting in a spot below your navel. Then, as you exhale, let your mind feel as much of your skin as possible. Imagine your chi is flowing over the entire surface of your body. Feel the heat as it builds. Picture a bubble of warmth surrounding yourself as it gradually grows larger and larger. Then breathe again. You may find at first that as you inhale, your skin feels cooler. That is because your chi is once again being sent to your Dan Tien and away from the outer level of your skin. As you gain experience with this technique, you should be able to concentrate your mind on both your Dan Tien and your skin simultaneously. That way, as you build up a reservoir of energy, you are also keeping a certain amount of it circulating to keep yourself warm.

Cooling Off

When you are too hot, you use the opposite technique to cool off. Use Buddhist Breathing and focus your mind on inhaling. As you inhale, try to be aware of your skin, because this will help to cool you. Imagine energy from the environment entering into your skin, and try to draw it deep into your body. Let it sink to your bones. As you concentrate on inhaling chi through your skin, notice if you can sense anything cool in your environment. Perhaps there is a slight breeze blowing, or maybe there is a small puddle of water nearby. Possibly you can sense some plants near you, and you can take some of their chi to help cool yourself.

Remember, though, that if you ever take chi from anything, you must also give a little back. It is the law of natural balance. You can give chi back by using either Wai Dan or Nei Dan. Let's say you took chi from a plant to cool yourself. Once you are cool, gently place your palm on the plant and practice the Three Regulations and Buddhist Breathing. As your mind relaxes, see if you pick up any sensations from the plant. Does it need water? Are there insects on it? Is there garbage around it? The plant helped you, so see if there is anything you can do for it. By gently touching the plant, you are sharing your chi with it using Wai Dan.

You could also give it energy or determine its needs using Nei Dan. To do this, you would have to know Grand Circulation, Environmental Breathing, and Chi Projection. The way you do it is to point your palm toward the plant from a distance. Inhale and take some of its chi to cool yourself and also to determine if it needs anything. After you are cool, thank the plant for helping you and then project some of your chi out of your palm and into the plant. If its leaves are damaged, send chi there to heal them. If the plant has pests, use your chi to make them leave the plant alone.

Reducing Pain

Chi Gung can also help you to reduce pain. By sending chi into an injured area you can heal faster than normal. With practice, healing six times faster is not uncommon. It is even possible to heal almost instantly once you achieve extremely high levels of skill.

Another way Chi Gung can help you with pain is by teaching you how to relax the area that is stressed. When something hurts, there is a natural tendency to tense muscles in the vicinity, which creates a paradox. On the one hand, chi is sent to the area, yet it has a difficult time flowing freely. If you can use your training to help relax your muscles, then your chi will help you heal much more quickly.

Another thing you can experience is the mental elimination of pain. You can eliminate pain by focusing your mind on a random part of your body that doesn't hurt and send chi there. Regardless of your pain, try to pay attention to moving your chi to the new location. You will find that by concentrating on something other than the pain, it will diminish rather quickly.

An awareness of cold, heat, and pain are vital for us to remain healthy. Just because we are aware of them doesn't mean we have to submit ourselves to adverse situations. Of course, you can use slightly uncomfortable situations as training tools. For instance, take a walk on a cool day with a minimum amount of protective clothing. As you walk, try to heat yourself with chi. On a hot day, wear extra clothes and try to cool yourself. You can also ease little pains you get while doing common activities. For example, if you start to get side cramps while running or sore legs while biking, use your chi training to see if you can eliminate the pain on the spot.

Don't let discomfort rule your life. Instead, learn to use it as a training ground for developing your Chi Gung skills. You will discover these skills will make life considerably more tolerable. You will feel happier, healthier, and more optimistic, which will in turn enable your chi skills to grow even stronger.

Reading the Thought Vibrations of a Place or an Object

With advanced training and awareness you can learn to pick up the thoughts of people who have been in particular locations or who have handled certain objects. This is called psychometry. For example, it is possible to put on someone else's shoes to get an idea of who their owner was, what that person thought, and where he or she has been.

Psychometry is a way to understand psychic imprints. Because everything in the universe vibrates, these vibrations leave certain identifiable patterns, similar to the way humans leave fingerprints. With Chi Gung training, you can increase your chances of reading any vibration.

How does it work? Just as with all the other exercises in this book, you first need to relax your mind, your body, and your emotions by practicing the Three Regulations. Then you need to breathe slowly through your nose using Buddhist Breathing. Thought vibrations are extremely subtle, so you will have to really pay attention to each of your senses. Try not to think about anything in particular. Just concentrate on relaxing. Loosen your muscles. Calm your emotions. Slow down your mind. Just breathe. If you have enough training you should suddenly get an image or thought in your mind—not in words, necessarily; it will probably be a feeling. Let it come, don't try to control it, and don't doubt it. Basically, it is like a gut feeling, a hunch, a fleeting thought. Try to remember it and see where it leads you.

A good place to initially practice this type of exercise is in a church or some important spiritual shrine. You could even go to a major historical location where extreme emotions were played out, such as the Alamo in San Antonio, Texas. Often, at least a few of the people who have been there before you have been extremely spiritual or had high levels of energy vibration. If you are sensitive enough, you can detect this.

With extensive practice, you will be able to pick up thoughts almost anywhere you go. Don't necessarily limit yourself by thinking that the only thoughts around come from people. Every living thing has some sort of thought process, and even inanimate objects give off certain unusual vibrational patterns that simulate alternative thought.

Defending Yourself With Chi Gung

Most martial arts teach you how to fight only after trouble has begun. Chi Gung goes a step beyond this. It teaches you how to avoid trouble in the first place. By paying attention to your senses, you are indirectly on the offense, probing the environment for potential danger rather than merely waiting for something bad to happen to you. As you gain skills in Chi Gung, you will increase your sensory awareness, which will enable you to see, hear, and smell things sooner than you normally would. This, of course, will allow you to avoid trouble that is relatively close to you.

With lots of practice, you will eventually be able to sense danger quite a distance away from the actual trouble spot. It is also possible to sense that trouble will happen long before it does. This skill is related to predicting the future. You can learn to detect the negative vibrational patterns from someone or something, and therefore decide not to place yourself in their proximity. Thus, you avoid trouble. An example of this would be driving your car into a mall parking lot and feeling something dangerous will happen. So you leave. Later that night on the news, you hear how a criminal was apprehended at that particular store shortly after you left.

There are going to be times when you can't just leave, because someone may need your help. Because defensive Chi Gung gives you a sort of danger radar, you should have time to call the police before trouble begins. You could tell them you saw a suspicious character and they could check it out. Of course, sometimes there isn't time to call for help and it is up to you to intervene. That is when defensive Chi Gung can be used offensively.

Once you have detected the criminals, you could alter the outcome of what they might do by manipulating their chi. This should only be done when you have achieved an advanced level, the level of knowing without any doubt what will happen. If you are asking yourself how you will know, you are not yet ready to take on this kind of responsibility. Keep practicing. After extensive practice, you will reach the level of chi skill where you can know what people will do, how they will do it, and even why they will attempt something. That will be the time when you can morally defend yourself and others with chi.

There are a number of ways you can do this. The first is to direct your energy at the people so they feel uncomfortable and stop doing whatever it is that was wrong. You have probably had the experience where you felt someone was watching you. This skill is kind of like that. You have to generate some energy. You can use either Wai Dan or Nei Dan. With Wai Dan, raise your arms for a few minutes as you rapidly contract and relax your shoulder, arm, and hand muscles. When your entire arm feels warm and tingly, point your palm at the person and relax your arm as you exhale using Taoist Reverse Breathing. Focus your mind on your palm, then on your target. If you have built up enough energy and you relax enough, your chi will leave your palm and travel to the people. When they feel it enter them, they will generally stop doing whatever they were doing and look around. Usually, they will sense danger or just get an eerie feeling, which will make most people move away. As you get better at this skill, you will be able to project more energy, which can literally bounce someone away as though they have been pushed.

Once you have learned to send your chi in a general sort of way by directing it at someone's entire body, then you need to learn how to aim it at specific parts. You can aim it at the head and make the person dizzy and disoriented, or you could direct it into a particular muscle, such as one of the legs, causing the person to collapse. If the person is holding a weapon, such as a gun or a knife, you could aim your chi at the hand so he or she would have to drop the weapon.

The next method involves taking people's energy. In a sense, you are draining the energy out of them. The way you do it is by pointing your palm at someone, and as you inhale, imagine you are absorbing their chi. When you first start practicing this, you will probably have to actually touch the people. Using this method, you can eventually drop a person on the spot by lightly brushing against him or her with your hand. The next level involves learning to take someone's chi from a distance. The main disadvantage of learning this skill is that it is possible to take too much energy and literally drain someone of life. Fortunately, though, when you are at that level, you should have gained the control and spirituality to avoid this mistake.

The last way you can defend yourself with chi is by calling nature to help you. By learning how to communicate with plants and animals you can ask them if they will come to your aid. Likewise, you have to be willing to help them. I'll give you an example. I once saw someone violently and unnecessarily destroying a grove of trees. Intuitively, I felt the trees calling for help, so I answered. I sent them chi to strengthen and energize them, and this chi also made the man leave.

You can learn the basics of sensing danger in a relatively short period of time once you have learned Grand Circulation, but mastering the full art of defensive Chi Gung can take a lot of time and concentrated practice. It is a worthy goal to strive for though, because it is important to know how to defend yourself and others. Remember, Chi Gung is a defensive art that is best used by learning to avoid or eliminate a problem before it occurs. If, however, you find yourself in a situation where you need to use it offensively, use your skills with as much discretion as possible. In fact, it would be quite difficult to use defensive Chi Gung inappropriately, because it requires relaxation in order to work at peak effectiveness. Because relaxation requires a calm state of mind, the chances of having someone develop this skill and maliciously use it effectively against you or someone else is almost impossible.

Reading People's Minds

Most of you at one time or another have probably felt that you knew what someone was going to say before they said it. The next time this happens, try to remember what it feels like. Where do you sense this awareness? In your head? Where specifically? Does it come across as words or in pictures? Perhaps you sensed it as an emotion.

The ability to know what someone is thinking involves being able to attune your brain waves to the same vibration pattern as his or hers. This, as you can imagine, is an extremely subtle skill, which is why it is often difficult to do if you try too hard. By trying, you create tension, and that very tension is enough to hinder your progress.

When you are a beginner, the way to start developing this skill is by carefully watching other people. How do they move? Does their color change? Do their pupils dilate? Do they emit any smell or sound? You must really learn to pay attention to details. For instance, you might learn that someone who is close to you always looks slightly to the left when he is confused, or you might see a slight twinkle in her eyes when she gets an idea. It is the little things you have to notice. If you read about the character Sherlock Holmes in books written by Sir Arthur Conan Doyle, you will get an idea of the type of attention to detail you must strive to develop.

Once you have an idea of how people behave in certain situations, you can then start to predict what type of responses they may make. When you can do this successfully, observe if you feel any sense of chi moving, changing temperature, or altering its volume anywhere in your body.

At this point, it is important to follow the principles of Chi Gung breathing, especially Buddhist Breathing. Slow your respiration rate. Let your stomach move freely and rhythmically. This is critical, because in order to pick up someone's thoughts, you need to relax totally. Don't try to read someone's mind, or the sheer act of trying will make you tense and you will fail.

With time, practice, and increased sensitivity, you may become more sensitive to the thoughts of strangers. At first, you will probably notice this ability when you are totally relaxed and not really thinking of anything at all. After that, it may happen more often, and you will begin to be able to direct your talents at particular people. You do this by noticing someone, relaxing, and focusing on your breathing. As you become more sensitive to the way people think and feel, you will probably find yourself becoming more receptive to random thoughts from others. For example, you might be in a grocery store, standing near someone debating on buying some fruit. Suddenly you find yourself receiving an image of bananas, then you will see that the person reaches out and grabs a bunch.

Gathering Distant Thoughts

Next, you will want to try long-distance telepathy. The easiest way to do this is to start letting your mind explore the thoughts of people who are far away.

For example, you might try reaching family or close friends living in another city or state. When you first try this, you will probably have a greater chance of success by working with people you are very familiar with.

After you can pick up other people's thoughts, you might want to try sending your thoughts to others. Start out with a family member or a good friend. Generally, it is more difficult to send thoughts than to receive them, so you should initially practice this skill when you are relatively close to your target person. One good place to try this is when you and a friend are at a party. When you are ready to leave, try letting the other person know. You will have a greater chance of success if you pick a time to transmit your message when the other person appears to be unoccupied. That way, your friend will be more receptive to your message.

Reading people's minds is an extremely advanced skill that requires a high degree of sensitivity and chi awareness. There are, of course, disadvantages to knowing what others think. It can make it more challenging for you to be objective, and it can hurt if their thoughts are negative and directed at you. (But when you think about it, both of these situations are really growth opportunities for you anyway.)

Reading People's Spirits

Reading people's spirits involves a deep sense of awareness of who someone really is. This skill goes a lot deeper than merely reading someone's mind and knowing what he or she is thinking at any given moment. It enables you to develop a sense of what people have done, where they have been, and what kind of people they are.

Essentially, you have to look deep within someone to see who he or she really is. Look into someone's eyes. The eyes are the mirror of our soul. It is interesting to note that by merely seeing someone's eyes, even if you can't see the rest of the face or body, you can often identify the person. An interesting example is in the movie *Mrs. Doubtfire* (Twentieth Century Fox, 1993), starring Robin Williams. In this movie, Williams masquerades at times as a woman, and he wears body-altering padding and a very convincing wig and woman's makeup. Yet, by looking into his eyes, you know it is Robin Williams.

Before you delve deeply into this aspect of chi training, you must be told that there is a drawback. Over the years I've met several people who tell me they feel very uneasy around me because they feel as though I'm looking directly into their spirits. Therefore, they feel they can't lie to me or hide anything from me. To a certain degree, this scares them. This feeling can make social situations rather awkward. When this happens, I try to put people at ease by trying to project positive, caring chi so they feel more comfortable.

In order to see who people really are, you need to ignore their outer appearance. It doesn't matter what they look like. You have to open your mind to the possibilities of really knowing someone. Try putting yourself in his or her place. Imagine, for a moment, you are that person.

This is an extremely advanced technique and it requires lots of practice, but there are some things you can do as a beginner to start developing this skill. You need to send chi out of your forehead, but first you have to collect it there. The way to do that is to tighten the muscles at the bridge of your nose. Once you can do that, then you can try contracting the muscles in your forehead by raising and lowering your eyebrows. After your forehead starts to perspire and feel warm, you will have built up enough chi. Next, breathe deeply using Buddhist Breathing. Relax your body and calm your emotions. Now you need to utilize Environmental Breathing and Chi Projection. Picture chi coming out of your forehead and entering someone's eyes. Instead of sending it straight at him or her, imagine the chi gently spiraling in wide, purple arcs.

Look the other person directly in the eyes, but do it without staring. Try to keep your eyes as relaxed as possible. Image absorbing the person's chi along the same path you just projected yours. Imagine your eyes and forehead are capable of absorbing chi. As you inhale, picture the energy from the person's eyes entering your forehead. This should make your forehead feel slightly cool. When you do this right, you should get a sense of who that person is.

You should reserve this skill for those times when you need to really know who a person is. In times of danger, you may need to know if someone is going to attack you, or you may need to know if someone is troubled and requires comforting. In this case, this skill should be used to help people, to share their joy, and to ease their sadness.

There is one extremely important point to remember. Once you have learned to read people's spirit, you still need to accept them for who they are. You don't have to like them or their behavior, but you must respect their individuality and humanity.

Becoming One With Everything

As your chi flow increases you will begin to realize that everything—every bird, fish, animal, tree, plant, rock, cloud, river, lake, desert, and mountain—gives off chi. It all feels slightly different, yet it is all the same, because it is all energy.

Everything in the universe, including the universe itself, vibrates. By learning how to interpret these vibrations, you can listen to every note and hear all the music. It just so happens that the symphony is everything you see, hear, smell, taste, touch, and sense. Life itself becomes a study of rhythms and harmony.

Once you realize this, everything suddenly becomes very important in and of itself. Because everything consists of vibrations, and all vibrations influence each other, we all vibrate with a little bit of everything within us. Thus, we are everything, and everything is us.

At this stage, you will begin to understand the relationships of nature. For example, if we cut down a rain forest in South America, then we are, in a sense, destroying a part of ourselves. The more we destroy the Earth, the more we destroy our own essence.

It is easy to walk through life while randomly pulling leaves from trees, stepping on ants, and dumping garbage everywhere. After all, it is not our problem, right? We are big, important people with things to do. Well, if we're so important, then why not take a little responsibility for our actions? Think about it for a moment. We are living in the pitifully ridiculous "Age of the Victim," a time of the "poor pitiful me" syndrome, where people feel that everybody owes them something. People with this attitude often feel that when bad things happen it is always someone else's fault and not their own. What they don't realize is that everybody is important and everybody can make a difference, if they choose to act. We need to become stewards of the Earth instead of destroyers or helpless victims.

If you are interested in saving the Earth, if you want peace among all people, if you want to ensure our future, learn as much about Chi Gung as you can, then put what you learn to work. Listen to the cries of nature and help her whenever you can, in any way you can. The best way to make a difference is by seeing and understanding the connection between everything. Then, and only then, will life truly begin to make sense.

Tips, Tentations, and Tales

This chapter contains a variety of personal stories and suggestions that are primarily intended to show you what types of experiences you might have when you practice Chi Gung for a long period of time. Chi in one's life is very personal, and everyone's experiences differ. By sharing some of the stories about things I have seen and done, I hope to encourage you with your own efforts and progress in Chi Gung.

The different sections contain some activities and skills for you to attempt. Unlike the rest of this book, which is intended to be an instruction manual, the main purpose of this chapter is to show what is possible with Chi Gung.

Controlling Body Temperature

My partner frequently gets extremely hot feet when she sleeps at night. Of course, this wakes both of us up rather quickly. Unless we deal with it, it keeps us awake. This warm feeling can get irritating if you are not used to it. I use chi to cool my partner's feet so she can sleep better.

As a beginner, you can alter your own temperature by practicing Wai Dan exercises. For instance, if you are cold, you can start moving your muscles to warm yourself while simultaneously practicing Taoist Reverse Breathing. When you get too cold, your body's natural defenses come into action by making you shiver, which is a form of muscular stimulation and energy consumption. Likewise, if you are hot, you can sit still and increase the length of your inhalations when you breathe. If you are really hot, try making them as much as twice as long as your exhalations.

Once you know Grand Circulation and how to project and absorb chi, it is possible to warm other people up or cool them off. By absorbing my partner's chi from her feet, for example, I'm not only able to cool her body temperature, but I'm also eliminating some of the excess energy she may have generated while feeling frustrated about waking up in the first place. When done properly, this method can help a person fall asleep almost immediately.

To cool someone's foot, gently place one of your palms against the sole of the other person's foot. Relax your whole body, particularly your hand, arm, and shoulder. Inhale slowly through your nose and imagine breathing through your palm as you practice Taoist Reverse Breathing. Picture yourself actually inhaling your partner's chi. Draw it into your hand, up your arm, and down to your Dan Tien, or center. If you don't want to keep the energy yourself, continue its journey by sending it up your back, along your opposite arm and out your free hand. By the way, if you are going to discard the chi, you might as well send it into a plant, animal, or something you cherish. That way, you are helping the energy flow of your household. You can use the same technique to cool people down when they have a fever.

Once you become skilled at this technique, you don't have to literally touch your partner to alter his or her chi. In fact, you can be quite a distance away. If you're just starting out, though, it is a little easier to be in physical contact, and frankly, it is more fun.

You don't only have to absorb heat from outside yourself, however. You can generate it from within. The easiest way to do this is by vigorously exercising, which is an example of Wai Dan. You can also achieve the same results by just using your mind. Increase your exhalations until they are up to twice the length of your inhalations as you practice Taoist Reverse Breathing. Concentrate on sending chi to your skin by focusing your mind on your skin as your exhale. If you need warmth in a hurry, perhaps because you are in a survival situation, pump your stomach muscles like a bellows as you breathe. Be very careful using this technique, because if you use it too much you can get too much energy and potentially damage your internal organs. That is the reason Chi Gung almost always emphasizes soft, delicate breathing.

Learning to control body temperature is a valuable skill. Its primary purpose is for helping people, but you can also use it to alter the minor temperature discomforts you experience from your environment.

Stopping Hiccups

Hiccups can be really annoying, especially if they last for more than a few moments. I'll bet that over the years you have tried innumerable solutions for getting rid of them. Some of them have probably been rather comical. Perhaps you drank a glass of water while holding a spoon laterally in your mouth. Maybe you have imagined a horse race where the hiccups are one kind of horse, and the non-hiccups are another. By the time you run the race in your mind, the hiccups are usually gone. While these solutions may have worked, there is another much more effective way to cure hiccups.

If you have hiccups, run your chi back and forth through your throat and they will go away almost immediately. First practice the Three Regulations, then use Buddhist Breathing. Next, slowly contract and relax your throat and neck muscles. This will collect chi in your throat and the hiccups will go away.

If a friend has the hiccups, after asking permission, gently place your hand against the side of his or her neck. By holding your arm at shoulder height, you will build chi in your arm. Rapidly tense and relax your arm muscles about a dozen times, then do the same thing with your hand. This will send chi to your hand and into the person's neck. This technique works equally well on animals. It usually takes only a few seconds for results.

Stopping Sneezing

Sometimes my partner gets incredible sneezing fits. She will start sneezing and may keep it up for ten or fifteen minutes. As you can imagine, these fits are very draining. If you ever experience these types of sneezing bouts, there is something you can try to do about it.

First, relax and practice the Three Regulations. This may be a little difficult, but concentrate and you should be able to do it. Next, inhale slowly using Buddhist Breathing with a slight variation. Imagine the air and chi coming into your nostrils in a rolling pattern, as though a small ball or marble was rolling toward your nose, then directly into it. More than likely, this will tickle. Let this rolling ball of energy sink down to your lungs and into your Dan Tien. As you exhale, imagine pushing the rolling ball of energy down your legs and out through the soles of your feet.

If someone you know sneezes a lot and he or she does not know how to do The Flowing themselves, you might want to give this next technique a try. After asking permission, place the palm of your hand against the side of the sneezing person's neck. Relax, breathe, and focus your mind on sending chi into the person's neck. By holding your arm about shoulder height, you will build Wai Dan Chi in your shoulder. To build it up even quicker, try rapidly tensing and relaxing your shoulder a dozen times. Next, lightly brush your free hand across the person's face a few times while picturing your chi penetrating his or her face. If done properly, this method can work almost immediately.

Healing Broken Bones

If we happen to break a bone when we're young, it generally heals rather quickly, often in just a matter of weeks. For the majority of people, though, it typically takes about six weeks to heal. As we get older, it usually takes longer and longer periods of time to heal a broken bone. It often takes elderly people months to heal. There is a way, though, to speed up the healing process substantially.

Not long ago I broke my thumb severely. I went to a Western doctor who said it would be more than a year before I had normal use of it again. The break was such that the doctor felt that the bone could actually separate and shift or float up my finger.

I wore the required splint on my thumb, but at the same time, I also began sending chi into the area and imagining the bones were healing. I did this by regulating my body, breath, and mind, while flowing my chi to the damaged spot. Once it was there, I used my mind to spiral the chi around and around as though I were wrapping my thumb up in a long piece of string. By using every spare minute I had, I was able to do this daily for hours at a time. I directed chi into my thumb while I waited in lines at stores, while I ate, while I read, and before drifting off to sleep at night. After one week of intensive self-healing, my thumb felt normal, but just in case, I continued to wear the splint. After two weeks, the doctor x-rayed my thumb again just to check on its healing progress. When he read the pictures, he was completely surprised to find that not only had the break healed, there wasn't any sign at all that the bone had ever been broken. I also had full functionality of my thumb.

The skill required for healing broken bones is advanced, and to use the method I did you would have to know how to do Nei Dan Grand Circulation, enabling you to send chi in a controlled manner throughout your body. This level of training generally takes extensive training to achieve, but there are things you can do for broken bones right now, even as a beginner, to help bones heal at least a little faster.

The way to heal a bone is to send energy to it, and the best way for beginners to do this is by using Wai Dan Chi Gung. Obviously, you will have to alter any exercise for your specific situation. If, for instance, you have a broken arm, wrist, or hand, you could very slightly elevate your arm for short periods of time in order to build up just a little tension in your shoulder muscles. Because you will probably have the added weight of a cast, you won't need to lift your arm very high. Once you have raised your arm, hold it steady as you relax your body, breathing, and mind as much as possible. At the same time, try to focus your mind on the specific area of the break. Do this exercise as often as possible until the fracture has healed.

If the break happens to be in a location you can't elevate, such as your hip, then you can use muscular tension created by flexing your muscles in the general area. If you experience pain and can't flex your muscles, try focusing your mind on the damaged area instead. Because your chi flows where your mind directs, this should help.

So, if you find yourself with the misfortune of having a broken bone, try sending chi into it. The sooner you start, the better. In fact, it is best to start the minute the accident occurs. Obviously, you need to go to a doctor and get it treated, but keep up with your chi therapy on your own.

Bonding With Cats

As you practice Chi Gung, sometimes you will discover you have developed some rather interesting and unusual skills. One I have a lot of fun with is an ability to bond with felines of all types.

I first noticed this particular skill when I was seven years old. I was walking around the Chicago Zoo when I found myself near the black panther exhibit. For some reason, I felt drawn to this particular animal. As I watched him, he casually turned his back on me and urinated. Actually, he sprayed me. He hit me full in the chest from about six or seven feet away. The rest of the day was most interesting, because everyone wanted to know what that strange smell was. Since then, I have been sprayed by ten big game cats, including lions, tigers, leopards, and panthers. It has happened at zoos, parks, animal exhibits, and anywhere I have been in proximity to them. Of course, domestic cats have done this to me, too, numerous times.

Another type of bonding I have experienced is my ability to call literally any cat, domestic or wild, from a considerable distance. I do this in a number of ways. One way is by imitating their calls. Another is by focusing on them and sending out chi. The third is simply by walking within 200 yards or so of them. Apparently, they sense my chi and are attracted to it. There have been times when I've taken walks around the block and had a dozen or so cats following me.

I also frequently go into the woods with my guitar or Celtic harp and play music. I've noticed that any cat, domestic or wild, within hearing distance will come and listen. Once, as I played, seven cats formed a circle around me. As they listened, they began sticking out their tongues in a feline sign of contentment, and soon started lying down. After about a half hour, I stopped and got up to leave. As one, the cats stirred and started meowing. Obviously, they wanted more. I told them I could play for a few more minutes. Once I finished the second time, they got up by ones and twos and wandered off into the forest.

The point of all of this is to show you that sometimes Chi Gung can cause some interesting and fun situations to arise. Therefore, practice diligently and open yourself up to any new experiences that might affect you. Who knows? Maybe you will develop a bonding with something unique. Perhaps it will be an animal, plant, or maybe even the opposite sex. It could be anything.

Sensing Bad Chi

Chi is energy and energy is inherently neutral, but how that energy is used definitely affects it. There is good chi and bad chi, and sensing the difference is a valuable skill. It allows you to accurately read people, as well as to know if something dangerous is going to happen in a particular place. Many times I have gone to stores, restaurants, or parks, and suddenly started sensing something was wrong. The chi in the area just didn't feel right. I then respond according to the demands of the situation.

You have probably sensed bad chi at some time or another in your life. You might have had a gut feeling, an awareness that something was wrong. Perhaps you felt it when people were looking at you. How many times have you been somewhere when suddenly you feel watched? Kind of eerie, isn't it? When you feel this, you need to listen to yourself instead of ignoring your senses. Of course, this also applies to people. You can learn to sense if people are lying to you or planning something sinister.

One time I went to a used bookstore filled with rare books, and as soon as I walked in I felt something terrible had happened there. The bad chi emanated from somewhere down in the basement. The owner of the store didn't even want to walk into the basement with me to turn on the lights. He told me that if I wanted to go down there, I could find the switch myself. Being the lover of books that I am, and wanting to see his collection downstairs, I decided to go down anyway. I walked down a series of dark rickety steps covered from floor to ceiling with cobwebs. When I got to the bottom, I found a single light bulb to turn on. It cast eerie shadows along the seven-foot-high rows of bookshelves. Following a sense of terror, I made my way through a confusing, irrational maze until I found the spot where it happened. Rape—I knew it in an instant. My breathing accelerated for a moment or two as my pulse soared. The horror happened a long time before, but its energy permeated everything. It was almost overwhelming. Fleeing the store, I vowed never to go back.

Learning to become aware of your feelings and intuition, and acting upon them, can make your life a lot easier and safer. If you ever sense bad chi, trust your gut. Leave immediately, unless someone needs your help.

Mastering the Night

Night training is an excellent way to hone your skills. Many people have a slight apprehension about darkness. If you have this fear, you will probably be more aware of all your senses, so it will be easier for you to learn about them at such a time. You will probably be able to hear, smell, taste, and touch with much greater clarity and precision.

Go outside at night and find a safe place to sit. Get yourself into a comfortable position. Relax and practice the Three Regulations. Breathe using Buddhist Breathing. As you sit still, let all of your senses come alive. Embrace them. What can you detect? If you know a dog is walking in your yard, can you hear the sound of its footsteps or its breathing? Can you smell it? Can you smell what the dog ate? Do you feel its footsteps vibrating against the ground? What about the dog's energy? Can you sense it?

Night is a perfect time to train, because you won't have as many people wandering aimlessly around you trying to figure out why you are standing like a tree or practicing one of the other Chi Gung techniques. Also, it gives you the chance to experience a time of the world that you seldom explore.

Practice The Flowing every night. The darkness will increase your awareness and concentration. This will help you gain deeper enlightenment into yourself, the environment, and the universe.

Spontaneous Experimentation

One of the best things you can do with your Chi Gung training is to follow your instincts. That way, you will progress at a natural pace based on your own capabilities. Remember, never rush your training. Whatever happens will happen when it happens.

Before you can start experimenting, you should have a strong grounding in the basics, but from there, you can go wherever The Flowing beckons you. Personally, though, I suggest you continue to practice and review the basic techniques of breathing and relaxing every day. Specifically, you should practice the Three Regulations and both Buddhist Breathing and Taoist Reverse Breathing as you practice the exercise called "Hugging a Tree." In addition, you should do some spontaneous Tai Chi Chuan and seated Nei Dan meditation. That should be your primary training. Anything else you try is secondary. In this way, your Chi Gung skills will grow in a natural progression.

As you go about your daily life, there will be times when you suddenly get the urge to do something, go somewhere, or even to try something you have never attempted before. Follow your hunches because someone or something just might need your help.

Here is an example. I had just dropped my partner off at work and was on my way home when I felt a strong urge to go to the Magic Kingdom at Walt

Disney World. When I got there, I followed my feelings until I got near the Peter Pan exhibit. Just as I walked up, a bird nest with two sparrows came crashing down within a foot of me. They needed help. Both of them were shaken up and disoriented by the fall. I had never given birds chi before to help them build a nest, but I followed my instincts. First, I gently gave them some chi to revitalize them, then I gave them more energy so they would have the strength to rebuild. As they went to work, I sat down on the bench where the nest landed and both birds flew repeatedly within inches of me to pick up material and carry it up to their home.

When you begin experimenting you will probably notice that the more things you try, the more ideas you will get for attempting even further pursuits. In other words, one thing leads to another. And you never know where any given path may ultimately lead you. Be willing to follow your intuition whenever you can by practicing spontaneous experimentation.

Chi Gung Exacts a Price

Everything in life costs something. It is not necessarily money—it can be time, energy, or anything else for that matter. In the case of Chi Gung, particularly at advanced levels, the payment is increased sensory awareness.

Now you may be asking yourself, how can that be a problem? In fact, it seems like a good trade off. You put in a little time and effort, which then enables you to sense things you never even knew existed. You gain new skills, improve your health, and enjoy a more interesting life. So what is the price?

The price, as I mentioned, is the increased acuteness of your senses. As you get better at Chi Gung, there comes a point where you can feel overwhelmed by common experiences and especially extreme ones. Going to a rock concert might be way too intense unless you learn how to shield your increased sensitivity from the excessive noise and light. With advanced Chi Gung training, you might learn to hear your heartbeat. In fact, it is possible that your hearing can get so sensitive that some sounds you listen to require you to hold your breath and listen between heartbeats in order to distinguish them. With proper practice, all of your senses can become increased in similar ways.

This increased sensory sensitivity can lead to a lifestyle change. You may find your life becoming simpler, slower paced, and more relaxed. Instead of feeling the need to pursue high-intensity adrenaline pumping sports, you may find yourself seeking solitude in quiet meadows as you watch plants move with the sun.

Now don't get me wrong. You are not doomed to a life of monotony—far from it. You will just become more aware of everything, which in turn, means you won't need as much to stimulate your senses. On the other hand, if you do choose to pursue extreme sports, for example, then they will seem even more intense than you ever dreamed. Instead of virtual reality, you will have super reality.

Don't let this discourage you from your training. Generally, this type of sensory experience only occurs after many years at the advanced levels of practice. By that time, you should have learned how to use selective chi attention. Essentially, this means you will be able to turn your senses on or off.

Mastering
The Flowing

Chi Gung is the art of mastering universal energy. At a basic level, its main purpose is to learn how to prevent disease. As you become more advanced, however, Chi Gung training can teach you how to treat disease, increase strength, increase intelligence, increase your sensory awareness, prolong life, and develop latent abilities such as psychic skills. Once you have learned the basic principles, you can take your new chi skills and apply them to almost any other area of your life.

To maintain your health and prolong the aging process, it is important for you to keep your twelve meridians open so that your chi can run smoothly and efficiently. To open your meridians, you should first learn how to regulate your body, breath, and mind—the Three Regulations. After you have learned the deep state of relaxation obtained by following these exercises, you then will be ready to sense the chi that is in your body.

At this point, you begin Wai Dan exercises, which help you generate chi by using muscular effort. Once you have built up a supply of chi, you can begin to manipulate it through your body. You can also use a series of mental exercises called Nei Dan to manipulate your chi.

It is very important to practice the basics first and master them. These are the foundation upon which your success and skill in this field will be based. Once you have thoroughly learned the basics, you can work on developing some of the more advanced skills.

Use this book as a reference. Refer to it often, concentrating on those sections where you might need extra work. Remember, the actual act of reading this book can be an exercise in developing your chi. Relax, close your eyes, and let your chi guide you to what you should read. As you try the exercises, feel free to personalize them to fit your specific needs.

If you are really serious about your training, you should experiment as much as possible. Don't merely take someone's word for how something is supposed to work, go out and try it yourself.

This book teaches you more than a hundred different exercises and skills you can use to develop your chi. The point of this book is not to limit yourself merely to these exercises, but to use them as stepping stones to develop your own exercises. Use your imagination. Branch out. Once you realize you can generate and manipulate your chi by following almost any activity, then you will be able to practice for many hours every day without really thinking of it as practice.

The Earth is facing a time of major crisis as we continue to pollute it and waste its resources. The future of our world requires a great need for more energy specialists who concentrate on improving themselves and therefore improving the world. Practice diligently. Master The Flowing.

Glossary

Acupressure—Using the hands and fingers to press on the chi cavities in the body in order to manipulate chi.

Acupuncture—Using needles to penetrate the chi cavities of the body in order to manipulate chi. This requires a highly trained specialist to perform.

Astral projection—Letting your spirit and mind leave your body and travel to other locations in order to find out information.

Auras—Fields of energy that surround the outside edges of the body.

Bio-magnetic electro-chemical energy—What chi is often referred to as in the West.

Bonsai—The Japanese art of growing miniature trees.

Buddhist Breathing—As you inhale, let your belly extend and push out. As you exhale, slowly let your stomach go back to its normal position.

Chakras—Balls of energy. According to the traditions of India, there are seven energy spheres in the body.

Channels—Chi runs through these twelve paths in the body. Channels are also called meridians.

Chi—The Chinese word for a variety of forms of energy containing infrared radiation, static electricity, infrasound, and magnetic fields. Basically, chi can be thought of as your breath, spirit, or vitality. You can learn to control chi by generating it in your body. You can also learn to project it from you and send it into someone or something else, primarily for healing purposes.

Chi Gung—An art emphasizing learning how to deliberately develop and utilize the energy that is within your own body. It is also spelled *Chi Kung* or *Qigong*, and pronounced *chee goong*.

Conception Vessel—The meridian that runs down the front of your body from your lower jaw to a spot midway between your legs called the Huiyin Cavity. Also called the Ren Mai. *See also:* meridians

Dan Tien—Your center of gravity, located about an inch and a half below your navel. It is the primary spot where chi is built up and collected.

Didjeridoo—An Australian Aborigine instrument made from a termite-hollowed eucalyptus tree branch. It is used for making music as well as for healing and generating the Aboriginal version of chi.

Du Mai—Another name for the Governing Vessel.

Earth chi—Chi that comes from everything on the Earth, such as land, seas, wind, plants, and animals.

Energy—Your chi. It is your vitality, spirit, and alertness.

Environmental Breathing—Absorbing chi from and projecting chi into the environment. It is an advanced skill.

Fire Path—The path chi follows as it goes down the front of your body through the Conception Vessel, then up your back in through the Governing Vessel.

Five Elements—The Chinese theory that states that everything is made up of either wood, fire, earth, metal, or water. These five things represent the traits of any object, and they all interconnect and influence each other. This theory is a study of relationships and patterns.

The Flowing—A type of universal Chi Gung that incorporates principles and concepts from energy systems from around the world. It specializes in healing and self-development.

Governing Vessel—The meridian that starts at your Huiyin Cavity between your legs, then goes up your back, over your head, to your upper jaw. Also called the Du Mai.

Grand Circulation—A method of circulating chi throughout your entire body.

Heaven chi—The energies of the universe, such as sunlight, gravity, and magnetism.

Heavenly Cycle—Another name for Grand Circulation.

Huiyin Cavity—A chi cavity located between your legs in front of the anus. It is an area where the muscles need to be relaxed in order to complete Small Circulation and Grand Circulation.

Human chi—The kind of Chi that humans have.

Jivaro shaman—A shaman from the Jivaro Indian tribe in Brazil.

Kahuna—A spiritual leader and teacher of the art of Huna in Hawaii.

Ki—The Japanese word for Chi.

Laogong Cavities—The chi cavities located in the center of the palms of the hands. Also called the Labor Palaces.

Magick—A New Age reference to the use of energy to achieve goals. It is literally chi and, simultaneously, the use of chi.

Maucht—The ancient Pict word for chi. It means *power*.

Meridians—Pathways in the body that chi travels along. There are eight vessels and twelve channels.

Micro Cosmic Cycle—Another name for Small Circulation.

Moving Wai Dan Chi Gung— A series of exercises that use muscular exertion and movement to generate chi.

Nei Dan Chi Gung—A series of mental exercises that are used to generate and manipulate chi.

Normal Breathing—The breathing that you generally do every day. Essentially, it means breathing without conscious awareness.

Power—What chi is called by practitioners of Voodoo.

Prana—The name for Chi in India.

Ren Mai—Another name for the Conception Vessel.

Santero mayor—A spiritual healer and leader in the Cuban art of Santeria.

The Seven Emotions—Joy, anger, sadness, pensiveness, grief, fear, and fright.

Shaman—A spiritual person who uses out-of-body experiences for aid in healing others.

The Shining—What chi is called by hill folk of the Appalachian Mountains.

The Six Desires—Sex, money, fame, wealth, gain, and avoidance of loss.

Small Circulation—The path chi follows from the lower jaw, down the front of the body to the Dan Tien, between the legs, up the back, over the head, and to the upper jaw. The tongue acts as a link between both jaws.

Still Wai Dan Chi Gung—A series of exercises that involve stationary postures. The most important one that you should practice every day is called "Hugging a Tree."

Tai Chi Chuan—Both a martial art and a form of moving meditation involving the principles of Moving Wai Dan Chi Gung. It is a method of generating and identifying energy in the body.

Taoist Reverse Breathing—As you inhale, contract your stomach muscles and pull your stomach in. As you exhale, let your stomach muscles relax and your belly will return to its normal position.

Telekinesis—The ability of moving objects with your mind.

Three Regulations—Regulating the body, regulating the mind, and regulating the breath. These three methods of achieving harmonious relaxation are vital in learning Chi Gung.

Vessels—There are eight vessels in the body. The two most commonly used ones in Chi Gung are the Conception Vessel and the Governing Vessel.

Water Path—An extremely advanced Nei Dan method involving having your chi circulate in the same direction it traveled on the Fire Path, but this time, as it travels up your back it does so from inside of the spinal column instead of merely next to it.

Wind Path—Chi goes down your Governing Vessel on your back and up your Conception Vessel on the front of your body.

Yang—The half of the yin-yang theory that represents things such as masculinity, the sun, movement, and left. Yin and yang complement each other, making a whole.

Yin—The half of the yin-yang theory that represents things such as femininity, the moon, stillness, and right.

Yoga—A style of exercise and meditation from India. Instead of focusing on meridians, it uses chakras.

Yongquan Cavities—Chi cavities located on the center of the soles of the feet. Also called the Bubbling Wells.

Zhan Zhuang—A form of Wai Dan training that uses the body's muscles to hold a relaxed position in order to build chi. Once the chi is generated, Nei Dan can be used to circulate it through the meridians.

Suggested Reading

Chin, Richard M. M.D., O.M.D. *The Energy Within: The Science Behind Eastern Healing Techniques*. New York, New York: Marlowe & Company, 1995.

Chuen, Lam Kam. *The Way Of Energy: Mastering The Chinese Art of Internal Strength With Chi Kung Exercise*. New York, New York: Simon & Schuster Inc., 1991.

Jwing-Ming, Yang Dr. *The Root of Chinese Chi Kung: The Secrets of Chi Gung Training*. Jamaica Plain, Massachusetts: Yang's Martial Arts Association, 1989.

———. *Chinese Qigong Massage: General Massage*. Jamaica Plain, Massachusetts: Yang's Martial Arts Association, 1989.

Kit, Wong Kiew. *The Art of Chi Kung: Making The Most of Your Vital Energy*. Rockport, Massachusetts: Element Books Limited, 1993.

MacRitchie, James. *The Chi Gung Way: Alive With Energy*. London: Thorsons, 1997.

———. *Chi Kung: Cultivating Personal Energy*. Rockport, Massachusetts: Element Books Limited, 1993.

Wang, Simon M.D., Ph.D. & Julius L. Liu, M.D. *Qi Gong: The Ancient Chinese Art of Relaxation/Meditation/Physical Fitness*. Tustin, California: The East Health Development Group, 1994.

Index

C

D

E

rocks, 115, 156, 166–167, 170, 181, 183–184, 189–190, 205, 207–208, 212, 231, 244, 253

running, 107, 117, 156, 184, 199, 212, 237

S

salt, 152

sexuality, 21, 145–146

Small Circulation, 11, 26, 33, 47, 62–63, 103, 105–108, 221

shaman, 8, 109, 160

shoulders, 28–30, 34, 38, 44, 47, 52, 54–56, 61, 67–70, 72–76, 78–85, 88–89, 91–94, 96, 99, 101–102, 106–107, 110, 118, 122, 124–128, 158, 164, 169, 172, 176, 187, 190, 199, 208, 210, 213, 219, 221–222, 228, 230, 235, 239, 246–249

sight, 195–197

skin, 14, 26, 34, 44, 60, 62–64, 118, 120–121, 127, 131–133, 157, 166, 182, 190, 198, 213, 217–218, 224, 229, 235–236, 246

skirt, 134–135

sky, 41, 72, 75, 99–100, 144, 154, 184, 212–214

slow, 45–46, 48, 52, 60, 69, 88, 91, 94, 118, 121, 127, 149, 164, 173–174, 198, 219–220, 226, 237, 241

smell, 44, 49, 67, 69, 133, 166, 183, 191–192, 197–198, 214, 238, 241, 244, 250–252

smiling, 53, 202–203

smoking, 160–161

sneezing, 247–248

snow, 115, 132–133, 213

soles, 40, 62–63, 97–98, 110, 116, 118–119, 132, 147, 167, 246, 248

soul, 192, 242

speech, 200

spinach, 226

spirit, 3, 7–8, 10, 17, 21, 124, 146, 148, 167–168, 177, 192, 203, 206, 208, 229, 233–234, 242–243

strength, 10, 19–20, 22, 41, 51, 54, 60, 62, 90–91, 93, 95, 119, 124, 153, 155–156, 183, 186, 217, 219, 253, 255

stretching, 6, 142, 157, 160, 219

sugar, 152

swimming, 117–118, 128, 130–131, 141–142, 156, 177

T

Tai Chi Chuan, 9–10, 127–129, 131, 252

taste, 39, 44, 50, 67, 69, 133, 142, 191, 194, 244, 251

tea, 226

telekinesis, 227

temperature, 69, 131, 186, 189, 194, 197, 207, 241, 245–247

tennis, 5, 156

thoughts, 21, 44–46, 48–50, 60–62, 105, 140, 147–148, 155, 190, 206, 209, 217, 231, 237–238, 241–242

toe, 35, 37, 142

tomatoes, 226

tongue, 35–37, 44, 68, 82–83, 90, 105, 117, 235

Z

V

W

☽ LOOK FOR THE CRESCENT MOON

Llewellyn publishes hundreds of books on your favorite subjects! To get these exciting books, including the ones on the following pages, check your local bookstore or order them directly from Llewellyn.

ORDER BY PHONE
- Call toll-free within the U.S. and Canada, 1-800-THE MOON
- In Minnesota, call (612) 291-1970
- We accept VISA, MasterCard, and American Express

ORDER BY MAIL
- Send the full price of your order (MN residents add 7% sales tax) in U.S. funds, plus postage & handling to:

  Llewellyn Worldwide
  P.O. Box 64383, Dept. K113-9
  St. Paul, MN 55164–0383, U.S.A.

POSTAGE & HANDLING
(For the U.S., Canada, and Mexico)
- $4 for orders $15 and under
- $5 for orders over $15
- No charge for orders over $100

We ship UPS in the continental United States. We ship standard mail to P.O. boxes. Orders shipped to Alaska, Hawaii, The Virgin Islands, and Puerto Rico are sent first-class mail. Orders shipped to Canada and Mexico are sent surface mail.

International orders: Airmail—add freight equal to price of each book to the total price of order, plus $5.00 for each non-book item (audio tapes, etc.).

Surface mail—Add $1.00 per item.

Allow 4–6 weeks for delivery on all orders.
Postage and handling rates subject to change.

DISCOUNTS

We offer a 20% discount to group leaders or agents. You must order a minimum of 5 copies of the same book to get our special quantity price.

FREE CATALOG

Get a free copy of our color catalog, *New Worlds of Mind and Spirit*. Subscribe for just $10.00 in the United States and Canada ($30.00 overseas, airmail). Many bookstores carry *New Worlds*—ask for it!

Visit our website at www.llewellyn.com for more information.

A Chakra & Kundalini Workbook

Psycho-Spiritual Techniques for Health, Rejuvenation, Psychic Powers and Spiritual Realization

Dr. John Mumford
(Swami Anandakapila Saraswati)

Spend just a few minutes each day on the remarkable psycho-physiological techniques in this book and you will quickly build a solid experience of drugless inner relaxation that will lead towards better health, a longer life, and greater control over your personal destiny. Furthermore, you will lay a firm foundation for the subsequent chapters leading to the attainment of super-normal powers (i.e., photographic memory, self-anesthesia and mental calculations), an enriched Inner Life, and ultimate transcendence. Learn techniques to use for burn-out, mild to moderate depression, insomnia, general anxiety and panic attacks, and reduction of mild to moderate hypertension. Experience sex for consciousness expansion, ESP development, and positive thinking. The text is supplemented with tables and illustrations to bridge the distance from information to personal understanding. In addition, the author has added a simple outline of a 12-week practice schedule referenced directly back to the first nine chapters.

A Chakra & Kundalini Workbook is one of the clearest, most approachable books on Yoga there is. Tailored for the Western mind, this is a practical system of personal training suited for anyone in today's active and complex world.

1-56718-473-1, 296 pp., 7 x 10, 8 color plates, softcover **$17.95**

To order call 1–800 THE MOON

Yoga for Every Athlete
Secrets of an Olympic Coach

Aladar Kogler, Ph.D.

Whether you train for competition or participate in a sport for the pure pleasure of it, here is a holistic training approach that unifies body and mind through yoga for amazing results. The yoga exercises in this book not only provide a greater sense of well being and deeper unity of body, mind and spirit, they also increase your body's ability to rejuvenate itself for overall fitness. Use the yoga asanas for warm-up, cool-down, regeneration, compensation of muscle dysbalances, prevention of injuries, stimulation of internal organs, or for increasing your capacity for hard training. You will experience the remarkable benefits of yoga that come from knowing yourself and knowing that you have the ability to control your autonomic, unconscious functions as you raise your mental and physical performance to new heights. Yoga is also the most effective means for accomplishing the daily practice of concentration. Yoga training plans are outlined for 27 different sports.

1-56718-387-5, 320 pp., 6 x 9, softcover $16.95

To order call 1–800 THE MOON

The Tao and the Tree of Life
Alchemical and Sexual Mysteries of the East and West

Eric Steven Yudelove

Until 1981, Taoist Yoga, or Taoist Internal Alchemy, remained a secret to the Western World. All of that changed when Master Mantak Chia emigrated from Thailand to the United States and began practicing openly. The complete Taoist Yoga system is now revealed—by one of Master Chia's first American students—in *The Tao and The Tree of Life*. Going beyond any previously published work, this book describes the entire structure of Taoist Yoga by comparing it with the Western Tradition of the Kaballah.

The Taoists developed the potential of human sexuality to a higher level than any other group. Uncover the secrets of single and dual cultivation, self-intercourse and the immortal child, as well as other mystical techniques never before available. Journey safely into the unknown through guided practice. Beginners can benefit almost immediately from the practical exercises in *The Tao and the Tree of Life*. Seasoned Kabbalists will marvel at actual alchemical formulas uncovered from The Sepher Yetzirah. There is a growing trend among Western Kabbalists to absorb the lower formulas of Taoist Yoga into their Tradition, and on the cusp of this rising tide is *The Tao and the Tree of Life*.

1-56718-250-X, 256 pp., 5$\frac{1}{4}$ x 8, illus., softcover $14.95

To order call 1–800 THE MOON

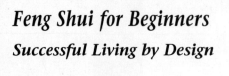

Feng Shui for Beginners

Successful Living by Design

Richard Webster

Not advancing fast enough in your career? Maybe your desk is located in a "negative position." Wish you had a more peaceful family life? Hang a mirror in your dining room and watch what happens. Is money flowing out of your life rather than into it? You may want to look to the construction of your staircase!

For thousands of years, the ancient art of feng shui has helped people harness universal forces and lead lives rich in good health, wealth and happiness. The basic techniques in *Feng Shui for Beginners* are very simple, and you can put them into place immediately in your home and work environments. Gain peace of mind, a quiet confidence, and turn adversity to your advantage with feng shui remedies.

1-56718-803-6, 240 pp., 5 $^{1}/_{4}$ x 8, photos, diagrams, softcover $12.95